PLAYFAIR

ANNUAL 1984

Compiled and edited by Touchdown Magazine

Queen Anne Press

A *Queen Anne Press* BOOK

First published in Great Britain in 1984 by
Queen Anne Press, a division of
Macdonald & Co (Publishers) Ltd
London and Sydney
A BPCC plc Company

Cover photograph: Dwight Clark of San Francisco 49ers

British Library Cataloguing in Publication Data
Playfair American Football Annual – 1984
1. Football – Periodicals
796.332'05 GV937
ISBN 0 356 10595 4

Typeset by SIOS Limited, London NW6 and Visage Typesetting Ltd., London SW19
Reproduced, printed and bound in Great Britain by
Hazell, Watson & Viney Limited,
Member of the BPCC Group,
Aylesbury, Bucks.

CONTENTS

AMERICAN FOOTBALL

What is American Football? It's not all that different from rugby, indeed, that's how it all started in the American Universities round about 1870. Just like rugby, it's a game of gaining territory, moving down the field and somehow getting the ball across the opposing team's goal line.

How does a team move the ball? *The 4-Down System*: The team in possession (the Offense) is allowed four downs (attempts) to gain 10 or more yards' progress towards the opposing goal line. These 10 or more yards may be gained on just one down (attempt) or, if necessary, by using all four downs. The immediate reward for gaining the 10 yards is that the offense retains the possession of the ball and is allowed another series of four downs to gain 10 or more yards, and so on

Scoring *Touchdown and Conversion*: Of course, the object is to score more points than your opponent. The most valuable score is a Touchdown, rather like a try in rugby. The difference is that, unlike a try, the ball need not be placed down onto the playing surface. Rather, it has simply to be taken over the goal line – into the so-called End Zone. A touchdown, which is worth six points, is immediately followed by a kick from directly in front of the goal posts. This is equivalent to the conversion in rugby and is known as an Extra Point Attempt, Point After Touchdown (PAT for short); a PAT is worth one point. It may not seem much but it is very important as many games are decided by just one point.

Field Goal: This is exactly like a penalty kick at goal in rugby, though in American football a team doesn't need to be awarded a penalty to have a go. In fact, a team can take a field goal kick on any one of its four downs, but they usually wait until the fourth down and even then, only when they're no more than 40 yards from their opponent's goal line. If the kick is successful, it's worth three points.

Safety: A safety is *given up* by a team when one of its players who has the ball is tackled *inside his own end zone*. In this case, the unlucky team gives up two points to the opposition.

The Playing Field The playing surface can be AstroTurf, Tartan Turf, (both man-made fibre) or grass. The field of play is 120 yards long and 53 1/3rd yards wide. The end zones take up 10 yards at each end of the field. In addition to the obvious gridiron markings, there are two lines of marks stretching the length of the field. These are called 'Hashmarks' and define a strip of ground in the middle of the field where all the downs begin

Starting the Game The captains toss a coin and the winner decides *either* to kick off or to face the kick, *or* the direction in which to play. The action starts when the kicker boots the ball as far as possible down the field. The man who makes the catch runs as far as possible up the field until he is tackled. His team keeps possession of the ball and they set off on their first series of four downs.

The Squads Each 45-man squad has three teams of 11 men plus a few reserves. They are known as the Offense, the Defense and the Special Team. The offense tries to score points, the defense tries to stop the opposition from scoring and the special team comes on when attempting or facing a kick. So there is a great deal of coming and going as the different teams enter and leave the field.

The League System All 28 professional teams form the National Football League but for competition (and historical reasons) they are divided into two 14-team Conferences, the American Football Conference and the National Football Conference. Each Conference is divided into three Divisions, not first, second and third, as in the Football League, but Eastern, Central and Western Divisions. All the divisions are meant to be of the same standard, the object being to group local teams together.

The Road to the Super Bowl There is a 16-week regular season in which the teams play normal league football. At the end of this, the top four teams in each Conference go into a knockout competition to decide the 'World Championship'. One week after the whole season is over the best players in each Conference form teams who play in the Pro Bowl, held in Hawaii. To be selected for the Pro Bowl is a great honour, even though both teams ease off a bit and the tackling isn't quite as tough.

PLAYERS' NUMBERS

All NFL players are numbered according to their position*

  1 – 19   Quarterbacks and Kickers
20 – 49   Running Backs and Defensive Backs
50 – 59   Centers and Linebackers
60 – 79   Defensive Linemen and Interior Offensive Linemen
80 – 89   Wide Receivers and Tight Ends
90 – 99   Defensive Linemen

*All players who had been in the National Football League
prior to 1972 may use their old number.

OFFENSE

Quarterback: He directs the play by 'handing off' to a
Running Back or throwing a forward pass.
Center. Guards and Tackles: The interior line – they pave the way for the Running Back or protect
the Quarterback on passing plays.
Tight End: He has the dual role of blocking like an Interior Lineman or catching medium range
passes.
The Wide Receiver: The 'flyer' who catches the full range of passes.
The Half Back*: The lighter more elusive runner
The Full Back*: The heavyweight power runner
* Known as the Running Backs who 'rush' with the ball and catch short passes.

DEFENSE

Tackles and Ends: The defensive line – they tackle the Running Back or kill the play at source by
'sacking' the Quarterback.
Linebackers: They pursue the Running Back on rushing plays or, on obvious passing plays, drop
back to reinforce the Defensive Backs.
Cornerbacks and Safeties: The Defensive Backs – primarily defend against the pass, they also
advance to assist the Linebackers on rushing plays.

KEY TO DEPTH CHART

OFFENSE
WR	– wide receiver
OLT	– offensive left tackle
OLG	– offensive left guard
C	– center
ORG	– offensive right guard
ORT	– offensive right tackle
TE	– tight end
QB	– quarterback
RB	– running back (general term)
HB	– half-back
H-B	– H-back
FB	– full back

DEFENSE
DLE	– defensive left end
DLT	– defensive left tackle
NT	– nose tackle
MG	– middle guard
DRT	– defensive right tackle
DRE	– defensive right end
LOLB	– left outside linebacker
LLB	– left linebacker
LILB	– left inside linebacker
MLB	– middle linebacker
RILB	– right inside linebacker
RLB	– right linebacker
ROLB	– right outside linebacker
LCB	– left cornerback
SS	– strong safety
LS	– left-side safety
RS	– right-side safety
FS	– free safety
RCB	– right cornerback

SPECIAL TEAMS
K	– kicker
P	– punter
H	– holder
KR	– kick returner
PR	– punt returner
LSN	– long snapper

* indicates players on injured reserve or non-football injury reserve
** indicates a player who will not return next season
*** indicates a player just returned from injury or suspension
**** indicates a suspended player

AMERICAN FOOTBALL CONFERENCE

TEAMS

BUFFALO BILLS

AFC Eastern Division

Address: One Bills Drive, Orchard Park, NY 14127
Telephone: (716) 648 1800

CLUB OFFICIALS
President: Ralph C. Wilson, Jr.
Executive Vice President: Patrick J. McGroder, Jr.
Vice President, Administration and General Manager:
Terry Bledsoe
Vice President, Football Operations: Kay Stephenson
Vice President, Player Personnel: Norm Pollom
Vice President, General Counsel and Secretary: Ralph L. Halpern
Vice President: Richard O. Morrison
Vice President, Public Relations: L. Budd Thalman
Head Coach: Kay Stephenson
Assistant Coaches: John Becker, Milt Jackson, Monte Kiffin, Don Lawrence, Perry Moss,
Andy MacDonald, Jim Niblack, Miller McCalmon, Bob Zeman
Assistant Director of Player Personnel: Bruce Nicholas
Administrative Assistant: Mike McDonnell
Head Trainer: Eddie Abramoski
Assistant Trainer: Bud Tice
Strength and Conditioning Coordinator: Jim Speros
Equipment Manager: Dave Hojnowski
Assistant Equipment Manager: Randy Ribbeck
Ticket Director: Jim Cipriano
Assistant Ticket Director: Adam Ziccardi
Assistant Director of Public Relations: Dave Senko

Stadium: Rich Stadium (Capacity 80,020)
Playing Surface: AstroTurf
Stadium Address: One Bills Drive, Orchard Park, NY 14127
Colors: Royal Blue, Scarlet Red & White
Summer Training Camp: Fredonia State University College, Fredonia, NY 14063

BUFFALO BILLS 1984 SCHEDULE

PRE-SEASON

Aug.	4	at Seattle Seahawks	7:30
Aug.	11	NEW ENGLAND PATRIOTS	6:00
Aug.	18	DETROIT LIONS	6:00
Aug.	24	Chicago Bears at Indianapolis	12:00

REGULAR SEASON

Sep.	2	NEW ENGLAND PATRIOTS	1:00
Sep.	9	at St Louis Cardinals	12:00
Sep.	17	MIAMI DOLPHINS	9:00
Sep.	23	NEW YORK JETS	1:00
Sep.	30	at Indianapolis Colts	1:00
Oct.	7	PHILADELPHIA EAGLES	1:00
Oct.	14	at Seattle Seahawks	1:00
Oct.	21	DENVER BRONCOS	1:00
Oct.	28	at Miami Dolphins	4:00
Nov.	4	CLEVELAND BROWNS	1:00
Nov.	11	at New England Patriots	1:00
Nov.	18	DALLAS COWBOYS	1:00
Nov.	25	at Washington Redskins	1:00
Dec.	2	INDIANAPOLIS COLTS	1:00
Dec.	8	at New York Jets	12:30
Dec.	16	at Cincinnati Bengals	1:00

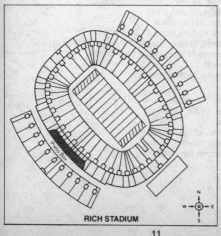

RICH STADIUM

BUFFALO BILLS END OF SEASON DEPTH CHART

OFFENSE

WR	— 81 Perry Tuttle, 89 Julius Dawkins, 80 Jerry Butler*, 88 Mike Mosley*
OLT	— 72 Ken Jones, 67 Darryl Caldwell
OLG	— 51 Jim Ritcher, 65 Tim Vogler
C	— 53 Will Grant, 65 Tim Vogler
ORG	— 73 Jon Borchardt, 65 Tim Vogler
ORT	— 61 Tom Lynch, 63 Justin Cross, 70 Joe Devlin*
TE	— 87 Tony Hunter, 86 Mark Brammer, 84 Buster Barnett
WR	— 82 Frank Lewis, 85 Byron Franklin, Robert Holt*
QB	— 12 Joe Ferguson, 10 Matt Kofler, 11 Joe Dufek
HB	— 20 Joe Cribbs**, 40 Robb Riddick, 23 Van Williams, 25 Roland Hooks*
FB	— 34 Booker Moore, 48 Roosevelt Leaks

DEFENSE

DLE	— 77 Ben Williams, 93 Scott Virkus
NT	— 76 Fred Smerlas, 75 Bill Acker, 99 Mark Roopenian*
DRE	— 91 Ken Johnson, 90 Scott Hutchinson, 83 Sherm White*
LOLB	— 57 Lucius Sanford, 56 Darryl Talley, 41 Phil Villapiano*
LILB	— 52 Chris Keating, 59 Joey Lumpkin, 55 Jim Haslett***
RILB	— 54 Eugene Marve, 58 Mark Merrill
ROLB	— 62 Ervin Parker, 50 Trey Junkin
LCB	— 29 Mario Clark, 43 David Kilson, 27 Chris Williams
SS	— 21 Mike Kennedy, 22 Steve Freeman, Judson Flint, 42 Rod Kush*
FS	— 22 Steve Freeman, 47 Bill Hurley, 27 Chris Williams, 45 Len Waltersheid*
RCB	— 26 Charles Romes, 24 Gary Thompson

SPECIAL TEAMS

K	— 18 Joe Danelo, 7 Greg Cater
P	— 7 Greg Cater, 59 Joey Lumpkin
H	— 10 Matt Kofler
KR	— 23 Van Williams, 40 Robb Riddick
PR	— 40 Robb Riddick, 43 David Kilson
LSN	— 63 Justin Cross, 50 Trey Junkin

BUFFALO BILLS

INDIVIDUAL RUSHERS

	Att	Yards	Avg	Long	TD
Cribbs, Joe	263	1131	4.3	45	3
Moore, Booker	60	275	4.6	21	0
Leaks, Roosevelt	58	157	2.7	12	1
Ferguson, Joe	20	88	4.4	19	0
Hunter, Tony	2	28	14.0	24	0
Kofler, Matt	4	25	6.3	11	0
Riddick, Robb	4	18	4.5	12	0
Williams, Van	3	11	3.7	5	0
Franklin, Byron	1	3	3.0	3	0

Leader based on most yards gained

INDIVIDUAL PASSING

	Att	Comp	% Comp	Yards	Avg Gain	TD	% TD	Long	Int	% Int	Rating Points
Ferguson, Joe	508	281	55.3	2995	5.90	26	5.1	t43	25	4.9	69.3
Kofler, Matt	61	35	57.4	440	7.21	4	6.6	t28	3	4.9	81.3
Cribbs, Joe	2	1	50.0	3	1.50	0	0.0	3	0	0.0	

INDIVIDUAL RECEIVERS

	No	Yards	Avg	Long	TD
Cribbs, Joe	57	524	9.2	t33	7
Lewis, Frank	36	486	13.5	t27	3
Hunter, Tony	36	402	11.2	t40	3
Butler, Jerry	36	385	10.7	25	3
Moore, Booker	34	199	5.9	21	1
Franklin, Byron	30	452	15.1	t43	4
Brammer, Mark	25	215	8.6	21	2
Tuttle, Perry	17	261	15.4	38	3
Mosley, Mike	14	180	12.9	35	3
Dawkins, Julius	11	123	11.2	t28	1
Barnett, Buster	10	94	9.4	14	0
Leaks, Roosevelt	8	74	9.3	12	0
Riddick, Robb	3	43	14.3	24	0

Leader based on most passes caught

INDIVIDUAL INTERCEPTORS

	No	Yards	Avg	Long	TD
Freeman, Steve	3	40	13.3	29	0
Williams, Chris	3	6	2.0	4	0
Sanford, Lucius	2	39	19.5	20	0
Romes, Charles	2	27	13.5	27	0
Keating, Chris	2	20	10.0	17	0
Kennedy, Mike	1	22	22.0	t22	1

Leader based on most interceptions

INDIVIDUAL KICKOFF RETURNERS

	No	Yards	Avg	Long	TD
Williams, Van	22	494	22.5	60	0
Riddick, Robb	28	568	20.3	49	0
Mosley, Mike	9	236	26.2	33	0
Williams, Ben	3	56	18.7	23	0
Talley, Darryl	2	9	4.5	5	0

Leader based on average return

INDIVIDUAL PUNTERS	No	Yards	Long	Avg	Total Punts	TB	Blk	Opp Ret	Ret Yds	In 20	Net Avg
Cater, Greg	89	3533	60	39.7	89	7	0	42	403	24	33.6

INDIVIDUAL PUNT RETURNERS	No	FC	Yards	Avg	Long	TD
Riddick, Robb	42	5	241	5.7	24	0
Hurley, Bill	1	0	0	0.0	0	0
Williams, Van	1	0	0	0.0	0	0

Leader based on average return

INDIVIDUAL SCORERS

KICKERS	XP	XPA	FG	FGA	PTS
Danelo, Joe	33	34	10	20	63

NON-KICKERS	TD	TDR	TDP	TDM	PTS
Cribbs, Joe	10	3	7	0	60
Franklin, Byron	4	0	4	0	24
Butler, Jerry	3	0	3	0	18
Hunter, Tony	3	0	3	0	18
Lewis, Frank	3	0	3	0	18
Mosley, Mike	3	0	3	0	18
Tuttle, Perry	3	0	3	0	18
Brammer, Mark	2	0	2	0	12
Dawkins, Julius	1	0	1	0	6
Kennedy, Mike	1	0	0	1	6
Kilson, David	1	0	0	1	6
Leaks, Roosevelt	1	1	0	0	6
Moore, Booker	1	0	1	0	6

t=Touchdown

CINCINNATI BENGALS

AFC Central Division

Address: 200 Riverfront Stadium, Cincinnati, OH 45202
Telephone: (513) 621 3550

CLUB OFFICIALS
President: John Sawyer
General Manager: Paul E. Brown
Head Coach: Sam Wyche
Assistant Coaches: Hank Bullough, Bruce Coslet, Lindy Infante, Dick LeBeau, Jim McNally, Dick Modzelewski, George Sefcik, Kim Wood
Assistant General Manager: Michael Brown
Business Manager: John Murdough
Director of Public Relations: Allan Heim
Director of Player Personnel: Pete Brown
Ticket Manager: Paul Kelly
Trainer: Marv Pollins
Equipment Manager: Tom Gray

Stadium: Riverfront Stadium (Capacity 59,754)
Playing Surface: AstroTurf
Stadium Address: 200 Riverfront Stadium, Cincinnati, OH 45202
Colors: Black, Orange & White
Summer Training Camp: Wilmington College, Wilmington, OH 45177

CINCINNATI BENGALS 1984 SCHEDULE

PRE-SEASON
Aug.	4	at New York Jets	8:30
Aug.	11	at Tampa Bay Buccaneers	8:00
Aug.	18	at Chicago Bears	6:00
Aug.	24	DETROIT LIONS	7:00

REGULAR SEASON
Sep.	2	at Denver Broncos	12:00
Sep.	9	KANSAS CITY CHIEFS	1:00
Sep.	16	at New York Jets	1:00
Sep.	23	LOS ANGELES RAMS	1:00
Oct.	1	at Pittsburgh Steelers	9:00
Oct.	7	HOUSTON OILERS	4:00
Oct.	14	at New England Patriots	1:00
Oct.	21	CLEVELAND BROWNS	1:00
Oct.	28	at Houston Oilers	12:00
Nov.	4	at San Francisco 49ers	1:00
Nov.	11	PITTSBURGH STEELERS	1:00
Nov.	18	SEATTLE SEAHAWKS	1:00
Nov.	25	ATLANTA FALCONS	1:00
Dec.	2	at Cleveland Browns	1:00
Dec.	9	at New Orleans Saints	12:00
Dec.	16	BUFFALO BILLS	1:00

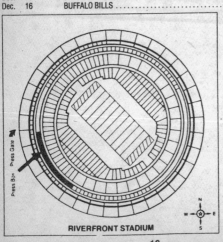

RIVERFRONT STADIUM

CINCINNATI BENGALS END OF SEASON DEPTH CHART

OFFENSE

WR	—	80 Cris Collinsworth, 81 David Verser, 87 Pat McInally
OLT	—	78 Anthony Munoz, 68 Mike Obrovac
OLG	—	62 Dave Lapham**, 68 Mike Obrovac
C	—	64 Dave Rimington, 60 Blake Moore
ORG	—	65 Max Montoya, 68 Mike Obrovac
ORT	—	77 Mike Wilson, 66 Jim Hannula
TE	—	89 Dan Ross**, 82 Rodney Holman, 48 Andy Gibler, 83 M.L. Harris*
WR	—	85 Isaac Curtis, 86 Steve Kreider
QB	—	14 Ken Anderson, 15 Turk Schonert, 11 Jeff Christensen
HB	—	40 Charles Alexander, 23 Rodney Tate, 32 Stanley Wilson, 45 Archie Griffin**
FB	—	46 Pete Johnson, 28 Larry Kinnebrew

DEFENSE

DLE	—	73 Eddie Edwards, 67 Gary Burley
NT	—	61 Jerry Boyarsky, 69 Tim Krumrie, 67 Gary Burley, 70 Emanuel Weaver*
DRE	—	79 Ross Browner, 76 Glen Collins, 67 Gary Burley
LOLB	—	49 Guy Frazier, 52 Tom Dinkel**, 59 Jeff Schuh
LILB	—	55 Jim LeClair**, 51 Rick Razzano, 47 Steve Maidlow
RILB	—	50 Glenn Cameron, 56 Ron Simpkins
ROLB	—	57 Reggie Williams, 52 Tom Dinkel**
LCB	—	34 Louis Breeden, 44 Ray Griffin, 35 Jimmy Turner
SS	—	26 Bobby Kemp, 22 James Griffin
FS	—	37 Robert Jackson, 22 James Griffin, 27 Bryan Hicks*
RCB	—	13 Ken Riley**, 20 Ray Horton, 25 John Simmons

SPECIAL TEAMS

K	—	10 Jim Breech
P	—	87 Pat McInally
H	—	86 Steve Kreider
KR	—	25 John Simmons, 20 Ray Horton
PR	—	25 John Simmons, 20 Ray Horton
LSN	—	66 Jim Hannula, 64 Dave Rimington

CINCINNATI BENGALS

INDIVIDUAL RUSHERS

	Att	Yards	Avg	Long	TD
Johnson, Pete	210	763	3.6	t16	14
Alexander, Charles	153	523	3.4	12	3
Wilson, Stanley	56	267	4.8	18	1
Kinnebrew, Larry	39	156	4.0	17	3
Anderson, Ken	22	147	6.7	29	1
Schonert, Turk	29	117	4.0	15	2
Tate, Rodney	25	77	3.1	13	0
Verser, David	2	31	15.5	29	0
Martin, Mike	2	21	10.5	15	0
Collinsworth, Cris	2	2	1.0	8	0
Kreider, Steve	1	2	2.0	2	0
Christensen, Jeff	1	−2	−2.0	−2	0

Leader based on most yards gained

INDIVIDUAL PASSING

	Att	Comp	% Comp	Yards	Avg Gain	TD	% TD	Long	Int	% Int	Rating Points
Anderson, Ken	297	198	66.7	2333	7.86	12	4.0	t80	13	4.4	85.6
Schonert, Turk	156	92	59.0	1159	7.43	2	1.3	54	5	3.2	73.1
Kreider, Steve	1	0	0.0	0	0.00	0	0.0	0	0	0.0	

INDIVIDUAL RECEIVERS

	No	Yards	Avg	Long	TD
Collinsworth, Cris	66	1130	17.1	63	5
Curtis, Issac	42	571	13.6	t80	2
Kreider, Steve	42	554	13.2	54	1
Ross, Dan	42	483	11.5	30	3
Alexander, Charles	32	187	5.8	14	0
Tate, Rodney	18	142	7.9	25	0
Johnson, Pete	15	129	8.6	18	0
Wilson, Stanley	12	107	8.9	19	1
Harris, M.L.	8	66	8.3	14	2
Verser, David	7	82	11.7	22	0
Martin, Mike	2	22	11.0	12	0
Holman, Rodney	2	15	7.5	10	0
Kinnebrew, Larry	2	4	2.0	2	0

Leader based on most passes caught

INDIVIDUAL INTERCEPTORS

	No	Yards	Avg	Long	TD
Riley, Ken	8	89	11.1	t42	2
Horton, Ray	5	121	24.2	t55	1
Kemp, Bobby	3	26	8.7	26	0
Breeden, Louis	2	47	23.5	39	0
Griffin, Ray	2	24	12.0	24	0
Jackson, Robert	2	21	10.5	15	0
Griffin, James	1	41	41.0	t41	1

Leader based on most interceptions

INDIVIDUAL KICKOFF RETURNERS

	No	Yards	Avg	Long	TD
Simmons, John	14	317	22.6	36	0
Verser, David	13	253	19.5	29	0
Tate, Rodney	13	218	16.8	23	0
Wilson, Stanley	7	161	23.0	32	0
Horton, Ray	5	128	25.6	49	0
Martin, Mike	1	19	19.0	19	0
Dinkel, Tom	1	1	1.0	1	0

Leader based on average return

INDIVIDUAL PUNTERS

	No	Yards	Long	Avg	Total Punts	TB	Blk	Opp Ret	Ret Yds	In 20	Net Avg
McInally, Pat	67	2804	60	41.9	69	9	2	41	310	13	33.5

INDIVIDUAL PUNT RETURNERS

	No	FC	Yards	Avg	Long	TD
Martin, Mike	23	3	227	9.9	19	0
Simmons, John	25	2	173	6.9	43	0
Horton, Ray	1	1	10	10.0	10	0

Leader based on average return

INDIVIDUAL SCORERS

KICKERS	XP	XPA	FG	FGA	PTS
Breech, Jim	39	41	16	23	87

NON-KICKERS	TD	TDR	TDP	TDM	PTS
Johnson, Pete	14	14	0	0	84
Collinsworth, Cris	5	0	5	0	30
Alexander, Charles	3	3	0	0	18
Kinnebrew, Larry	3	3	0	0	18
Ross, Dan	3	0	3	0	18
Curtis, Issac	2	0	2	0	12
Harris, M.L.	2	0	2	0	12
Riley, Ken	2	0	0	2	12
Schonert, Turk	2	2	0	0	12
Wilson, Stanley	2	1	1	0	12
Anderson, Ken	1	1	0	0	6
Griffin, James	1	0	0	1	6
Horton, Ray	1	0	0	1	6
Kreider, Steve	1	0	1	0	6
Williams, Reggie	1	0	0	1	6
Browner, Ross	0	0	0	0	#1

#=Scored extra point
t=Touchdown

CLEVELAND BROWNS

AFC Central Division

Address: Tower B, Cleveland Stadium, Cleveland,
OH 44114
Telephone: (216) 696 5555

CLUB OFFICIALS
President: Arthur B. Modell
Assistant to the President: Ernie Accorsi
Vice President, Legal and Administration: Jim Bailey
Vice President, Finance: Mike Poplar
Director of Operations: Dennis Lynch
Director of Public Relations: Kevin Byrne
Vice President, Head Coach: Sam Rutigliano
Assistant Coaches: Dave Adolph, Joe Daniels, Jim Garrett, Howard Mudd, John Petercuskie, Tom Pratt, Dave Redding, Joe Scannella, Marty Schottenheimer, Larrye Weaver, Darvin Wallace
Director of Player Personnel: Bill Davis
Special Scouts: Dave Beckman, Tom Heckert, Mike Nixon
Film Coordinator: Ed Ulinski
Ticket Manager: Bill Breit
Head Trainer: Bill Tessendorf
Equipment Manager: Charles Cusick

Stadium: Cleveland Stadium (Capacity 80,098)
Playing Surface: Grass
Stadium Address: West 3rd Street, Cleveland, OH 44114
Colors: Seal Brown, Orange & White
Summer Training Camp: Lakeland Community College, Mentor, OH 44060

CLEVELAND BROWNS 1984 SCHEDULE

PRE-SEASON

Aug.	4	PITTSBURGH STEELERS	7:30
Aug.	13	at Los Angeles Rams	7:00
Aug.	18	at Kansas City Chiefs	7:30
Aug.	23	at Philadelphia Eagles	7:00

REGULAR SEASON

Sep.	2	at Seattle Seahawks	1:00
Sep.	9	at Los Angeles Rams	1:00
Sep.	16	DENVER BRONCOS	9:00
Sep.	23	PITTSBURGH STEELERS	1:00
Sep.	30	at Kansas City Chiefs	12:00
Oct.	7	NEW ENGLAND PATRIOTS	1:00
Oct.	14	NEW YORK JETS	1:00
Oct.	21	at Cincinnati Bengals	1:00
Oct.	28	NEW ORLEANS SAINTS	1:00
Nov.	4	at Buffalo Bills	1:00
Nov.	11	SAN FRANCISCO 49ers	1:00
Nov.	18	at Atlanta Falcons	1:00
Nov.	25	HOUSTON OILERS	1:00
Dec.	2	CINCINNATI BENGALS	1:00
Dec.	9	at Pittsburgh Steelers	1:00
Dec.	16	at Houston Oilers	12:00

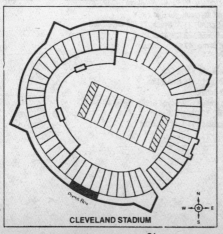

CLEVELAND STADIUM

CLEVELAND BROWNS END OF SEASON DEPTH CHART

OFFENSE

WR	—	80 Willis Adams, 89 Bobby Jones, Duriel Harris
OLT	—	73 Doug Dieken, 75 Bill Contz
OLG	—	68 Robert Jackson, 61 Mike Baab, 74 Paul Farren
C	—	61 Mike Baab, 54 Tom DeLeone, 74 Paul Farren
ORG	—	64 Joe DeLamielleure, 61 Mike Baab
ORT	—	63 Cody Risien, 78 Thomas Hopkins
TE	—	82 Ozzie Newsome, 81 Harry Holt, 87 Tim Stracka
WR	—	85 Dave Logan, 83 Ricky Feacher, 88 Rocky Belk
QB	—	17 Brian Sipe**, 16 Paul McDonald, 12 Rick Trocano, Tom Flick
HB	—	30 Boyce Green, 42 Dwight Walker, 26 Dino Hall, 25 Charles White*
FB	—	43 Mike Pruitt, 38 Johnny Davis

DEFENSE

DLE	—	96 Reggie Camp, 97 Thomas Brown
NT	—	79 Bob Golic, 72 Dave Puzzuoli
DRE	—	94 Elvis Franks, 99 Keith Baldwin, Carl Hairston
LOLB	—	56 Chip Banks, 59 Dale Carver
LILB	—	58 Scott Nicolas, 51 Eddie Johnson, 52 Dick Ambrose*
RILB	—	50 Tom Cousineau, 51 Eddie Johnson
ROLB	—	57 Clay Matthews, 55 Curtis Weathers
LCB	—	48 Lawrence Johnson, 40 Rod Perry
SS	—	49 Clinton Burrell, 31 Al Gross, 22 Clarence Scott
FS	—	21 Mike Whitwell, 22 Clarence Scott
RCB	—	29 Hanford Dixon, 47 Larry Braziel

SPECIAL TEAMS

K	—	9 Matt Bahr, 15 Steve Cox
P	—	7 Jeff Gossett**, 15 Steve Cox
H	—	16 Paul McDonald
KR	—	42 Dwight Walker, 30 Boyce Green, 26 Dino Hall
PR	—	26 Dino Hall, 42 Dwight Walker
LSN	—	58 Scott Nicolas, 54 Tom DeLeone

CLEVELAND BROWNS

INDIVIDUAL RUSHERS

	Att	Yards	Avg	Long	TD
Pruitt, Mike	293	1184	4.0	27	10
Green, Boyce	104	497	4.8	29	3
Walker, Dwight	19	100	5.3	15	0
Sipe, Brian	26	56	2.2	9	0
Davis, Johnny	13	42	3.2	16	0
Jones, Bobby	1	19	19.0	19	0
McDonald, Paul	3	17	5.7	10	0
Holt, Harry	3	8	2.7	4	0
Adams, Willis	1	2	2.0	2	0
Hall, Dino	1	2	2.0	2	0
Belk, Rocky	1	−5	−5.0	−5	0

Leader based on most yards gained

INDIVIDUAL PASSING

	Att	Comp	% Comp	Yards	Avg Gain	TD	% TD	Long	Int	% Int	Rating Points
Sipe, Brian	496	291	58.7	3566	7.19	26	5.2	t66	23	4.6	79.1
McDonald, Paul	68	32	47.1	341	5.01	1	1.5	27	4	5.9	42.6
Walker, Dwight	3	1	33.3	25	8.33	0	0.0	25	1	33.3	

INDIVIDUAL RECEIVERS

	No	Yards	Avg	Long	TD
Newsome, Ozzie	89	970	10.9	t66	6
Logan, Dave	37	627	16.9	34	2
Jones, Bobby	36	507	14.1	t32	4
Pruitt, Mike	30	157	5.2	21	2
Holt, Harry	29	420	14.5	t48	3
Walker, Dwight	29	273	9.4	35	1
Green, Boyce	25	167	6.7	33	1
Adams, Willis	20	374	18.7	59	2
Feacher, Ricky	13	217	16.7	t42	3
Belk, Rocky	5	141	28.2	t64	2
Davis, Johnny	5	20	4.0	10	0
Hall, Dino	4	33	8.3	18	0
Dieken, Doug	1	14	14.0	t14	1
Stracka, Tim	1	12	12.0	12	0

Leader based on most passes caught

INDIVIDUAL INTERCEPTORS

	No	Yards	Avg	Long	TD
Cousineau, Tom	4	47	11.8	15	0
Banks, Chip	3	95	31.7	t65	1
Whitwell, Mike	3	67	22.3	28	0
Dixon, Hanford	3	41	13.7	35	0
Burrell, Clinton	2	0	0.0	0	0
Johnson, Lawrence	2	0	0.0	0	0
Scott, Clarence	2	0	0.0	0	0
Perry, Rod	1	21	21.0	21	0
Gross, Al	1	18	18.0	18	0
Golic, Bob	1	7	7.0	t7	1

Leader based on most interceptions

INDIVIDUAL KICKOFF RETURNERS

	No	Yards	Avg	Long	TD
Walker, Dwight	29	627	21.6	38	0
Green, Boyce	17	350	20.6	30	0
Hall, Dino	11	237	21.5	28	0
Ferguson, Vagas	2	36	18.0	27	0
Nicolas, Scott	2	29	14.5	15	0
Davis, Johnny	1	8	8.0	8	0
Contz, Bill	1	3	3.0	3	0

Leader based on average return

INDIVIDUAL PUNTERS

	No	Yards	Long	Avg	Total Punts	TB	Blk	Opp Ret	Ret Yds	In 20	Net Avg
Gossett, Jeff	70	2854	60	40.8	70	8	0	30	309	17	34.1

INDIVIDUAL PUNT RETURNERS

	No	FC	Yards	Avg	Long	TD
Hall, Dino	39	12	284	7.3	19	0
Walker, Dwight	3	0	26	8.7	13	0

Leader based on average return

INDIVIDUAL SCORERS

KICKERS

	XP	XPA	FG	FGA	PTS
Bahr, Matt	38	40	21	24	101
Cox, Steve	0	0	1	1	3

NON-KICKERS

	TD	TDR	TDP	TDM	PTS
Pruitt, Mike	12	10	2	0	72
Newsome, Ozzie	6	0	6	0	36
Green, Boyce	4	3	1	0	24
Jones, Bobby	4	0	4	0	24
Feacher, Ricky	3	0	3	0	18
Holt, Harry	3	0	3	0	18
Adams, Willis	2	0	2	0	12
Belk, Rocky	2	0	2	0	12
Logan, Dave	2	0	2	0	12
Banks, Chip	1	0	0	1	6
Dieken, Doug	1	0	1	0	6
Golic, Bob	1	0	0	1	6
Walker, Dwight	1	0	1	0	6

t=Touchdown

DENVER BRONCOS

AFC Western Division

Address: 5700 Logan Street, Denver, CO 80216
Telephone: (303) 296 1982

CLUB OFFICIALS

Chairman of the Board: Edgar F. Kaiser, Jr.
General Manager: Hein Poulus
Director of Football Operations: John Beake
Director of Administration: Sandy Waters
Coordinator of College Scouting: Reed Johnson
Coordinator of Combine Scouting: Carroll Hardy
Head Coach: Dan Reeves
Assistant Coaches: Marvin Bass, Joe Collier, John Hadl,
Stan Jones, Myrel Moore, Nick Nicolau, Fran Polsfoot, Dan Radakovich, Charlie West
Director of Public Relations: Charlie Lee
Publicity Director: Jim Saccomano
Treasurer: Robert M. Hurley
Ticket Manager: Gail Stuckey
Equipment Manager: Bill Harpole
Trainer: Steve Antonopulos

Stadium: Denver Mile High Stadium (Capacity 75,103)
Playing Surface: Grass (PAT)
Stadium Address: 1900 West Eliot, Denver, CO 80204
Colors: Orange, Royal Blue & White
Summer Training Camp: University of Northern Colorado, Greeley, CO 80521

DENVER BRONCOS 1984 SCHEDULE

PRE-SEASON

Aug.	4	WASHINGTON REDSKINS	7:00
Aug.	11	SAN FRANCISCO 49ers	7:00
Aug.	18	INDIANAPOLIS COLTS	7:00
Aug.	24	at Atlanta Falcons	8:00

REGULAR SEASON

Sep.	2	CINCINNATI BENGALS	2:00
Sep.	9	at Chicago Bears	12:00
Sep.	16	at Cleveland Browns	9:00
Sep.	23	KANSAS CITY CHIEFS	2:00
Sep.	30	LOS ANGELES RAIDERS	2:00
Oct.	7	at Detroit Lions	1:00
Oct.	15	GREEN BAY PACKERS	7:00
Oct.	21	at Buffalo Bills	1:00
Oct.	28	at Los Angeles Raiders	1:00
Nov.	4	NEW ENGLAND PATRIOTS	2:00
Nov.	11	at San Diego Chargers	1:00
Nov.	18	MINNESOTA VIKINGS	2:00
Nov.	25	SEATTLE SEAHAWKS	2:00
Dec.	2	at Kansas City Chiefs	12:00
Dec.	9	SAN DIEGO CHARGERS	2:00
Dec.	15	at Seattle Seahawks	1:00

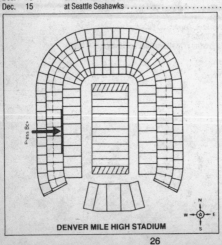

DENVER MILE HIGH STADIUM

26

DENVER BRONCOS END OF SEASON DEPTH CHART

OFFENSE

WR	— 84 Clinton Sampson, 82 Zac Thomas, 80 Rick Upchurch*
OLT	— 70 Dave Studdard, 67 Keith Uecker
OLG	— 54 Keith Bishop, 62 Tom Glassic**, 73 Shawn Hollingsworth*
C	— 64 Bill Bryan, 54 Keith Bishop
ORG	— 60 Paul Howard, 63 Mark Cooper
ORT	— 76 Ken Lanier, 74 Jerry Baker
TE	— 85 Ron Egloff, 83 John Sawyer, 88 Riley Odoms**, 87 Jim Wright*, 89 Dean Barnett*, 41 Rob Lytle*, Eason Ramson
WR	— 81 Steve Watson, 82 Zac Thomas
QB	— 17 Steve DeBerg, 7 John Elway, 8 Gary Kubiak
RB	— 23 Sammy Winder, 47 Gerald Willhite, 46 Dave Preston
RB	— 34 Nathan Poole, 39 Jesse Myles, 24 Rick Parros*

DEFENSE

DLE	— 79 Barney Chavous, 66 Brison Manor, 65 Walt Bowyer
NT	— 68 Rubin Carter, 72 Don Latimer**, 78 Rich Stachowski
DRE	— 75 Rulon Jones, 66 Brison Manor, 77 Karl Mecklenburg
LOLB	— 50 Jim Ryan, 59 Darren Comeaux, 51 Bob Swenson*
LILB	— 58 Steve Busick, 55 Rick Dennison
RILB	— 53 Randy Gradishar**, 58 Steve Busick, Stan Blinka
ROLB	— 57 Tom Jackson, 52 Ken Woodard
LCB	— 20 Louis Wright, 28 Roger Jackson, 29 Wilbur Myers
SS	— 49 Dennis Smith, 21 Myron Dupree
FS	— 43 Steve Foley, 28 Roger Jackson, 37 Steve Trimble**
RCB	— 31 Mike Harden, 45 Steve Wilson

SPECIAL TEAMS

K	— 3 Rich Karlis
P	— 11 Luke Prestridge
H	— 11 Luke Prestridge, 8 Gary Kubiak
KR	— 82 Zac Thomas, 45 Steve Wilson
PR	— 82 Zac Thomas, 45 Steve Wilson, 80 Rick Upchurch*
LSN	— 54 Keith Bishop, 64 Bill Bryan

DENVER BRONCOS

INDIVIDUAL RUSHERS

	Att	Yards	Avg	Long	TD
Winder, Sammy	196	757	3.9	52	3
Poole, Nathan	81	246	3.0	19	4
Preston, Dave	57	222	3.9	28	1
Willhite, Gerald	43	188	4.4	t24	3
Elway, John	28	146	5.2	23	1
Parros, Rick	30	96	3.2	13	1
Myles, Jesse	8	52	6.5	16	0
DeBerg, Steve	13	28	2.2	11	1
Upchurch, Rick	6	19	3.2	9	1
Kubiak, Gary	4	17	4.3	8	1
Watson, Steve	3	17	5.7	10	0
Prestridge, Luke	1	7	7.0	7	0
Wright, James	1	−11	−11.0	−11	0

Leader based on most yards gained

INDIVIDUAL PASSING

	Att	Comp	% Comp	Yards	Avg Gain	TD	% TD	Long	Int	% Int	Rating Points
DeBerg, Steve	215	119	55.3	1617	7.52	9	4.2	54	7	3.3	79.9
Elway, John	259	123	47.5	1663	6.42	7	2.7	t49	14	5.4	54.9
Kubiak, Gary	22	12	54.5	186	8.45	1	4.5	t78	1	4.5	79.0
Upchurch, Rick	2	0	0.0	0	0.00	0	0.0	0	0	0.0	
Willhite, Gerald	1	0	0.0	0	0.00	0	0.0	0	0	0.0	

INDIVIDUAL RECEIVERS

	No	Yards	Avg	Long	TD
Watson, Steve	59	1133	19.2	t78	5
Upchurch, Rick	40	639	16.0	40	2
Winder, Sammy	23	150	6.5	17	0
Egloff, Ron	20	205	10.3	32	2
Poole, Nathan	20	184	9.2	23	0
Preston, Dave	17	137	8.1	25	1
Willhite, Gerald	14	153	10.9	t26	1
Wright, James	13	134	10.3	23	0
Thomas, Zack	12	182	15.2	44	0
Parros, Rick	12	126	10.5	t33	1
Sampson, Clinton	10	200	20.0	t49	2
Myles, Jesse	7	119	17.0	33	1
Odoms, Riley	4	62	15.5	21	0
Sawyer, John	3	42	14.0	17	0

Leader based on most passes caught

INDIVIDUAL INTERCEPTORS

	No	Yards	Avg	Long	TD
Wright, Louis	6	50	8.3	34	0
Wilson, Steve	5	91	18.2	36	0
Foley, Steve	5	28	5.6	16	0
Harden, Mike	4	127	31.8	48	0
Smith, Dennis	4	39	9.8	23	0
Jackson, Roger	1	15	15.0	15	0
Gradishar, Randy	1	5	5.0	5	0
Jackson, Tom	1	0	0.0	0	0

Leader based on most interceptions

INDIVIDUAL KICKOFF RETURNERS

	No	Yards	Avg	Long	TD
Thomas, Zack	28	573	20.5	42	0
Wilson, Steve	24	485	20.2	32	0
Studdard, Dave	2	8	4.0	8	0
Harden, Mike	1	9	9.0	9	0
Jackson, Tom	1	2	2.0	2	0

Leader based on average return

INDIVIDUAL PUNTERS

	No	Yards	Long	Avg	Total Punts	TB	Blk	Opp Ret	Ret Yds	In 20	Net Avg
Prestridge, Luke	87	3620	60	41.6	87	7	0	55	524	19	34.0

INDIVIDUAL PUNT RETURNERS

	No	FC	Yards	Avg	Long	TD
Thomas, Zack	33	9	368	11.2	t70	1
Upchurch, Rick	4	1	52	13.0	17	0
Wright, Louis	1	0	0	0.0	0	0

Leader based on average return

INDIVIDUAL SCORERS

KICKERS	XP	XPA	FG	FGA	PTS
Karlis, Rich	33	34	21	25	96

NON-KICKERS	TD	TDR	TDP	TDM	PTS
Watson, Steve	5	0	5	0	30
Poole, Nathan	4	4	0	0	24
Willhite, Gerald	4	3	1	0	24
Parros, Rick	3	1	2	0	18
Sampson, Clinton	3	0	3	0	18
Winder, Sammy	3	3	0	0	18
Egloff, Ron	2	0	2	0	12
Preston, Dave	2	1	1	0	12
Upchurch, Rick	2	0	2	0	12
Chavous, Barney	1	0	0	1	6
DeBerg, Steve	1	1	0	0	6
Elway, John	1	1	0	0	6
Kubiak, Gary	1	1	0	0	6
Myles, Jesse	1	0	1	0	6
Thomas, Zack	1	0	0	1	6
Jones, Rulon	0	0	0	0	*2

*=Safety
t=Touchdown

HOUSTON OILERS

AFC Central Division

Address: Box 1516, Houston, TX 77251-1516
Telephone: (713) 797 9111

CLUB OFFICIALS
Owner/President: K.S. 'Bud' Adams, Jr.
Executive Vice-President/General Manager: Ladd K. Herzeg
Vice President, Player Personnel: Mike Holovak
Director of Administration: Rick Nichols
Media Relations Director: Bob Hyde
Marketing/Media Relations Assistant: Gregg Stengel
Controller: Marilan Logan
Ticket Manager: David Fuqua
Head Coach: Hugh Campbell
Offensive Coordinator: O. Kay Dalton
Defensive Coordinator: Jerry Glanville
Receivers: Bruce Lemmerman
Offensive Line: Bill Walsh
Offensive Backs: Al Roberts
Defensive Line: Bob Padilla
Linebackers: John Devlin
Defensive Backs: Ken Houston
Special Teams: Gene Gaines
Scouts: Bill Bell, C.O. Brocato, Dub Fesperman, Bill Young
Coordinator/Pro Scouting: Walt Schlinkman
Strength and Conditioning: Bill Allerheiligen
Head Trainer: Jerry Meins
Assistant Trainer: Joel Krekelberg
Equipment Manager: Gordon Batty
Equipment Assistant: Bill Lackey

Stadium: Astrodome (Capacity 50,496)
Playing Surface: AstroTurf
Stadium Address: Loop 610, Kirby and Fannin Streets, Houston, TX 77202
Colors: Columbia Blue, Scarlet & White
Summer Training Camp: Angelo State University, San Angelo, TX 76901

HOUSTON OILERS 1984 SCHEDULE

PRE-SEASON

Aug.	4	at Tampa Bay Buccaneers	8:00
Aug.	11	NEW YORK JETS	8:00
Aug.	18	NEW ORLEANS SAINTS	8:00
Aug.	25	at Dallas Cowboys	8:00

REGULAR SEASON

Sep.	2	LOS ANGELES RAIDERS	3:00
Sep.	9	INDIANAPOLIS COLTS	3:00
Sep.	16	at San Diego Chargers	1:00
Sep.	23	at Atlanta Falcons	1:00
Sep.	30	NEW ORLEANS SAINTS	3:00
Oct.	7	at Cincinnati Bengals	4:00
Oct.	14	at Miami Dolphins	1:00
Oct.	21	SAN FRANCISCO 49ers	3:00
Oct.	28	CINCINNATI BENGALS	12:00
Nov.	4	at Pittsburgh Steelers	1:00
Nov.	11	at Kansas City Chiefs	12:00
Nov.	18	NEW YORK JETS	3:00
Nov.	25	at Cleveland Browns	1:00
Dec.	2	PITTSBURGH STEELERS	12:00
Dec.	9	at Los Angeles Rams	1:00
Dec.	16	CLEVELAND BROWNS	12:00

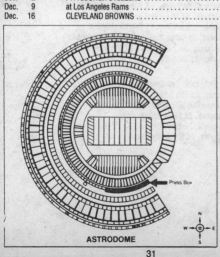

Press Box

ASTRODOME

HOUSTON OILERS END OF SEASON DEPTH CHART

OFFENSE

WR	—	81 Steve Bryant, 86 Herkie Walls, 82 Mike Renfro**
OLT	—	77 Doug France, 76 Morris Towns, 62 John Schuhmacher*
OLG	—	63 Mike Munchak, 66 Pat Howell
C	—	58 David Carter, 68 Les Studdard
ORG	—	74 Bruce Matthews, 66 Pat Howell
ORT	—	73 Harvey Salem, 76 Morris Towns
TE	—	88 Chris Dressel, 89 Mike McCloskey, 87 Walt Arnold
WR	—	83 Tim Smith, 84 Mike Holston, Butch Johnson
QB	—	10 Oliver Luck, 14 Gifford Nielsen, 12 Brian Ramson, Warren Moon
RB	—	30 Larry Moriarty, 35 Stan Edwards
RB	—	34 Earl Campbell, 40 Donnie Craft, 45 Dwayne Crutchfield**

DEFENSE

DLE	—	90 Bob Hamm, 70 Malcolm Taylor**, 71 Ken Kennard*
MG	—	72 Brian Sochia, 67 Mike Stensrud, 79 Wilson Whitley*
DRE	—	75 Jesse Baker, 78 Jerome Foster, 65 Elvin Bethea**
LOLB	—	53 Avon Riley, 57 Tim Joiner
LILB	—	54 Gregg Bingham, 51 Ted Thompson
RILB	—	50 Daryl Hunt, Kevin Turner, 56 Robert Abraham*
ROLB	—	52 Robert Brazile, 57 Tim Joiner
LCB	—	24 Steve Brown, 22 Bill Kay, 21 Derrick Hatchett
SS	—	25 Keith Bostic, 36 Carter Hartwig, 26 Darryl Meadows
FS	—	36 Carter Hartwig, 33 J.C. Wilson, 37 Mike Reinfeldt*
RCB	—	20 Willie Tullis, 23 Greg Hill

SPECIAL TEAMS

K	—	4 Florian Kempf, 51 Ted Thompson
P	—	6John James, 83 Tim Smith
H	—	6 John James, 14 Gifford Nielsen
KR	—	85 Carl Roaches, 24 Steve Brown
PR	—	85 Carl Roaches, 24 Steve Brown
LSN	—	58 David Carter, 74 Bruce Matthews

HOUSTON OILERS

INDIVIDUAL RUSHERS

	Att	Yards	Avg	Long	TD
Campbell, Earl	322	1301	4.0	42	12
Crutchfield, Dwayne, Jets-Hou.	140	578	4.1	17	3
Moriarty, Larry	65	321	4.9	80	3
Craft, Donald	55	147	2.7	8	0
Luck, Oliver	17	55	3.2	17	0
Walls, Herkie	5	44	8.8	14	0
Nielsen, Gifford	8	43	5.4	20	0
Edwards, Stan	16	40	2.5	9	0
Smith, Tim	2	16	8.0	9	0
Allen, Gary	1	5	5.0	5	0
Dressel, Chris	1	3	3.0	3	0
Renfro, Mike	1	3	3.0	3	0
Brown, Curtis	3	0	0.0	t1	1
James, John	1	0	0.0	0	0

Leader based on most yards gained

INDIVIDUAL PASSING

	Att	Comp	% Comp	Yards	Avg Gain	TD	% TD	Long	Int	% Int	Rating Points
Luck, Oliver	217	124	57.1	1375	6.34	8	3.7	66	13	6.0	63.4
Nielsen, Gifford	175	90	51.4	1125	6.43	5	2.9	48	8	4.6	62.2
Manning, Archie	88	44	50.0	755	8.58	2	2.3	t47	8	9.1	49.2
Bryant, Steve	1	1	100.0	24	24.00	1	100.0	t24	0	0.0	
James, John	1	1	100.0	7	7.00	0	0.0	7	0	0.0	

INDIVIDUAL RECEIVERS

	No	Yards	Avg	Long	TD
Smith, Tim	83	1176	14.2	t47	6
Dressel, Chris	32	316	9.9	t35	4
Renfro, Mike	23	316	13.7	t38	2
Campbell, Earl	19	216	11.4	66	0
Bryant, Steve	16	211	13.2	26	0
McCloskey, Mike	16	137	8.6	20	1
Holston, Michael	14	205	14.6	43	0
Walls, Herkie	12	276	23.0	48	1
Arnold, Walt	12	137	11.4	37	1
Craft, Donald	12	99	8.3	14	0
Edwards, Stan	9	79	8.8	20	1
Moriarty, Larry	4	32	8.0	12	0
Kempf, Florian	1	7	7.0	7	0

Leader based on most passes caught

INDIVIDUAL INTERCEPTORS

	No	Yards	Avg	Long	TD
Tullis, Willie	5	65	13.0	44	0
Kay, Bill	2	31	15.5	27	0
Bostic, Keith	2	0	0.0	0	0
Reinfeldt, Mike	1	19	19.0	19	0
Brown, Steve	1	16	16.0	16	0
Bingham, Gregg	1	4	4.0	4	0
Abraham, Robert	1	0	0.0	0	0
Riley, Avon	1	0	0.0	0	0

Leader based on most interceptions

P.A.F.A. 84/85.—2

INDIVIDUAL KICKOFF RETURNERS

	No	Yards	Avg	Long	TD
Brown, Steve	31	795	25.6	t93	1
Roaches, Carl	34	641	18.9	t97	1
Walls, Herkie	9	110	12.2	25	0
Dressel, Chris	4	40	10.0	13	0
Moriarty, Larry	2	25	12.5	16	0
Tullis, Willie	1	16	16.0	16	0
Hunt, Daryl	1	12	12.0	12	0
McCloskey, Mike	1	11	11.0	11	0
Riley, Avon	0	26	---	26	0

Leader based on average return

INDIVIDUAL PUNTERS

	No	Yards	Long	Avg	Total Punts	TB	Blk	Opp Ret	Ret Yds	In 20	Net Avg
James, John	79	3136	53	39.7	80	8	1	47	354	12	32.8

INDIVIDUAL PUNT RETURNERS

	No	FC	Yards	Avg	Long	TD
Roaches, Carl	20	9	159	8.0	23	0

INDIVIDUAL SCORERS

KICKERS	XP	XPA	FG	FGA	PTS
Kempf, Florian	33	34	17	21	84

NON-KICKERS	TD	TDR	TDP	TDM	PTS
Campbell, Earl	12	12	0	0	72
Smith, Tim	6	0	6	0	36
Dressel, Chris	4	0	4	0	24
Moriarty, Larry	3	3	0	0	18
Renfro, Mike	2	0	2	0	12
Arnold, Walt	1	0	1	0	6
Brown, Curtis	1	1	0	0	6
Brown, Steve	1	0	0	1	6
Edwards, Stan	1	0	1	0	6
McCloskey, Mike	1	0	1	0	6
Roaches, Carl	1	0	0	1	6
Walls, Herkie	1	0	1	0	6

t=*Touchdown*

INDIANAPOLIS COLTS
(formerly Baltimore Colts)

AFC Eastern Division

Address: P.O. Box 20000, Indianapolis, IN 46220
Telephone: (317) 252 2658

CLUB OFFICIALS
President-Treasurer: Robert Irsay
Vice President-General Manager: James Irsay
Vice President-General Counsel: Michael G. Chernoff
Assistant General Manager: Bob Terpening
Director of Player Personnel: Jack Bushofsky
Director of College Scouting: Clyde Powers
Controller: Joe Dezelan
Director of Operations: Pete Ward
Director of Public Relations: Bob Walters
Assistant Director of Public Relations: Bob Eller
Purchasing Administrator: David Filer
Head Coach: Frank Kush
Equipment Manager: Jon Scott
Assistant Equipment Manager: John Starliper
Cheerleader Director: Meg Irsay

Stadium: Hoosier Dome (Capacity 61,000)
Playing Surface: Astro Turf
Stadium Address: 100 South Capitol Avenue, Indianapolis, IN 46225
Colors: Royal Blue, White & Silver
Summer Training Camp: Anderson College, Anderson, IN 46011

INDIANAPOLIS COLTS 1984 SCHEDULE

PRE-SEASON

Aug.	4	at Miami Dolphins	8:00
Aug.	11	NEW YORK GIANTS	7:00
Aug.	18	at Denver Broncos	7:00
Aug.	25	at Green Bay Packers	7:00

REGULAR SEASON

Sep.	2	NEW YORK JETS	4:00
Sep.	9	at Houston Oilers	3:00
Sep.	16	ST LOUIS CARDINALS	1:00
Sep.	23	at Miami Dolphins	4:00
Sep.	30	BUFFALO BILLS	1:00
Oct.	7	WASHINGTON REDSKINS	1:00
Oct.	14	at Philadelphia Eagles	1:00
Oct.	21	PITTSBURGH STEELERS	1:00
Oct.	28	at Dallas Cowboys	12:00
Nov.	4	SAN DIEGO CHARGERS	1:00
Nov.	11	at New York Jets	1:00
Nov.	18	NEW ENGLAND PATRIOTS	1:00
Nov.	25	at Los Angeles Raiders	1:00
Dec.	2	at Buffalo Bills	1:00
Dec.	9	MIAMI DOLPHINS	1:00
Dec.	16	at New England Patriots	1:00

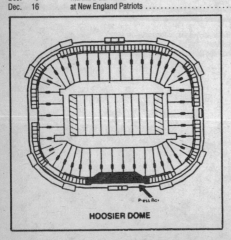

Press Box

HOOSIER DOME

INDIANAPOLIS COLTS END OF SEASON DEPTH CHART

OFFENSE

WR	—	87 Tracy Porter, 84 Victor Oatis, 85 Matt Bouza*, Phil Smith*
OLT	—	72 Karl Baldischwiler, 74 Sid Abramowitz
OLG	—	75 Chris Hinton, 64 Ben Utt, 50 Grant Feasel
C	—	53 Ray Donaldson, 50 Grant Feasel
ORG	—	64 Ben Utt, 73,Steve Wright, 50 Grant Feasel
ORT	—	68 Jeff Hart**, 79 Lindsey Mason**, 76 Jim Mills*
TE	—	83 Tim Sherwin, 81 Pat Beach, 86 Dave Young
WR	—	88 Bernard Henry, 21 Aundra Thompson, 80 Ray Butler*
QB	—	18 Mike Pagel, 9 Mark Herrmann, 8 Mark Reed, 12 Jim Bob Taylor, 10 Art Schlichter****
HB	—	33 Curtis Dickey, 23 Alvin Moore, 20 Rick Porter
FB	—	32 Randy McMillan, 39 Newton Williams

DEFENSE

DLE	—	99 Donnell Thompson, 90 Mark Bell
NT	—	69 Leo Wisniewski, 97 Quinton Ballard
DRE	—	78 Steve Parker, 71 Henry Waechter
LOLB	—	52 Greg Bracelin, 54 Sanders Shiver
LILB	—	98 Johnie Cooks, 49 Cliff Odom
RILB	—	55 Barry Krauss, 60 Gary Padjen
ROLB	—	56 Vernon Maxwell, 51 Ricky Jones
LCB	—	45 Jim Burroughs, 44 Kendall Williams
SS	—	30 Larry Anderson, 34 Jeff Delaney**, 29 Mark Kafentzis
FS	—	25 Nesby Glasgow, 26 Kim Anderson
RCB	—	35 Tate Randle, 44 Kendall Williams

SPECIAL TEAMS

K	—	2 Raul Allegre
P	—	3 Rohn Stark
H	—	3 Rohn Stark, 18 Mike Pagel
KR	—	30 Larry Anderson, 44 Kendall Williams
PR	—	30 Larry Anderson, 44 Kendall Williams
LSN	—	81 Pat Beach, 53 Ray Donaldson

INDIANAPOLIS COLTS

INDIVIDUAL RUSHERS

	Att	Yards	Avg	Long	TD
Dickey, Curtis	254	1122	4.4	56	4
McMillan, Randy	198	802	4.1	t39	5
Pagel, Mike	54	441	8.2	33	0
Moore, Alvin	57	205	3.6	13	1
Williams, Newton	28	77	2.8	13	0
Reed, Mark	2	27	13.5	18	0
Stark, Rohn	1	8	8.0	8	0
Herrmann, Mark	1	0	0.0	0	0
Krauss, Barry	1	−1	−1.0	−1	0

Leader based on most yards gained

INDIVIDUAL PASSING

	Att	Comp	% Comp	Yards	Avg Gain	TD	% TD	Long	Int	% Int	Rating Points
Pagel, Mike	328	163	49.7	2353	7.17	12	3.7	t72	17	5.2	64.0
Herrmann, Mark	36	18	50.0	256	7.11	0	0.0	35	3	8.3	38.7
Reed, Mark	10	6	60.0	34	3.40	0	0.0	16	1	10.0	26.7
Taylor, Jim Bob	2	1	50.0	20	10.00	0	0.0	20	1	50.0	
Stark, Rohn	1	0	0.0	0	0.00	0	0.0	0	0	0.0	

INDIVIDUAL RECEIVERS

	No	Yards	Avg	Long	TD
Henry, Bernard	30	416	13.9	t40	4
Porter, Tracy	28	384	13.7	38	0
Bouza, Matt	25	385	15.4	26	0
Sherwin, Tim	25	358	14.3	30	0
Dickey, Curtis	24	483	20.1	t72	3
McMillan, Randy	24	195	8.1	27	1
Butler, Raymond	10	207	20.7	60	3
Oatis, Victor	6	93	15.5	25	0
Moore, Alvin	6	38	6.3	16	0
Beach, Pat	5	56	11.2	16	1
Williams, Newton	4	46	11.5	19	0
Dixon, Zachary	1	2	2.0	2	0

Leader based on most passes caught

INDIVIDUAL INTERCEPTORS

	No	Yards	Avg	Long	TD
Hatchett, Derrick	4	36	9.0	25	0
Glasgow, Nesby	3	35	11.7	18	0
Anderson, Kim	2	81	40.5	t71	1
Bracelin, Greg	2	19	9.5	19	0
Delaney, Jeff	2	16	8.0	11	0
Burroughs, Jim	2	8	4.0	8	0
Randle, Tate	1	41	41.0	41	0
Williams, Kendall	1	32	32.0	18	0
Maxwell, Vernon	1	31	31.0	31	0
Cooks, Johnie	1	15	15.0	15	0
Anderson, Larry	1	0	0.0	0	0

Leader based on most interceptions

INDIVIDUAL KICKOFF RETURNERS

	No	Yards	Avg	Long	TD
Williams, Kendall	20	490	24.5	90	0
Porter, Ricky	18	340	18.9	28	0
Anderson, Larry	18	309	17.2	26	0
Moore, Alvin	2	40	20.0	23	0
Beach, Pat	1	0	0.0	0	0
Bouza, Matt	1	−4	−4.0	−4	0

Leader based on average return

INDIVIDUAL PUNTERS

	No	Yards	Long	Avg	Total Punts	TB	Blk	Opp Ret	Ret Yds	In 20	Net Avg
Stark, Rohn	91	4124	68	45.3	91	9	0	55	642	20	36.3

INDIVIDUAL PUNT RETURNERS

	No	FC	Yards	Avg	Long	TD
Anderson, Larry	20	4	138	6.9	20	0
Porter, Ricky	14	5	104	7.4	50	0
Williams, Kendall	9	4	43	4.8	13	0
Glasgow, Nesby	1	1	9	9.0	9	0

Leader based on average return

INDIVIDUAL SCORERS

KICKERS	XP	XPA	FG	FGA	PTS
Allegre, Raul	22	24	30	35	112

NON-KICKERS	TD	TDR	TDP	TDM	PTS
Dickey, Curtis	7	4	3	0	42
McMillan, Randy	6	5	1	0	36
Henry, Bernard	4	0	4	0	24
Butler, Raymond	3	0	3	0	18
Anderson, Kim	1	0	0	1	6
Anderson, Larry	1	0	0	1	6
Beach, Pat	1	0	1	0	6
Cooks, Johnie	1	0	0	1	6
Moore, Alvin	1	1	0	0	6
Thompson, Donnell	0	0	0	0	*2

*=Safety
t=Touchdown

KANSAS CITY CHIEFS

AFC Western Division

Address: One Arrowhead Drive, Kansas City, MO 64129
Telephone: (816) 924 9300

CLUB OFFICIALS
Owner: Lamar Hunt
President: Jack Steadman
Vice President and General Manager: Jim Schaaf
Head Coach: John Mackovic
Assistant Coaches: Bud Carson, Walt Corey, Dan Daniel,
Doug Graber, J.D. Helm, C.T. Hewgley, Rod Humeniuk,
Pete McCulley, Willie Peete, Jim Vechiarella, Richard Williamson
Director of Player Personnel: Les Miller
Director of Research and Development: Ron Waller
Treasurer: Roger Peyton
Secretary: Jim Siegfried
Manager of Administration: Don Steadman
Stadium Manager: Bob Wachter
Ticket Manager: Joe Mazza
Public Relations Director: Bob Sprenger
Assistant Director of Public Relations: Gary Heise
Promotions Director: Russ Cline
Director of Sales: David Smith
Trainer: Wayne Rudy
Assistant Trainer: Dave Kendall
Equipment Coordinator: Jon Phillips

Stadium: Arrowhead (Capacity 78,067)
Playing Surface: Tartan Turf
Stadium Address: One Arrowhead Drive, Arrowhead Stadium, Kansas City, MO 64129
Colors: Red, Gold & White
Summer Training Camp: William Jewell College, Liberty, MO 64068

KANSAS CITY CHIEFS 1984 SCHEDULE

PRE-SEASON

Aug.	4	NEW ORLEANS SAINTS	7:30
Aug.	10	at St Louis Cardinals	7:30
Aug.	18	CLEVELAND BROWNS	7:30
Aug.	24	at New England Patriots	7:30

REGULAR SEASON

Sep.	2	at Pittsburgh Steelers	1:00
Sep.	9	at Cincinnati Bengals	1:00
Sep.	16	LOS ANGELES RAIDERS	12:00
Sep.	23	at Denver Broncos	2:00
Sep.	30	CLEVELAND BROWNS	12:00
Oct.	7	NEW YORK JETS	12:00
Oct.	14	SAN DIEGO CHARGERS	12:00
Oct.	21	at New York Jets	4:00
Oct.	28	TAMPA BAY BUCCANEERS	12:00
Nov.	4	at Seattle Seahawks	1:00
Nov.	11	HOUSTON OILERS	12:00
Nov.	18	at Los Angeles Raiders	1:00
Nov.	25	at New York Giants	1:00
Dec.	2	DENVER BRONCOS	12:00
Dec.	9	SEATTLE SEAHAWKS	12:00
Dec.	16	at San Diego Chargers	1:00

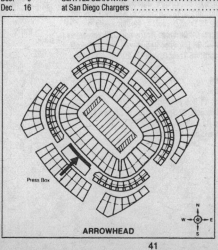

Press Box

N
W ✦ E
S

ARROWHEAD

KANSAS CITY CHIEFS END OF SEASON DEPTH CHART

OFFENSE
WR   — 88 Carlos Carson, 83 Stephone Paige, 86 J.T. Smith
OLT   — 60 Matt Herkenhoff, 77 Rich Baldinger, 70 Jim Rourke
OLG   — 66 Brad Budde, 73 Bob Simmons**, 64 Mark Kirchner
C   — 53 Bob Rush, 62 Adam Lingner
ORG   — 73 Bob Simmons**, 75 Ellis Gardner, 65 Tom Condon*
ORT   — 72 David Lutz, 77 Rich Baldinger, 75 Ellis Gardner
TE   — 85 Ed Beckman, 81 Willie Scott, 87 Ron Wetzel
WR   — 82 Anthony Hancock, 83 Stephone Paige, 89 Henry Marshall*
QB   — 9 Bill Kenney, 14 Todd Blackledge, 11 Bob Gagliano**
HB   — 27 Theotis Brown, 42 Lawrence Ricks, 31 Jewerl Thomas
FB   — 43 Billy Jackson, 35 Ken Thomas*, Ken Lacy

DEFENSE
DLE   — 67 Art Still, 71 Dave Lindstrom
NT   — 74 Dino Mangiero, 91 Ken Kremer, Ray Yakavonis
DRE   — 99 Mike Bell, 79 Dean Prater, 71 Dave Lindstrom
LOLB   — 52 Thomas Howard, 50 Calvin Daniels, Ken McAlister
LILB   — 57 Jerry Blanton, 58 Steve Potter, 55 Dave Klug*, 54 James Walker*
RILB   — 59 Gary Spani, 61 John Zamberlin, 58 Steve Potter
ROLB   — 51 Charles Jackson, 50 Calvin Daniels, 56 Louis Haynes*
LCB   — 24 Gary Green, 45 Trent Bryant**, 22 Van Jakes
SS   — 34 Lloyd Burruss, 38 Durwood Roquemore, 22 Van Jakes
FS   — 20 Deron Cherry, 38 Durwood Roquemore, Isaac Metcalf
RCB   — 23 Lucious Smith, 45 Trent Bryant**, 29 Albert Lewis

SPECIAL TEAMS
K   — 8 Nick Lowery
P   — 6 Jim Arnold
H   — 9 Bill Kenney, 11 Bob Gagliano**
KR   — 82 Anthony Hancock, 27 Theotis Brown, 35 Ken Thomas*
PR   — 86 J.T. Smith, 82 Anthony Hancock
LSN   — 62 Adam Lingner, 53 Bob Rush

KANSAS CITY CHIEFS

INDIVIDUAL RUSHERS

	Att	Yards	Avg	Long	TD
Jackson, Billy	152	499	3.3	19	2
Brown, Theotis, Sea.-K.C.	130	481	3.7	t49	8
Thomas, Jewerl	44	115	2.6	11	0
Kenney, Bill	23	59	2.6	11	3
Thomas, Ken	15	55	3.7	28	0
Ricks, Lawrence	21	28	1.3	10	0
Carson, Carlos	2	20	10.0	18	0
Hadnot, James	4	10	2.5	7	0
Scott, Willie	1	1	1.0	1	0
Blackledge, Todd	1	0	0.0	0	0

Leader based on most yards gained

INDIVIDUAL PASSING

	Att	Comp	% Comp	Yards	Avg Gain	TD	% TD	Long	Int	% Int	Rating Points
Kenney, Bill	603	346	57.4	4348	7.21	24	4.0	53	18	3.0	80.8
Blackledge, Todd	34	20	58.8	259	7.62	3	8.8	43	0	0.0	112.3
Carson, Carlos	1	1	100.0	48	48.0	1	100.0	t48	0	0.0	
Brown, Theotis	1	1	100.0	11	11.00	0	0.0	11	0	0.0	
Thomas, Jewerl	2	1	50.0	18	9.0	1	50.0	t18	1	50.0	
Marshall, Henry	0	0	----	0	----	0	----	0	0	----	

INDIVIDUAL RECEIVERS

	No	Yards	Avg	Long	TD
Carson, Carlos	80	1351	16.9	t50	7
Marshall, Henry	50	788	15.8	52	6
Hancock, Anthony	37	584	15.8	50	1
Jackson, Billy	32	243	7.6	29	0
Paige, Stephone	30	528	17.6	43	6
Scott, Willie	29	247	8.5	22	6
Thomas, Ken	28	236	8.4	25	1
Beckman, Ed	13	130	10.0	20	0
Thomas, Jewerl	10	51	5.1	9	0
Smith, J.T.	7	85	12.1	18	0
Ricks, Lawrence	3	5	1.7	7	0
Hadnot, James	2	18	9.0	16	0
Kenney, Bill	1	0	0.0	0	0

Leader based on most passes caught

INDIVIDUAL INTERCEPTORS

	No	Yards	Avg	Long	TD
Cherry, Deron	7	100	14.3	41	0
Green, Gary	6	59	9.8	25	0
Roquemore, Durwood	4	117	29.3	t42	1
Burruss, Lloyd	4	46	11.5	27	0
Lewis, Albert	4	42	10.5	34	0
Smith, Lucious	3	99	33.0	t58	1
Bryant, Trent	1	19	19.0	19	0
Potter, Steve	1	0	0.0	0	0

Leader based on most interceptions

INDIVIDUAL KICKOFF RETURNERS

	No	Yards	Avg	Long	TD
Hancock, Anthony	29	515	17.8	33	0
Brown, Theotis	15	301	20.1	46	0
Roquemore, Durwood	3	36	12.0	13	0
Cherry, Deron	2	54	27.0	31	0
Carson, Carlos	1	12	12.0	12	0
Thomas, Ken	1	6	6.0	6	0
Smith, J.T.	1	5	5.0	5	0
Daniels, Calvin	1	0	0.0	0	0
Lindstrom, Dave	1	0	0.0	0	0
Burruss, Lloyd	0	0	----	0	0

Fair Catches: Burruss
Leader based on average return

INDIVIDUAL PUNTERS

	No	Yards	Long	Avg	Total Punts	TB	Blk	Opp Ret	Ret Yds	In 20	Net Avg
Arnold, Jim	93	3710	64	39.9	93	6	0	54	559	21	32.6

INDIVIDUAL PUNT RETURNERS

	No	FC	Yards	Avg	Long	TD
Smith, J.T.	26	5	210	8.1	19	0
Hancock, Anthony	14	9	81	5.8	18	0

Leader based on average return

INDIVIDUAL SCORERS

KICKERS	XP	XPA	FG	FGA	PTS
Lowery, Nick	44	45	24	30	116

NON-KICKERS	TD	TDR	TDP	TDM	PTS
Brown, Theotis	10	8	2	0	60
Carson, Carlos	7	0	7	0	42
Marshall, Henry	6	0	6	0	36
Paige, Stephone	6	0	6	0	36
Scott, Willie	6	0	6	0	36
Kenney, Bill	3	3	0	0	18
Jackson, Billy	2	2	0	0	12
Hancock, Anthony	1	0	1	0	6
Jackson, Charles	1	0	0	1	6
Roquemore, Durwood	1	0	0	1	6
Smith, Lucious	1	0	0	1	6
Thomas, Ken	1	0	1	0	6

t=Touchdown

LOS ANGELES RAIDERS

AFC Western Division

Address: 332 Center Street, El Segundo, CA 90245
Telephone: (213) 322 3451

CLUB OFFICIALS
General Partners: Al Davis, E.W. McGah
Managing General Partner: Al Davis
Executive Assistant: Al LoCasale
Director of Operations: Ron Wolf
Head Coach: Tom Flores
Assistant Coaches: Sam Boghosian, Willie Brown,
Chet Franklin, Larry Kennan, Earl Leggett, Bob Mischak,
Steve Ortmayer, Art Shell, Charlie Sumner, Tom Walsh,
Ray Willsey
Player Personnel: Ron Wolf
Business Manager: Ken LaRue
Senior Administrators: Tom Grimes, Irv Kazse
Publications: Bill Glazier
Marketing/Promotions: Gil Hernandez, Mike Ornstein
Ticket Operations: Peter Eiges
Comptroller: Dee Rutledge
Trainers: George Anderson, H. Rod Martin
Equipment Manager: Richard Romanski

Stadium: Los Angeles Memorial Coliseum (Capacity 92,498)
Playing Surface: Grass
Stadium Address: 3911 South Figueroa Street, Los Angeles, CA 90037
Colors: Silver, Black
Summer Training Camp: El Rancho Tropicana, Santa Rosa, CA 95401

LOS ANGELES RAIDERS 1984 SCHEDULE

PRE-SEASON

Aug.	4	at San Francisco 49ers	6:00
Aug.	10	at Washington Redskins	8:00
Aug.	19	MIAMI DOLPHINS	1:00
Aug.	24	NEW YORK JETS	6:00

REGULAR SEASON

Sep.	2	at Houston Oilers	3:00
Sep.	9	GREEN BAY PACKERS	1:00
Sep.	16	at Kansas City Chiefs	12:00
Sep.	24	SAN DIEGO CHARGERS	6:00
Sep.	30	at Denver Broncos	2:00
Oct.	7	SEATTLE SEAHAWKS	1:00
Oct.	14	MINNESOTA VIKINGS	1:00
Oct.	21	at San Diego Chargers	1:00
Oct.	28	DENVER BRONCOS	1:00
Nov.	4	at Chicago Bears	12:00
Nov.	12	at Seattle Seahawks	6:00
Nov.	18	KANSAS CITY CHIEFS	1:00
Nov.	25	INDIANAPOLIS COLTS	1:00
Dec.	2	at Miami Dolphins	4:00
Dec.	10	at Detroit Lions	9:00
Dec.	16	PITTSBURGH STEELERS	1:00

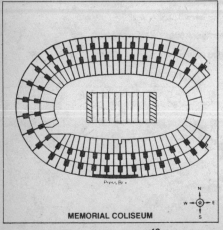

MEMORIAL COLISEUM

LOS ANGELES RAIDERS END OF SEASON DEPTH CHART

OFFENSE

WR	— 21 Cliff Branch, 82 Calvin Muhammad, 28 Cle Montgomery
OLT	— 79 Bruce Davis, 64 Shelby Jordan, 76 Ed Muransky***
OLG	— 73 Charley Hannah, 66 Steve Sylvester, 60 Curt Marsh*
C	— 50 Dave Dalby, 66 Steve Sylvester, 52 Jim Romano*
ORG	— 65 Mickey Marvin, 72 Don Mosebar
ORT	— 70 Henry Lawrence, 64 Shelby Jordan
TE	— 46 Todd Christensen, 87 Don Hasselback, 31 Derrick Jensen
WR	— 80 Malcolm Barnwell, 85 Dokie Williams, 28 Cle Montgomery
QB	— 16 Jim Plunkett, 6 Marc Wilson, 11 David Humm
RB	— 33 Kenny King, 27 Frank Hawkins, 38 Chester Willis***, 40 Rick Berns*
RB	— 32 Marcus Allen, 34 Greg Pruitt

DEFENSE

DLE	— 75 Howie Long, 93 Greg Townsend
NT	— 62 Reggie Kinlaw, 61 Dave Stalls**, 68 Johnny Robinson, 74 Archie Reese**
DRE	— 77 Lyle Alzado, 71 Bill Pickel
LOLB	— 83 Ted Hendricks, 56 Jeff Barnes
LILB	— 55 Matt Millen, 58 Jack Squirek, 54 Darryl Byrd
RILB	— 51 Bob Nelson, 58 Jack Squirek, 54 Darryl Byrd
ROLB	— 53 Rod Martin, 57 Tony Caldwell
LCB	— 37 Lester Hayes, 45 James Davis, 25 Irvin Phillips*
SS	— 36 Mike Davis, 48 Kenny Hill
FS	— 26 Vann McElroy, 23 Odis McKinney
RCB	— 22 Mike Haynes, 20 Ted Watts

SPECIAL TEAMS

K	— 10 Chris Bahr, 8 Ray Guy
P	— 8 Ray Guy, 10 Chris Bahr
H	— 11 David Humm, 8 Ray Guy, 26 Vann McElroy
KR	— 34 Greg Pruitt, 28 Cle Montgomery
PR	— 34 Greg Pruitt, 28 Cle Montgomery
LSN	— 46 Todd Christensen, 50 Dave Dalby, 73 Charley Hannah

LOS ANGELES RAIDERS

INDIVIDUAL RUSHERS

	Att	Yards	Avg	Long	TD
Allen, Marcus	266	1014	3.8	19	9
Hawkins, Frank	110	526	4.8	32	6
King, Kenny	82	294	3.6	16	1
Pruitt, Greg	26	154	5.9	18	2
Wilson, Marc	13	122	9.4	23	0
Plunkett, Jim	26	78	3.0	20	0
Berns, Rick	6	22	3.7	13	0
Branch, Cliff	1	20	20.0	20	0
Barnwell, Malcolm	1	12	12.0	12	0
Montgomery, Cleotha	2	7	3.5	5	0
Jensen, Derrick	1	5	5.0	5	0
Willis, Chester	5	0	0.0	4	0
Humm, David	1	−1	−1.0	−1	0
Guy, Ray	2	−13	−6.5	−3	0

Leader based on most yards gained

INDIVIDUAL PASSING

	Att	Comp	% Comp	Yards	Avg Gain	TD	% TD	Long	Int	% Int	Rating Points
Plunkett, Jim	379	230	60.7	2935	7.74	20	5.3	199	18	4.7	82.7
Wilson, Marc	117	67	57.3	864	7.38	8	6.8	t50	6	5.1	82.0
Allen, Marcus	7	4	57.1	111	15.86	3	42.9	t43	0	0.0	
Pruitt, Greg	1	0	0.0	0	0.00	0	0	0	0	0.0	

INDIVIDUAL RECEIVERS

	No	Yards	Avg	Long	TD
Christensen, Todd	92	1247	13.6	45	12
Allen, Marcus	68	590	8.7	36	2
Branch, Cliff	39	696	17.8	t99	5
Barnwell, Malcolm	35	513	14.7	41	1
Hawkins, Frank	20	150	7.5	28	2
Williams, Dokie	14	259	18.5	t50	3
Muhammad, Calvin	13	252	19.4	45	2
Hasselbeck, Don, N.E.-Raider	3	24	8.0	t13	2
Montgomery, Cleotha	2	29	14.5	15	0
Pruitt, Greg	1	6	6.0	6	0
Jensen, Derrick	1	2	2.0	t2	1

Leader based on most passes caught

INDIVIDUAL INTERCEPTORS

	No	Yards	Avg	Long	TD
McElroy, Vann	8	68	8.5	28	0
Martin, Rod	4	81	20.3	t40	2
Hayes, Lester	2	49	24.5	28	0
Millen, Matt	1	14	14.0	14	0
Watts, Ted	1	13	13.0	13	0
Davis, James	1	10	10.0	10	0
Davis, Mike	1	3	3.0	3	0
Haynes, Mike	1	0	0.0	0	0
McKinney, Odis	1	0	0.0	0	0

Leader based on most interceptions

INDIVIDUAL KICKOFF RETURNERS

	No	Yards	Avg	Long	TD
Montgomery, Cleotha	21	464	22.1	48	0
Pruitt, Greg	31	604	19.5	42	0
Williams, Dokie	5	88	17.6	19	0
Millen, Matt	2	19	9.5	10	0
Jensen, Derrick	1	0	0.0	0	0
Martin, Rod	1	0	0.0	0	0

Leader based on average return

INDIVIDUAL PUNTERS

	No	Yards	Long	Avg	Total Punts	TB	Blk	Opp Ret	Ret Yds	In 20	Net Avg
Guy, Ray	78	3336	67	42.8	78	10	0	35	334	17	35.9

INDIVIDUAL PUNT RETURNERS

	No	FC	Yards	Avg	Long	TD
Pruitt, Greg	58	18	666	11.5	t97	1

INDIVIDUAL SCORERS

KICKERS	XP	XPA	FG	FGA	PTS
Bahr, Chris	51	53	21	27	114

NON-KICKERS	TD	TDR	TDP	TDM	PTS
Allen, Marcus	12	9	2	1	72
Christensen, Todd	12	0	12	0	72
Hawkins, Frank	8	6	2	0	48
Branch, Cliff	5	0	5	0	30
Pruitt, Greg	3	2	0	1	18
Williams, Dokie	3	0	3	0	18
Hasselbeck, Don	2	0	2	0	12
King, Kenny	2	1	1	0	12
Martin, Rod	2	0	0	2	12
Muhammad, Calvin	2	0	2	0	12
Townsend, Greg	1	0	0	1	*8
Barnwell, Malcolm	1	0	1	0	6
Jensen, Derrick	1	0	1	0	6
Alzado, Lyle	0	0	0	0	*2

*=Safety
t=Touchdown

MIAMI DOLPHINS

AFC Eastern Division

Address: 4770 Biscayne Boulevard, Suite 1440, Miami,
FL 33137
Telephone: (305) 576 1000

CLUB OFFICIALS
President: Joseph Robbie
Vice President: Elizabeth L. Robbie
Executive Vice President, General Manager: J. Michael Robbie
Vice President, Head Coach: Don Shula
Vice President, Special Projects and Business Affairs: Don Poss
Director of Publicity: Chip Namias
Director of Player Personnel: Chuck Connor
Director of Pro Personnel: Charley Winner
Assistant Coaches: Chuck Studley, Tom Keane, Bob Matheson, John Sandusky, Mike Scarry,
David Shula, Carl Taseff, Junior Wade
Ticket Director: Ross Paul
Controller: Howard F. Rieman
Trainer: Bob Lundy
Equipment Manager: Danny Dowe

Stadium: Orange Bowl (Capacity 75,459)
Playing Surface: Grass (PAT)
Stadium Address: 1501 N.W. Third Street, Miami, FL 33125
Colors: Aqua, Coral & White
Training Centre: St Thomas of Villanova University, 16400-D N.W. 32nd Avenue,
Miami, FL 33054

MIAMI DOLPHINS 1984 SCHEDULE

PRE-SEASON

Aug.	4	INDIANAPOLIS COLTS	8:00
Aug.	11	at Minnesota Vikings	7:00
Aug.	19	at Los Angeles Raiders	1:00
Aug.	24	at Tampa Bay Buccaneers	8:00

REGULAR SEASON

Sep.	2	at Washington Redskins	1:00
Sep.	9	NEW ENGLAND PATRIOTS	1:00
Sep.	17	at Buffalo Bills	9:00
Sep.	23	INDIANAPOLIS COLTS	4:00
Sep.	30	at St Louis Cardinals	12:00
Oct.	7	at Pittsburgh Steelers	1:00
Oct.	14	HOUSTON OILERS	1:00
Oct.	21	at New England Patriots	1:00
Oct.	28	BUFFALO BILLS	4:00
Nov.	4	at New York Jets	4:00
Nov.	11	PHILADELPHIA EAGLES	1:00
Nov.	18	at San Diego Chargers	1:00
Nov.	26	NEW YORK JETS	9:00
Dec.	2	LOS ANGELES RAIDERS	4:00
Dec.	9	at Indianapolis Colts	1:00
Dec.	17	DALLAS COWBOYS	9:00

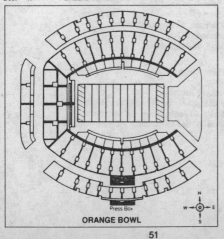

Press Box

ORANGE BOWL

MIAMI DOLPHINS END OF SEASON DEPTH CHART

OFFENSE

WR	— 85 Mark Duper, 82 Duriel Harris**, 88 Vince Heflin
OLT	— 79 Jon Giesler, 74 Cleveland Green
OLG	— 67 Bob Kuechenberg, 60 Jeff Toews
C	— 57 Dwight Stephenson, 60 Jeff Toews, 63 Mark Dennard**
ORG	— 64 Ed Newman, 60 Jeff Toews
ORT	— 68 Eric Laakso, 61 Roy Foster
TE	— 87 Dan Johnson, 84 Bruce Hardy, 80 Joe Rose
WR	— 89 Nat Moore, 83 Mark Clayton, 11 Jim Jensen, 81 Jimmy Cefalo*
QB	— 13 Dan Marino, 10 Don Strock, 16 David Woodley**, 11 Jim Jensen
HB	— 22 Tony Nathan, 20 David Overstreet, 31 Eddie Hill
FB	— 37 Andra Franklin, 34 Woody Bennett, 32 Tommy Vigorito*

DEFENSE

DLE	— 75 Doug Betters, 76 Steve Clark, 91 Charles Benson
NT	— 73 Bob Baumhower, 70 Bill Barnett
DRE	— 58 Kim Bokamper, 71 Mike Charles, 91 Charles Benson
LOLB	— 59 Bob Brudzinski, 54 Rodell Thomas, 53 Ron Hester*
LILB	— 77 A.J. Duhe, 52 Terry Tautolo, Emmett Tilley*
RILB	— 55 Earnie Rhone, 51 Mark Brown, Steve Shull*
ROLB	— 56 Charles Bowser, 54 Rodell Thomas
LCB	— 49 William Judson, 41 Fulton Walker, 28 Don McNeal*
SS	— 47 Glenn Blackwood, 40 Mike Kozlowski
FS	— 42 Lyle Blackwood, 44 Paul Lankford
RCB	— 48 Gerald Small, 45 Robert Sowell

SPECIAL TEAMS

K	— 5 Uwe Von Schamann
P	— 4 Reggie Roby
H	— 10 Don Strock, 11 Jim Jensen
KR	— 41 Fulton Walker, 83 Mark Clayton, 88 Vince Heflin
PR	— 83 Mark Clayton, 41 Fulton Walker, 88 Vince Heflin
LSN	— 84 Bruce Hardy, 67 Bob Kuechenberg, 63 Mark Dennard**

MIAMI DOLPHINS

INDIVIDUAL RUSHERS

	Att	Yards	Avg	Long	TD
Franklin, Andra	224	746	3.3	18	8
Nathan, Tony	151	685	4.5	40	3
Overstreet, David	85	392	4.6	44	1
Bennett, Woody	49	197	4.0	25	2
Woodley, David	19	78	4.1	15	0
Marino, Dan	28	45	1.6	15	2
Hill, Eddie	2	12	6.0	10	0
Clayton, Mark	2	9	4.5	9	0
Hardy, Bruce	1	2	2.0	2	0
Harris, Duriel	1	0	0.0	0	0
Strock, Don	6	−16	−2.7	0	0

Leader based on most yards gained

INDIVIDUAL PASSING

	Att	Comp	% Comp	Yards	Avg Gain	TD	% TD	Long	Int	% Int	Rating Points
Marino, Dan	296	173	58.4	2210	7.47	20	6.8	t85	6	2.0	96.0
Strock, Don	52	34	65.4	403	7.75	4	7.7	47	1	1.9	106.5
Woodley, David	89	43	48.3	528	5.93	3	3.4	t64	4	4.5	59.6
Clayton, Mark	1	1	100.0	48	48.00	1	100.0	t48	0	0.0	
Nathan, Tony	4	3	75.0	46	11.50	0	0.0	22	0	0.0	

INDIVIDUAL RECEIVERS

	No	Yards	Avg	Long	TD
Nathan, Tony	52	461	8.9	25	1
Duper, Mark	51	1003	19.7	t85	10
Moore, Nat	39	558	14.3	t66	6
Rose, Joe	29	345	11.9	37	3
Johnson, Dan	24	189	7.9	33	4
Hardy, Bruce	22	202	9.2	25	0
Harris, Duriel	15	260	17.3	t64	1
Overstreet, David	8	55	6.9	20	2
Clayton, Mark	6	114	19.0	39	1
Bennett, Woody	6	35	5.8	9	0
Vigorito, Tom	1	7	7.0	7	0
Woodley, David	1	6	6.0	6	0

Leader based on most passes caught

INDIVIDUAL INTERCEPTORS

	No	Yards	Avg	Long	TD
Judson, William	6	60	10.0	29	0
Small, Gerald	5	60	12.0	28	0
Blackwood, Lyle	4	77	19.3	45	0
Blackwood, Glenn	3	0	0.0	0	0
Kozlowski, Mike	2	73	36.5	t38	2
Bokamper, Kim	2	43	21.5	t24	0
Rhone, Earnest	1	15	15.0	15	0
Lankford, Paul	1	10	10.0	10	0
Walker, Fulton	1	7	7.0	7	0
Brown, Mark	1	0	0.0	0	0

Leader based on most interceptions

INDIVIDUAL KICKOFF RETURNERS

	No	Yards	Avg	Long	TD
Walker, Fulton	36	962	26.7	78	0
Kozlowski, Mike	4	50	12.5	23	0
Nathan, Tony	3	15	5.0	12	0
Heflin, Vince	1	27	27.0	27	0
Clayton, Mark	1	25	25.0	25	0
Bennett, Woody	1	6	6.0	6	0
Brown, Mark	1	0	0.0	0	0

Leader based on average return

INDIVIDUAL PUNTERS

	No	Yards	Long	Avg	Total Punts	TB	Blk	Opp Ret	Ret Yds	In 20	Net Avg
Roby, Reggie	74	3189	64	43.1	75	11	1	32	229	26	36.5

INDIVIDUAL PUNT RETURNERS

	No	FC	Yards	Avg	Long	TD
Clayton, Mark	41	11	392	9.6	t60	1
Walker, Fulton	8	0	86	10.8	23	0
Kozlowski, Mike	2	10	12	6.0	11	0
Vigorito, Tom	1	0	62	62.0	62	0
Heflin, Vince	1	0	19	19.0	19	0
Blackwood, Glenn	1	2	10	10.0	10	0
Sowell, Robert	1	0	0	0.0	0	0

Leader based on average return

INDIVIDUAL SCORERS

KICKERS

	XP	XPA	FG	FGA	PTS
von Schamann, Uwe	45	48	18	27	99

NON-KICKERS

	TD	TDR	TDP	TDM	PTS
Duper, Mark	10	0	10	0	60
Franklin, Andra	8	8	0	0	48
Moore, Nat	6	0	6	0	36
Johnson, Dan	4	0	4	0	24
Nathan, Tony	4	3	1	0	24
Overstreet, David	3	1	2	0	18
Rose, Joe	3	0	3	0	18
Bennett, Woody	2	2	0	0	12
Clayton, Mark	2	0	1	1	12
Kozlowski, Mike	2	0	0	2	12
Marino, Dan	2	2	0	0	12
Bokamper, Kim	1	0	0	1	6
Harris, Duriel	1	0	1	0	6
Charles, Mike	0	0	0	0	*2

*=Safety
t=Touchdown

NEW ENGLAND PATRIOTS

AFC Eastern Division

Address: Sullivan Stadium, Foxboro, MA 02035
Telephone: (617) 543 7911, 262 1776

CLUB OFFICIALS
President: William H. Sullivan, Jr.
Executive Vice President: Charles W. Sullivan
Vice President: Francis J. (Bucko) Kilroy
General Manager: Patrick J. Sullivan
Admin. Asst. to the General Manager: Judy Quimby
Business Manager: Phil Lynch
Director of Public Relations and Sales: Tom Hoffman
Director of Publications: Dave Wintergrass
Director of Ticket Sales: Peter Thompson
Director of Promotions: Claudia Smith
Public Relations Assistant: Kris Erickson
Cheerleaders Director: Susan Ouellette
Head Coach: Ron Meyer
Offensive Coordinator/Qbs.: Lew Erber
Defensive Coordinator: Rod Rust
Defensive Line: Tommy Brasher
Offensive Backs: Cleve Bryant
Strength/Conditioning: LeBaron Caruthers
Receivers: Steve Endicott
Special Teams: Dante Scarnecchia
Linebackers: Steve Sidwell
Secondary: Steve Walters
Offensive Line: Bill Muir

Stadium: Sullivan Stadium (Capacity 61,150)
Playing Surface: Super Turf
Stadium Address: Foxboro, MA 02035
Colors: Red, White and Blue
Summer Training Camp: Bryant College, Smithfield, RI 02917

NEW ENGLAND PATRIOTS 1984 SCHEDULE

PRE-SEASON

Aug.	3	NEW YORK GIANTS	7:30
Aug.	11	at Buffalo Bills	6:00
Aug.	17	at Washington Redskins	8:00
Aug.	24	KANSAS CITY CHIEFS	7:30

REGULAR SEASON

Sep.	2	at Buffalo Bills	1:00
Sep.	9	at Miami Dolphins	1:00
Sep.	16	SEATTLE SEAHAWKS	1:00
Sep.	23	WASHINGTON REDSKINS	1:00
Sep.	30	at New York Jets	1:00
Oct.	7	at Cleveland Browns	1:00
Oct.	14	CINCINNATI BENGALS	1:00
Oct.	21	MIAMI DOLPHINS	1:00
Oct.	28	NEW YORK JETS	1:00
Nov.	4	at Denver Broncos	2:00
Nov.	11	BUFFALO BILLS	1:00
Nov.	18	at Indianapolis Colts	1:00
Nov.	22	at Dallas Cowboys	3:00
Dec.	2	ST LOUIS CARDINALS	1:00
Dec.	9	at Philadelphia Eagles	1:00
Dec.	16	INDIANAPOLIS COLTS	1:00

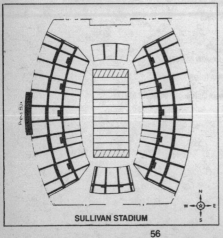

SULLIVAN STADIUM

NEW ENGLAND PATRIOTS END OF SEASON DEPTH CHART

OFFENSE

WR	— 86 Stanley Morgan, 82 Clarence Weathers
OLT	— 76 Brian Holloway, 68 Darryl Haley, 67 Steve Moore
OLG	— 73 John Hannah, 62 Dwight Wheeler
C	— 58 Pete Brock, 62 Dwight Wheeler, 78 Art Kuehn
ORG	— 61 Ron Wooten, 62 Dwight Wheeler
ORT	— 75 Bob Cryder, 68 Darryl Haley, 67 Steve Moore
TE	— 87 Lin Dawson, 88 Derrick Ramsey, 80 Brooks Williams
WR	— 81 Stephen Starring, 83 Cedric Jones, Darryal Wilson*
QB	— 11 Tony Eason, 19 Mike Kerrigan, 14 Steve Grogan***
HB	— 33 Anthony Collins, 24 Robert Weathers
FB	— 34 Mark Van Eeghen, 24 Robert Weathers, 30 Mosi Tatupu, 35 George Peoples

DEFENSE

DLE	— 77 Kenneth Sims, 90 Toby Williams, 91 George Crump*
NT	— 98 Dennis Owens, 72 Lester Williams, 70 Luther Henson*
DRE	— 85 Julius Adams, 74 Dave Browning**, 65 Doug Rogers
LOLB	— 50 Larry McGrew, 56 Andre Tippett, 94 Ed Reynolds
LILB	— 57 Steve Nelson, 52 Johnny Rembert, 59 Tim Golden
RILB	— 53 Clayton Weishuhn, 52 Johnny Rembert, 59 Tim Golden
ROLB	— 55 Don Blackmon, 50 Larry McGrew, 94 Ed Reynolds, 51 Brian Ingram*
LCB	— 42 Ronnie Lippett, 27 Ricky Smith
SS	— 38 Roland James, 22 Keith Lee
FS	— 25 Rick Sanford, 31 Fred Marion
RCB	— 26 Ray Clayborn, 47 Paul Dombroski

SPECIAL TEAMS

K	— 5 Joaquin Zendejas, Tony Franklin
P	— 3 Rich Camarillo
H	— 11 Tony Eason, 3 Rich Camarillo
KR	— 27 Ricky Smith, 82 Clarence Weathers
PR	— 27 Ricky Smith, 82 Clarence Weathers
LSN	— 62 Dwight Wheeler, 75 Bob Cryder

NEW ENGLAND PATRIOTS

INDIVIDUAL RUSHERS

	Att	Yards	Avg	Long	TD
Collins, Anthony	219	1049	4.8	t50	10
Tatupu, Mosi	106	578	5.5	55	4
Weathers, Robert	73	418	5.7	77	1
van Eeghen, Mark	95	358	3.8	11	2
Grogan, Steve	23	108	4.7	17	2
Eason, Tony	19	39	2.1	12	0
Weathers, Clarence	1	28	28.0	28	0
Kerrigan, Mike	1	14	14.0	14	0
Morgan, Stanley	1	13	13.0	13	0

Leader based on most yards gained

INDIVIDUAL PASSING

	Att	Comp	% Comp	Yards	Avg Gain	TD	% TD	Long	Int	% Int	Rating Points
Grogan, Steve	303	168	55.4	2411	7.96	15	5.0	t76	12	4.0	81.4
Eason, Tony	95	46	48.4	557	5.86	1	1.1	35	5	5.3	48.4
Kerrigan, Mike	14	6	42.9	72	5.14	0	0.0	19	1	7.1	29.5

INDIVIDUAL RECEIVERS

	No	Yards	Avg	Long	TD
Morgan, Stanley	58	863	14.9	t50	2
Collins, Anthony	27	257	9.5	20	0
Ramsey, Derrick	24	335	14.0	39	6
Weathers, Robert	23	212	9.2	19	0
Jones, Cedric	20	323	16.2	30	1
Weathers, Clarence	19	379	19.9	t58	3
Starring, Stephen	17	389	22.9	t76	2
van Eeghen, Mark	10	102	10.2	23	0
Tatupu, Mosi	10	97	9.7	17	1
Dawson, Lin	9	84	9.3	14	1
Williams, Brooks	1	0	0.0	0	0
Grogan, Steve	1	−8	−8.0	−8	0

Leader based on most passes caught

INDIVIDUAL INTERCEPTORS

	No	Yards	Avg	Long	TD
Sanford, Rick	7	24	3.4	16	0
James, Roland	5	99	19.8	46	0
Marion, Fred	2	4	2.0	4	0
Blackmon, Don	1	39	39.0	39	0
Nelson, Steve	1	6	6.0	6	0
McGrew, Larry	1	3	3.0	3	0
Weishuhn, Clayton	0	27	---	t27	1

Leader based on most interceptions

INDIVIDUAL KICKOFF RETURNERS

	No	Yards	Avg	Long	TD
Smith, Ricky	42	916	21.8	53	0
Jones, Cedric	4	63	15.8	23	0
Lee, Keith	4	40	10.0	19	0
Weathers, Robert	3	68	22.7	29	0
Weathers, Clarence	3	58	19.3	33	0
Golden, Tim	1	10	10.0	10	0

Fair Catches: Jones
Leader based on average return

INDIVIDUAL PUNTERS

	No	Yards	Long	Avg	Total Punts	TB	Blk	Opp Ret	Ret Yds	In 20	Net Avg
Camarillo, Rich	81	3615	70	44.6	81	11	0	48	392	25	37.1

INDIVIDUAL PUNT RETURNERS

	No	FC	Yards	Avg	Long	TD
Smith, Ricky	38	12	398	10.5	55	0
Weathers, Clarence	4	0	1	0.3	3	0
Lee, Keith	1	0	0	0.0	0	0
Sanford, Rick	1	2	0	0.0	0	0

Leader based on average return

INDIVIDUAL SCORERS

KICKERS

	XP	XPA	FG	FGA	PTS
Steinfort, Buff	17	18	7	21	38
Zendejas, Joaquin	3	4	0	1	3

NON-KICKERS

	TD	TDR	TDP	TDM	PTS
Collins, Anthony	10	10	0	0	60
Ramsey, Derrick	6	0	6	0	36
Tatupu, Mosi	5	4	1	0	30
Weathers, Clarence	3	0	3	0	18
Grogan, Steve	2	2	0	0	12
Morgan, Stanley	2	0	2	0	12
Starring, Stephen	2	0	2	0	12
van Eeghen, Mark	2	2	0	0	12
Dawson, Lin	1	0	1	0	6
Jones, Cedric	1	0	1	0	6
Weathers, Robert	1	1	0	0	6
Weishuhn, Clayton	1	0	0	1	6

t=Touchdown

NEW YORK JETS

AFC Eastern Division .

Address: 598 Madison Avenue, New York, NY 10022
Telephone: (212) 421 6600

CLUB OFFICIALS
Chairman of the Board: Leon Hess
President: Jim Kensil
Secretary and Administrative Manager: Steve Gutman
Comptroller: Phil Thaw
Assistant Comptroller: Michael Gerstle
Director of Public Relations: Frank Ramos
Assistant Director of Public Relations: Ron Cohen
Director of Operations: Tim Davey
Travelling Secretary: Mike Kensil
Ticket Manager: Bob Parente
Head Coach: Joe Walton
Assistant Head Coach and Defensive Coordinator: Joe Gardi
Defensive Backs: Billy Baird
Linebackers: Ralph Baker
Defensive Line: Ray Callahan
Special Assistant to the Head Coach: Mike Faulkiner
Running Backs: Bobby Hammond
Receivers and Passing Game Coordinator: Rich Kotite
Special Teams: Larry Pasquale
Offensive Line and Running Game Coordinator: Jim Ringo
Pro Personnel Director: Jim Royer
Pro Personnel Assistant: Gail Baldwin
Director of Player Personnel: Mike Hickey
Talent Scouts: Joe Collins, Don Grammer, Sid Hall, Marv Sunderland
College Scouting Assistant: John Griffin
Head Trainer: Bob Reese
Assistant Trainer: Pepper Burruss
Conditioning Coordinator: Jim Williams
Equipment Manager: Bill Hampton

Stadium: Giants Stadium (Capacity 76,891)
Playing Surface: AstroTurf
Stadium Address: East Rutherford, NJ
Colors: Kelly Green & White
Training Center: 1000 Fulton Avenue, Hempstead, NY 10022
Telephone: (516) 538 6600

NEW YORK JETS 1984 SCHEDULE

PRE-SEASON

Aug.	4	CINCINNATI BENGALS	8:30
Aug.	11	at Houston Oilers	8:00
Aug.	18	at New York Giants	8:00
Aug.	24	at Los Angeles Raiders	6:00

REGULAR SEASON

Sep.	2	at Indianapolis Colts	4:00
Sep.	6	PITTSBURGH STEELERS	9:00
Sep.	16	CINCINNATI BENGALS	1:00
Sep.	23	at Buffalo Bills	1:00
Sep.	30	NEW ENGLAND PATRIOTS	1:00
Oct.	7	at Kansas City Chiefs	12:00
Oct.	14	at Cleveland Browns	1:00
Oct.	21	KANSAS CITY CHIEFS	4:00
Oct.	28	at New England Patriots	1:00
Nov.	4	MIAMI DOLPHINS	4:00
Nov.	11	INDIANAPOLIS COLTS	1:00
Nov.	18	at Houston Oilers	3:00
Nov.	26	at Miami Dolphins	9:00
Dec.	2	NEW YORK GIANTS	1:00
Dec.	8	BUFFALO BILLS	12:30
Dec.	16	at Tampa Bay Buccaneers	1:00

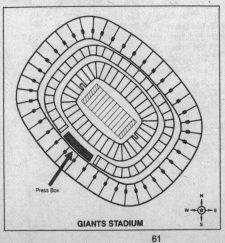

Press Box

N
W · E
S

GIANTS STADIUM

NEW YORK JETS END OF SEASON DEPTH CHART

OFFENSE

WR	— 85 Wesley Walker, 81 Derrick Gaffney, 89 Preston Brown
OLT	— 72 Chris Ward, 68 Reggie McElroy, 64 Guy Bingham
OLG	— 64 Guy Bingham, 62 Joe Pellegrini, 68 Reggie McElroy, 70 Stan Waldemore*
C	— 65 Joe Fields, 64 Guy Bingham, 59 George Lilja
ORG	— 60 Dan Alexander, 62 Joe Pellegrini, 64 Guy Bingham, 71 Jim Luscinski*
ORT	— 79 Marvin Powell, 68 Reggie McElroy, 64 Guy Bingham
TE	— 83 Jerome Barkum, 82 Mickey Shuler, 88 Tom Coombs
WR	— 80 Johnny 'Lam' Jones, 81 Derrick Gaffney, 86 Nick Bruckner
QB	— 14 Richard Todd**, 10 Pat Ryan, 16 Ken O'Brien
HB	— 24 Freeman McNeil, 42 Bruce Harper, 22 Kenny Lewis, 34 Johnny Hector
FB	— 31 Marion Barber, 25 Scott Dierking**, 30 Rocky Klever, 35 Mike Augustyniak*

DEFENSE

DLE	— 99 Mark Gastineau, 76 Ben Rudolph, 94 Rusty Guilbeau
DLT	— 73 Joe Klecko, 74 Abdul Salaam**, 76 Ben Rudolph
DRT	— 93 Marty Lyons, 78 Barry Bennett, 76 Ben Rudolph
DRE	— 77 Kenny Neil**, 73 Joe Klecko, 76 Ben Rudolph
LLB	— 57 John Woodring, 55 Ron Crosby**, 52 Jim Eliopolus, 51 Greg Buttle*
MLB	— 50 Bob Crable, 57 John Woodring, 54 Stan Blinka**
RLB	— 56 Lance Mehl, 55 Ron Crosby**, 52 Jim Eliopolus
LCB	— 40 Bobby Jackson, 29 Johnny Lynn, 20 Davlin Mullen
SS	— 48 Ken Schroy, 21 Kirk Springs, 29 Johnny Lynn, 27 Jesse Johnson**
FS	— 28 Darrol Ray, 21 Kirk Springs, 29 Johnny Lynn, 38 George Floyd*
RCB	— 47 Jerry Holmes**, 29 Johnny Lynn, 20 Davlin Mullen

SPECIAL TEAMS

K	— 5 Pat Leahy, 15 Chuck Ramsey
P	— 15 Chuck Ramsey, 5 Pat Leahy
H	— 10 Pat Ryan, 16 Ken O'Brien
KR	— 89 Preston Brown, 21 Kirk Springs, 34 Johnny Hector
PR	— 21 Kirk Springs, 20 Davlin Mullen
LSN	— 64 Guy Bingham, 65 Joe Fields, 62 Joe Pellegrini

NEW YORK JETS

INDIVIDUAL RUSHERS

	Att	Yards	Avg	Long	TD
McNeil, Freeman	160	654	4.1	19	1
Harper, Bruce	51	354	6.9	t78	1
Dierking, Scott	28	113	4.0	31	3
Todd, Richard	35	101	2.9	17	0
Hector, Johnny	16	85	5.3	42	0
Barber, Marion	15	77	5.1	13	1
Augustyniak, Mike	18	50	2.8	6	2
Lewis, Kenny	5	25	5.0	7	0
Ryan, Pat	4	23	5.8	25	0
Jones, Lam	4	10	2.5	9	0
Crosby, Ron	1	5	5.0	5	0

Leader based on most yards gained

INDIVIDUAL PASSING

	Att	Comp	% Comp	Yards	Avg Gain	TD	% TD	Long	Int	% Int	Rating Points
Todd, Richard	518	308	59.5	3478	6.71	18	3.5	t64	26	5.0	70.3
Ryan, Pat	40	21	52.5	259	6.48	2	5.0	36	2	5.0	68.6
McNeil, Freeman	1	1	100.0	5	5.00	1	100.0	t5	0	0.0	

INDIVIDUAL RECEIVERS

	No	Yards	Avg	Long	TD
Walker, Wesley	61	868	14.2	t64	7
Harper, Bruce	48	413	8.6	33	2
Jones, Lam	43	734	17.1	t50	4
Dierking, Scott	33	275	8.3	19	0
Barkum, Jerome	32	385	12.0	34	1
Shuler, Mickey	26	272	10.5	28	1
McNeil, Freeman	21	172	8.2	21	3
Crutchfield, Dwayne	19	133	7.0	15	0
Gaffney, Derrick	17	243	14.3	35	0
Augustyniak, Mike	10	71	7.1	17	1
Barber, Marion	7	48	6.9	12	1
Lewis, Kenny	6	62	10.3	23	0
Hector, Johnny	5	61	12.2	t22	1
Harmon, Mike	1	4	4.0	4	0
Coombs, Tom	1	1	1.0	1	0

Leader based on most passes caught

INDIVIDUAL INTERCEPTORS

	No	Yards	Avg	Long	TD
Mehl, Lance	7	57	8.1	t34	1
Holmes, Johnny	3	107	35.7	t43	1
Ray, Darrol	3	77	25.7	42	0
Lynn, Johnny	3	70	23.3	t42	1
Jackson, Bobby	2	8	4.0	8	0
Schroy, Ken	2	6	3.0	4	0
Buttle, Greg	1	17	17.0	17	0
Crable, Bob	1	0	0.0	0	0

Leader based on most interceptions

INDIVIDUAL KICKOFF RETURNERS

	No	Yards	Avg	Long	TD
Springs, Kirk	16	364	22.8	64	0
Brown, Preston	29	645	22.2	46	0
Hector, Johnny	14	274	19.6	45	0
Mullen, Davlin	3	57	19.0	26	0
Harper, Bruce	1	16	16.0	16	0
Barber, Marion	1	9	9.0	9	0
McElroy, Reggie	1	7	7.0	7	0
Shuler, Mickey	1	3	3.0	3	0

Leader based on average return

INDIVIDUAL PUNTERS

	No	Yards	Long	Avg	Punts	Total TB	Blk	Opp Ret	Ret Yds	In 20	Net Avg
Ramsey, Chuck	81	3218	56	39.7	82	5	1	47	367	17	33.5

INDIVIDUAL PUNT RETURNERS

	No	FC	Yards	Avg	Long	TD
Springs, Kirk	23	4	287	12.5	t76	1
Harmon, Mike	12	8	109	9.1	21	0
Mullen, Davlin	2	3	13	6.5	9	0
Schroy, Ken	1	0	11	11.0	11	0

Leader based on average return

INDIVIDUAL SCORERS

KICKERS	XP	XPA	FG	FGA	PTS
Leahy, Pat	36	37	16	24	84

NON-KICKERS	TD	TDR	TDP	TDM	PTS
Walker, Wesley	7	0	7	0	42
Jones, Lam	4	0	4	0	24
McNeil, Freeman	4	1	3	0	24
Augustyniak, Mike	3	2	1	0	18
Crutchfield, Dwayne	3	3	0	0	18
Dierking, Scott	3	3	0	0	18
Harper, Bruce	3	1	2	0	18
Barber, Marion	2	1	1	0	12
Holmes, Johnny	2	0	0	2	12
Barkum, Jerome	1	0	1	0	6
Gastineau, Mark	1	0	0	1	6
Hector, Johnny	1	0	1	0	6
Lynn, Johnny	1	0	0	1	6
Mehl, Lance	1	0	0	1	6
Shuler, Mickey	1	0	1	0	6
Springs, Kirk	1	0	0	1	6
Ryan, Pat	0	0	0	0	# 1

# = Scored extra point
t = *Touchdown*

PITTSBURGH STEELERS

AFC Central Division

Address: Three Rivers Stadium, 300 Stadium Circle,
Pittsburgh, PA 15212
Telephone: (412) 323 1200

CLUB OFFICIALS
Chairman of the Board: Arthur J. Rooney, Sr.
President: Daniel M. Rooney
Vice President: John R. McGinley
Vice President: Arthur J. Rooney, Jr.
Head Coach: Chuck Noll
Assistant Coaches: Ron Blackledge, Tony Dungy,
Dennis Fitzgerald, Dick Hoak, Jon Kolb, Tom Moore,
Jed Hughes, Bill Meyers
Travelling Secretary: Jim Boston
Controller: Dennis P. Thimons
Publicity Director: Joe Gordon
Assistant Publicity Director: John Evenson
Director of Player Personnel: Dick Haley
Director of Public Relations: Ed Kiely
Assistant Director of Player Personnel: William Nunn, Jr.
Pro Talent Scout: Tom Modrak
Talent Scout-West Coast: Bob Schmitz
College Talent Scout: Joe Krupa
Director of Ticket Sales: Geraldine R. Glenn
Trainer: Ralph Berlin
Equipment Manager: Anthony Parisi

Stadium: Three Rivers Stadium (Capacity 59,000)
Playing Surface: AstroTurf
Stadium Address: 300 Stadium Circle, Pittsburgh, PA 15212
Colors: Gold & Black
Summer Training Camp: St Vincent College, Latrobe, PA 15650

PITTSBURGH STEELERS 1984 SCHEDULE

PRE-SEASON

Aug.	4	at Cleveland Browns	7:30
Aug.	11	PHILADELPHIA EAGLES	6:00
Aug.	16	at Dallas Cowboys	8:00
Aug.	25	at New York Giants	8:00

REGULAR SEASON

Sep.	2	KANSAS CITY CHIEFS	1:00
Sep.	6	at New York Jets	9:00
Sep.	16	LOS ANGELES RAMS	4:00
Sep.	23	at Cleveland Browns	1:00
Oct.	1	CINCINNATI BENGALS	9:00
Oct.	7	MIAMI DOLPHINS	1:00
Oct.	14	at San Francisco 49ers	1:00
Oct.	21	at Indianapolis Colts	1:00
Oct.	28	ATLANTA FALCONS	4:00
Nov.	4	HOUSTON OILERS	1:00
Nov.	11	at Cincinnati Bengals	1:00
Nov.	19	at New Orleans Saints	8:00
Nov.	25	SAN DIEGO CHARGERS	1:00
Dec.	2	at Houston Oilers	12:00
Dec.	9	CLEVELAND BROWNS	1:00
Dec.	16	at Los Angeles Raiders	1:00

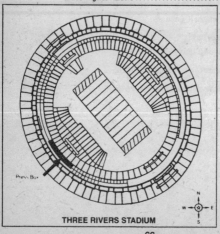

Press Box

THREE RIVERS STADIUM

PITTSBURGH STEELERS END OF SEASON DEPTH CHART

OFFENSE

WR	—	27 Greg Hawthorne, 86 Gregg Garrity, 82 John Stallworth***
OLT	—	62 Tunch Ilkin, 71 Emil Boures, 66 Ted Petersen*, John Meyer*
OLG	—	73 Craig Wolfley, 55 Rick Donnalley, 61 Blake Wingle
C	—	52 Mike Webster, 71 Emil Boures, 55 Rick Donnalley
ORG	—	77 Steve Courson, 71 Emil Boures, 55 Rick Donnalley
ORT	—	79 Larry Brown, 62 Tunch Ilkin, 71 Emil Boures
TE	—	89 Bennie Cunningham, 87 John Rodgers, 84 Craig Dunaway
WR	—	85 Calvin Sweeney, 80 Wayne Capers, 81 Paul Skansi
QB	—	18 Cliff Stoudt**, 16 Mark Malone, 12 Terry Bradshaw***, David Woodley
RB	—	30 Frank Pollard, 34 Walter Abercrombie, 44 Henry Odum, 43 Tim Harris
RB	—	32 Franco Harris, 30 Frank Pollard, 45 Russell Davis, Frank Wilson*

DEFENSE

DLE	—	95 John Goodman, 93 Keith Willis, 64 Ed Nelson
NT	—	67 Gary Dunn, 64 Ed Nelson, 65 Tom Beasley, 69 Gabe Rivera**
DRE	—	65 Tom Beasley, 92 Keith Gary
LOLB	—	57 Mike Merriweather, 53 Bryan Hinkle, 54 Craig Bingham
LILB	—	58 Jack Lambert, 50 David Little, 90 Bob Kohrs*
RILB	—	51 Loren Toews, 50 David Little, 53 Bryan Hinkle, Todd Seabaugh*
ROLB	—	56 Robin Cole, 53 Bryan Hinkle
LCB	—	49 Dwayne Woodruff, 41 Sam Washington
SS	—	31 Donnie Shell, 29 Ron Johnson, 25 Greg Best
FS	—	22 Rick Woods, 29 Ron Johnson, 21 Eric Williams*, 20 Ernie French**
RCB	—	47 Mel Blount**, 33 Harvey Clayton

SPECIAL TEAMS

K	—	1 Gary Anderson
P	—	5 Craig Colquitt
H	—	5 Craig Colquitt, 18 Cliff Stoudt**, 86 Greg Garrity
KR	—	44 Henry Odum, 43 Tim Harris, 33 Harvey Clayton
PR	—	81 Paul Skansi, 22 Rick Woods, 43 Tim Harris
LSN	—	52 Mike Webster, 71 Emil Boures

PITTSBURGH STEELERS

INDIVIDUAL RUSHERS

	Att	Yards	Avg	Long	TD
Harris, Franco	279	1007	3.6	19	5
Pollard, Frank	135	608	4.5	32	4
Stoudt, Cliff	77	479	6.2	23	4
Abercrombie, Walter	112	446	4.0	t50	4
Hawthorne, Greg	5	47	9.4	20	0
Harris, Tim	2	15	7.5	10	0
Odom, Henry	2	7	3.5	4	0
Bradshaw, Terry	1	3	3.0	3	0
Sweeney, Calvin	1	−2	−2.0	−2	0

Leader based on most yards gained

INDIVIDUAL PASSING

	Att	Comp	% Comp	Yards	Avg Gain	TD	% TD	Long	Int	% Int	Rating Points
Stoudt, Cliff	381	197	51.7	2553	6.70	12	3.1	52	21	5.5	60.6
Malone, Mark	20	9	45.0	124	6.20	1	5.0	38	2	10.0	42.5
Bradshaw, Terry	8	5	62.5	77	9.63	2	25.0	24	0	0.0	

INDIVIDUAL RECEIVERS

	No	Yards	Avg	Long	TD
Sweeney, Calvin	39	577	14.8	42	5
Cunningham, Bennie	35	442	12.6	29	3
Harris, Franco	34	278	8.2	t29	2
Abercrombie, Walter	26	391	15.0	t51	3
Hawthorne, Greg	19	300	15.8	52	0
Garrity, Gregg	19	279	14.7	38	1
Pollard, Frank	16	127	7.9	17	0
Capers, Wayne	10	185	18.5	36	1
Stallworth, John	8	100	12.5	20	0
Skansi, Paul	3	39	13.0	21	0
Rodgers, John	2	36	18.0	25	0

Leader based on most passes caught

INDIVIDUAL INTERCEPTORS

	No	Yards	Avg	Long	TD
Woods, Rick	5	53	10.6	31	0
Shell, Donnie	5	18	3.6	18	0
Blount, Mel	4	32	8.0	21	0
Woodruff, Dwayne	3	85	28.3	47	0
Johnson, Ron	3	84	28.0	t34	1
Merriweather, Mark	3	55	18.3	t31	1
Lambert, Jack	2	−1	−0.5	0	0
Clayton, Harvey	1	70	70.0	t70	1
Washington, Sam	1	25	25.0	25	0
Hinkle, Brian	1	14	14.0	t14	1

Leader based on most interceptions

INDIVIDUAL KICKOFF RETURNERS

	No	Yards	Avg	Long	TD
Odom, Henry	39	756	19.4	35	0
Harris, Tim	18	289	16.1	32	0
Bingham, Craig	1	15	15.0	15	0
Kohrs, Bob	1	6	6.0	6	0
Donnalleyk, Rick	0	2	----	2	0

Leader based on average return

INDIVIDUAL PUNTERS

	No	Yards	Long	Avg	Total Punts	TB	Blk	Opp Ret	Ret Yds	In 20	Net Avg
Colquitt, Craig	80	3352	58	41.9	80	7	0	44	418	20	34.9

INDIVIDUAL PUNT RETURNERS

	No	FC	Yards	Avg	Long	TD
Skansi, Paul	43	9	363	8.4	57	0
Woods, Rick	5	0	46	9.2	13	0
Harris, Tim	3	0	12	4.0	8	0

Leader based on average return

INDIVIDUAL SCORERS

KICKERS	XP	XPA	FG	FGA	PTS
Anderson, Gary	38	39	27	31	119

NON-KICKERS	TD	TDR	TDP	TDM	PTS
Abercrombie, Walter	7	4	3	0	42
Harris, Franco	7	5	2	0	42
Sweeney, Calvin	5	0	5	0	30
Pollard, Frank	4	4	0	0	24
Stoudt, Cliff	4	4	0	0	24
Cunningham, Bennie	3	0	3	0	18
Best, Greg	1	0	0	1	6
Blount, Mel	1	0	0	1	6
Capers, Wayne	1	0	1	0	6
Clayton, Harvey	1	0	0	1	6
Garrity, Gregg	1	0	1	0	6
Hinkle, Brian	1	0	0	1	6
Johnson, Ron	1	0	0	1	6
Merriweather, Mark	1	0	0	1	6
Woods, Rick	1	0	0	1	6
Kohrs, Bob	0	0	0	0	*2

*=Safety
t=Touchdown

SAN DIEGO CHARGERS

AFC Western Division

Address: San Diego Jack Murphy Stadium, P.O. Box 20666, San Diego, CA 92120
Telephone: (619) 280 2111

CLUB OFFICIALS
President: Eugene V. Klein
General Manager: John R. Sanders
Assistant General Manager: Paul (Tank) Younger
Assistant to the President: Jack Teele
Head Coach: Don Coryell
Assistant Coaches: Tom Bass, Marv Braden, Earnel Durden, Dave Levy, Al Saunders, Jerry Smith, Jim Wagstaff, Chuck Weber, Ernie Zampese
Administrative Assistant, Player Personnel: John Trump
Chief Scout: Aubrey (Red) Phillips
Director of Public Relations: Rick Smith
Business Manager: Pat Curran
Director of Advertising/Promotions: Rich Israel
Assistant Director of Public Relations: Rodney Knox
Public Relations Assistant: Bill Johnston
Director of Ticket Operations: John McConaha
Controller: Frances Beede
Trainer: Ric McDonald
Equipment Manager: Sid Brooks

Stadium: San Diego Jack Murphy (Capacity 52,675)
Playing Surface: Grass
Stadium Address: 9449 Friars Road, San Diego, CA 92108
Colors: Royal Blue, Gold & White
Summer Training Camp: University of California-San Diego, La Jolla, CA 92037

SAN DIEGO CHARGERS 1984 SCHEDULE

PRE-SEASON

Aug.	4	LOS ANGELES RAMS	6:00
Aug.	11	DALLAS COWBOYS	6:00
Aug.	18	SAN FRANCISCO 49ers	6:00
Aug.	23	at Los Angeles Rams	7:00

REGULAR SEASON

Sep.	2	at Minnesota Vikings	12:00
Sep.	9	at Seattle Seahawks	1:00
Sep.	16	HOUSTON OILERS	1:00
Sep.	24	at Los Angeles Raiders	6:00
Sep.	30	DETROIT LIONS	1:00
Oct.	7	at Green Bay Packers	3:00
Oct.	14	at Kansas City Chiefs	12:00
Oct.	21	LOS ANGELES RAIDERS	1:00
Oct.	29	SEATTLE SEAHAWKS	6:00
Nov.	4	at Indianapolis Colts	1:00
Nov.	11	DENVER BRONCOS	1:00
Nov.	18	MIAMI DOLPHINS	1:00
Nov.	25	at Pittsburgh Steelers	1:00
Dec.	3	CHICAGO BEARS	6:00
Dec.	9	at Denver Broncos	2:00
Dec.	16	KANSAS CITY CHIEFS	1:00

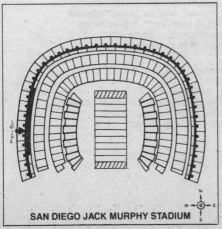

SAN DIEGO JACK MURPHY STADIUM

SAN DIEGO CHARGERS END OF SEASON DEPTH CHART

OFFENSE

WR	— 18 Charlie Joiner, 84 Hosea Fortune, 87 Dwight Scales**, 81 Roger Carr*
OLT	— 66 Billy Shields, 77 Sam Claphan
OLG	— 63 Doug Wilkerson, 60 Dennis McKnight, 68 Bill Elko
C	— 62 Don Macek, 60 Dennis McKnight, 69 Derrel Gofourth
ORG	— 67 Ed White, 69 Derrel Gofourth, 64 Chuck Loewen*
ORT	— 75 Drew Gissinger, 61 Don Brown
WR	— 89 Wes Chandler, 82 Bobby Duckworth, 84 Hosea Fortune
TE	— 80 Kellen Winslow, 85 Eric Sievers, 88 Pete Holohan
QB	— 14 Dan Fouts, 11 Ed Luther, 12 Bruce Mathison
HB	— 46 Chuck Muncie, 21 James Brooks, 41 Earnest Jackson, Mike Pleasant*
FB	— 85 Eric Sievers, 47 Sherman Smith, 40 Jim Jodat, 25 John Cappelletti**

DEFENSE

DLE	— 76 Keith Ferguson, 68 Leroy Jones**, 72 Kenny Neil
NT	— 91 Richard Ackerman, 68 Bill Elko, 74 Abdul Salaam
DRE	— 79 Gary Johnson, 78 Chuck Ehin, 72 Kenny Neil
LOLB	— 57 Linden King, 50 Carlos Bradley, 56 Larry Evans
LIBL	— 58 Mike Green, 59 Cliff Thrift
RILB	— 54 Billy Ray Smith, 55 Derrie Nelson, 53 Brian Kelley
ROLB	— 51 Woodrow Lowe, 52 Ray Preston, 56 Larry Evans
LCB	— 22 Gill Byrd, 20 Reuben Henderson, 24 Miles McPherson*
SS	— 49 Andre Young, 30 Bruce Laird**, 45 Henry Williams
FS	— 28 Ken Greene, 48 Tim Fox, 43 Bob Gregor***
RCB	— 23 Danny Walters, 20 Reuben Henderson

SPECIAL TEAMS

K	— 6 Rolf Benirschke
P	— 7 Maury Buford
H	— 11 Ed Luther, 88 Pete Holohan
KR	— 21 James Brooks, 30 Bruce Laird**, 41 Earnest Jackson
PR	— 21 James Brooks, 89 Wes Chandler
LSN	— 60 Dennis McKnight, 75 Drew Gissinger

SAN DIEGO CHARGERS

INDIVIDUAL RUSHERS

	Att	Yards	Avg	Long	TD
Muncie, Chuck	235	886	3.8	t34	12
Brooks, James	127	516	4.1	61	3
Smith, Sherman	24	91	3.8	20	0
Jackson, Ernest	11	39	3.5	6	0
Chandler, Wes	2	25	12.5	23	0
Cappelletti, John	1	5	5.0	5	0
Mathison, Bruce	1	0	0.0	0	0
Fouts, Dan	12	−5	−0.4	3	1
Sievers, Eric	1	−7	−7.0	−7	0
Luther, Ed	9	−14	−1.6	8	0

Leader based on most yards gained

INDIVIDUAL PASSING

	Att	Comp	% Comp	Yards	Avg Gain	TD	% TD	Long	Int	% Int	Rating Points
Fouts, Dan	340	215	63.2	2975	8.75	20	5.9	t59	15	4.4	92.5
Luther, Ed	287	151	52.6	1875	6.53	7	2.4	46	17	5.9	56.6
Mathison, Bruce	5	3	60.0	41	8.20	0	0.0	25	1	20.0	
Buford, Maury	1	0	0.0	0	0.00	0	0.0	0	0	0.0	
Chandler, Wes	0	0	---	0	----	0	---	0	0	---	
Holohan, Pete	1	0	0.0	0	0.00	0	0.0	0	0	0.0	
Smith, Sherman	1	0	0.0	0	0.00	0	0.0	0	0	0.0	

INDIVIDUAL RECEIVERS

	No	Yards	Avg	Long	TD
Winslow, Kellen	88	1172	13.3	46	8
Joiner, Charlie	65	960	14.8	t33	3
Chandler, Wes	58	845	14.6	t44	5
Muncie, Chuck	42	396	9.4	27	1
Sievers, Eric	33	452	13.7	28	3
Brooks, James	25	215	8.6	36	0
Holohan, Pete	23	272	11.8	35	2
Duckworth, Bobby	20	422	21.1	t59	5
Smith, Sherman	6	51	8.5	21	0
Jackson, Ernest	5	42	8.4	10	0
Carr, Roger	2	36	18.0	23	0
Scales, Dwight	2	28	14.0	14	0

Leader based on most passes caught

INDIVIDUAL INTERCEPTORS

	No	Yards	Avg	Long	TD
Walters, Danny	7	55	7.9	33	0
Young, Andre	2	49	24.5	t40	1
Fox, Tim	2	14	7.0	14	0
King, Linden	1	19	19.0	19	0
Preston, Ray	1	13	13.0	13	0
Green, Mike	1	3	3.0	3	0
Byrd, Gill	1	0	0.0	0	0
McPherson, Miles	1	0	0.0	0	0

Leader based on most interceptions

INDIVIDUAL KICKOFF RETURNERS

	No	Yards	Avg	Long	TD
Brooks, James	32	607	19.0	34	0
Laird, Bruce	15	342	22.8	41	0
Jackson, Ernest	11	201	18.3	32	0
McPherson, Miles	5	77	15.4	19	0
Jodat, Jim	3	45	15.0	18	0
Young, Andre	3	41	13.7	19	0
Smith, Sherman	2	32	16.0	21	0
Scales, Dwight	1	16	16.0	16	0
Smith, Billy Ray	1	10	10.0	10	0
Sievers, Eric	1	6	6.0	6	0

Leader based on average return

INDIVIDUAL PUNTERS

	No	Yards	Long	Avg	Total Punts	TB	Blk	Opp Ret	Ret Yds	In 20	Net Avg
Buford, Maury	63	2763	60	43.9	63	8	0	35	299	13	36.6

INDIVIDUAL PUNT RETURNERS

	No	FC	Yards	Avg	Long	TD
Brooks, James	18	4	137	7.6	30	0
Chandler, Wes	8	6	26	3.3	11	0
Fortune, Hosea	4	0	16	4.0	9	0
Scales, Dwight	2	0	34	17.0	30	0
Laird, Bruce	1	0	0	0.0	0	0

Leader based on average return

INDIVIDUAL SCORERS

KICKERS	XP	XPA	FG	FGA	PTS
Benirschke, Rolf	43	45	15	24	88

NON-KICKERS	TD	TDR	TDP	TDM	PTS
Muncie, Chuck	13	12	1	0	78
Winslow, Kellen	8	0	8	0	48
Chandler, Wes	5	0	5	0	30
Duckworth, Bobby	5	0	5	0	30
Brooks, James	3	3	0	0	18
Joiner, Charlie	3	0	3	0	18
Sievers, Eric	3	0	3	0	18
Holohan, Pete	2	0	2	0	12
Fouts, Dan	1	1	0	0	6
Nelson, Derrie	1	0	0	1	6
Young, Andre	1	0	0	1	6

t=*Touchdown*

SEATTLE SEAHAWKS

AFC Western Division

Address: 5305 Lake Washington Blvd., Kirkland, WA 98033
Telephone: (206) 827 9777

CLUB OFFICIALS
President, General Manager: Mike McCormack
Assistant General Manager: Chuck Allen
Business Manager: Mickey Loomis
Assistant Business Manager: Lynda Sides
Public Relations Director: Gary Wright
Assistant Public Relations Director: Dave Neubert
Head Coach: Chuck Knox
Asst. Head Coach, Def. Coordinator, Linebackers: Tom Catlin
Offensive Coordinator, Offensive Line: Ray Prochaska
Defensive Line: George Dyer
Offensive Backs: Chick Harris
Defensive Backs: Ralph Hawkins
Quarterbacks: Ken Meyer
Receivers: Steve Moore
Special Teams, Tight Ends: Rusty Tillman
Special Assignments: Joe Vitt
Player Personnel Director: Dick Mansperger
Staff Scouts: Ralph Goldston, Warren Harper, Doug Kretz, Jeff Smith
Training Camp Director, Scouting Assistant: Rick Thompson
Staff Assistant, Pro Personnel: Randy Mueller
Ticket Director: James Nagaoka
Head Trainer: Jim Whitesel
Assistant Trainer: John Kasik
Equipment Manager: Walt Loeffler
Assistant Equipment Manager: Terry Sinclair

Stadium: Kingdome (Capacity 64,984)
Playing Surface: AstroTurf
Stadium Address: 201 South King Street, Seattle, WA 98104
Colors: Blue, Green & Silver
Summer Training Camp: Eastern Washington University, Cheney, WA 99004

SEATTLE SEAHAWKS 1984 SCHEDULE

PRE-SEASON

Jul.	28	TAMPA BAY BUCCANEERS at Canton	3:00
Aug.	4	BUFFALO BILLS	7:30
Aug.	11	at Detroit Lions	7:00
Aug.	17	ST LOUIS CARDINALS	7:30
Aug.	24	at San Francisco 49ers	6:00

REGULAR SEASON

Sep.	2	CLEVELAND BROWNS	1:00
Sep.	9	SAN DIEGO CHARGERS	1:00
Sep.	16	at New England Patriots	1:00
Sep.	23	CHICAGO BEARS	1:00
Sep.	30	at Minnesota Vikings	12:00
Oct.	7	at Los Angeles Raiders	1:00
Oct.	14	BUFFALO BILLS	1:00
Oct.	21	Green Bay Packers at Milwaukee	12:00
Oct.	29	at San Diego Chargers	6:00
Nov.	4	KANSAS CITY CHIEFS	1:00
Nov.	12	LOS ANGELES RAIDERS	6:00
Nov.	18	at Cincinnati Bengals	1:00
Nov.	25	at Denver Broncos	2:00
Dec.	2	DETROIT LIONS	1:00
Dec.	9	at Kansas City Chiefs	12:00
Dec.	15	DENVER BRONCOS	1:00

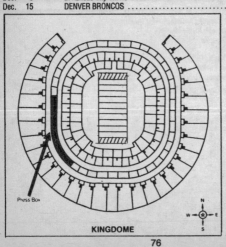

Press Box

KINGDOME

SEATTLE SEAHAWKS END OF SEASON DEPTH CHART

OFFENSE

WR	—	85 Paul Johns, 29 Harold Jackson, 83 Chris Castor
OLT	—	64 Ron Essink, 69 Matt Hernandez
OLG	—	67 Reggie McKenzie, 66 Bill Dugan, 65 Edwin Bailey
C	—	59 Blair Bush, 62 Kani Kauahi, 65 Edwin Bailey
ORG	—	61 Robert Pratt, 66 Bill Dugan
ORT	—	76 Steve August, 69 Matt Hernandez
TE	—	87 Charle Young, 88 Pete Metzelaars, 86 Mike Tice
WR	—	80 Steve Largent, 89 Byron Walker
QB	—	17 Dave Krieg, 10 Jim Zorn, 12 Sam Adkins**
HB	—	28 Curt Warner, 37 Eric Lane, 31 Zachary Dixon
FB	—	32 Cullen Bryant, 33 Dan Doornink, 46 David Hughes

DEFENSE

DLE	—	79 Jacob Green, 70 Darrell Irvin
NT	—	72 Joe Nash, 74 Manu Tuiasosopo**, 75 Robert Hardy*
DRE	—	77 Jeff Bryant, 70 Darrell Irvin, 84 Sam Clancy**
LOLB	—	58 Bruce Scholtz, 63 Mark Hicks
LILB	—	57 Shelton Robinson, 52 Joe Norman, Jim Youngblood
RILB	—	53 Keith Butler, 51 Sam Merriman
ROLB	—	55 Michael Jackson, 56 Greg Gaines, 63 Mark Hicks, 54 Eugene Williams*
LCB	—	26 Kerry Justin**, 42 Keith Simpson, Terry Jackson
SS	—	45 Kenny Easley, 21 Paul Moyer, 35 Dan Dufek
FS	—	44 John Harris, 21 Paul Moyer
RCB	—	22 Dave Brown, 27 Greggory Johnson**

SPECIAL TEAMS

K	—	9 Norm Johnson
P	—	8 Jeff West
H	—	10 Jim Zorn, 80 Steve Largent
KR	—	31 Zachary Dixon, 46 David Hughes
PR	—	85 Paul Johns, 45 Kenny Easley
LSN	—	59 Blair Bush, 62 Kani Kauahi

SEATTLE SEAHAWKS

INDIVIDUAL RUSHERS

	Att	Yards	Avg	Long	TD
Warner, Curt	335	1449	4.3	60	13
Hughes, David	83	313	3.8	26	1
Doornink, Dan	40	99	2.5	9	2
Bryant, Cullen	27	87	3.2	9	0
Zorn, Jim	30	71	2.4	t18	1
Krieg, Dave	16	55	3.4	t10	2
Dixon, Zachary, Balt.-Sea.	9	32	3.6	7	0
Johns, Paul	2	12	6.0	26	0
Lane, Eric	3	1	0.3	7	0

Leader based on most yards gained

INDIVIDUAL PASSING

	Att	Comp	% Comp	Yards	Avg Gain	TD	% TD	Long	Int	% Int	Rating Points
Krieg, Dave	243	147	60.5	2139	8.80	18	7.4	t50	11	4.5	95.0
Zorn, Jim	205	103	50.2	1166	5.69	7	3.4	43	7	3.4	64.8
Largent, Steve	1	1	100.0	11	11.00	0	0.0	11	0	0.0	

INDIVIDUAL RECEIVERS

	No	Yards	Avg	Long	TD
Largent, Steve	72	1074	14.9	t46	11
Brown, Theotis	47	418	8.9	53	2
Warner, Curt	42	325	7.7	28	1
Young, Charle	36	529	14.7	47	2
Johns, Paul	34	486	14.3	t30	4
Doornink, Dan	24	328	13.7	47	2
Walker, Byron	12	248	20.7	t50	2
Hughes, David	10	100	10.0	t33	1
Jackson, Harold	8	126	15.8	29	1
Metzelaars, Pete	7	72	10.3	t17	1
Bryant, Cullen	3	8	2.7	3	0
Lane, Eric	2	9	4.5	7	0
Krieg, Dave	1	11	11.0	11	0

Leader based on most passes caught

INDIVIDUAL INTERCEPTORS

	No	Yards	Avg	Long	TD
Easley, Ken	7	106	15.1	48	0
Brown, Dave	6	83	13.8	37	0
Simpson, Keith	4	39	9.8	14	0
Harris, John	2	15	7.5	10	0
Green, Jacob	1	73	73.0	t73	1
Moyer, Paul	1	19	19.0	t19	1
Robinson, Shelton	1	18	18.0	18	0
Scholtz, Bruce	1	8	8.0	8	0
Justin, Kerry	1	2	2.0	2	0
Butler, Keith	1	0	0.0	0	0
Williams, Eugene	1	0	0.0	0	0

Leader based on most interceptions

INDIVIDUAL KICKOFF RETURNERS

	No	Yards	Avg	Long	TD
Dixon, Zachary, Balt.-Sea.	51	1171	23.0	t94	1
Hughes, David	12	282	23.5	35	0
Lane, Eric	4	58	14.5	18	0
McAlister, Ken	3	59	19.7	22	0
Tice, Mike	2	28	14.0	19	0
Metzelaars, Pete	1	0	0.0	0	0

Leader based on average return

INDIVIDUAL PUNTERS

	No	Yards	Long	Avg	Total Punts	TB	Blk	Opp Ret	Ret Yds	In 20	Net Avg
West, Jeff	79	3118	56	39.5	79	10	0	36	185	25	34.6

INDIVIDUAL PUNT RETURNERS

	No	FC	Yards	Avg	Long	TD
Johns, Paul	28	5	316	11.3	t75	1
Johnson, Gregg	3	1	17	5.7	10	0
Harris, John	2	0	27	13.5	14	0
Easley, Ken	1	0	6	6.0	6	0

Leader based on average return

INDIVIDUAL SCORERS

KICKERS

	XP	XPA	FG	FGA	PTS
Johnson, Norm	49	50	18	25	103

NON-KICKERS

	TD	TDR	TDP	TDM	PTS
Warner, Curt	14	13	1	0	84
Largent, Steve	11	0	11	0	66
Johns, Paul	5	0	4	1	30
Doornink, Dan	4	2	2	0	24
Hughes, David	2	1	1	0	12
Krieg, Dave	2	2	0	0	12
Robinson, Shelton	2	0	0	2	12
Walker, Byron	2	0	2	0	12
Young, Charle	2	0	2	0	12
Dixon, Zachary, Balt.-Sea.	1	0	0	1	6
Green, Jacob	1	0	0	1	6
Jackson, Harold	1	0	1	0	6
Metzelaars, Pete	1	0	0	1	6
Moyer, Paul	1	0	0	1	6
Zorn, Jim	1	1	0	0	6

t=Touchdown

NATIONAL FOOTBALL CONFERENCE

TEAMS

ATLANTA FALCONS

NFC Western Division

Address: 1-85 at Suwanee Road, Suwanee, GA 30174
Telephone: (404) 588 1111

CLUB OFFICIALS

Chairman of the Board: Rankin M. Smith, Sr.
President: Rankin Smith, Jr.
Executive Vice President: Eddie LeBaron
General Manager: Tom Braatz
Corporate Secretary: Taylor Smith
Vice President, Chief Financial Officer: Jim Hay
Head Coach: Dan Henning
Assistant Coaches: Steve Crosby, George Dostal, Sam Elliott, Ted Fritsch, Bob Fry, Bob Harrison, Bobby Jackson, John Marshall, Garry Puetz, Dan Sekanovich, Jack Stanton
Director of Pro Personnel: Bill Jobko
Ticket Manager: Ken Grantham
Assistant Ticket Manager: Joan Nave
Public Relations Director: Charlie Dayton
Assistant Public Relations Director: Bob Dickinson
Assistant Director of Community Affairs: Carol Henderson
Head Trainer: Jerry Rhea
Assistant Trainer: Billy Brooks
Equipment Manager: Whitey Zimmerman
Assistant Equipment Manager: Horace Daniel
Scouts: Bob Cegelski, John Jelacic, Bob Riggle, Bill Striegel

Stadium: Atlanta-Fulton County Stadium (Capacity 60,748)
Playing Surface: Grass
Stadium Address: 521 Capitol Avenue S.W., Atlanta, GA 30312
Colors: Red, Black, White, Silver
Summer Training Camp: 1-85 at Suwanee Road, Suwanee, GA 30174

ATLANTA FALCONS 1984 SCHEDULE

PRE-SEASON

Aug. 4	at Minnesota Vikings	7:00
Aug. 11	at New Orleans Saints	7:00
Aug. 18	TAMPA BAY BUCCANEERS	8:00
Aug. 24	DENVER BRONCOS	8:00

REGULAR SEASON

Sep. 2	at New Orleans Saints	12:00
Sep. 9	DETROIT LIONS	1:00
Sep. 16	at Minnesota Vikings	12:00
Sep. 23	HOUSTON OILERS	1:00
Sep. 30	at San Francisco 49ers	1:00
Oct. 7	at Los Angeles Rams	1:00
Oct. 14	NEW YORK GIANTS	1:00
Oct. 22	LOS ANGELES RAMS	9:00
Oct. 28	at Pittsburgh Steelers	4:00
Nov. 5	at Washington Redskins	9:00
Nov. 11	NEW ORLEANS SAINTS	1:00
Nov. 18	CLEVELAND BROWNS	1:00
Nov. 25	at Cincinnati Bengals	1:00
Dec. 2	SAN FRANCISCO 49ers	1:00
Dec. 9	at Tampa Bay Buccaneers	1:00
Dec. 16	PHILADELPHIA EAGLES	4:00

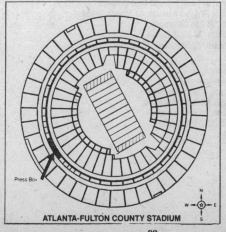

Press Box

ATLANTA-FULTON COUNTY STADIUM

ATLANTA FALCONS END OF SEASON DEPTH CHART

OFFENSE

WR	— 82 Stacey Bailey, 81 Billy Johnson, 85 Alfred Jackson*
OLT	— 78 Mike Kenn, 67 Eric Sanders, 62 Brett Miller
OLG	— 68 R.C. Thielemann, 71 Dan Dufour, 70 Ronnie Lee
C	— 57 Jeff Van Note, 68 R.C. Thielemann, 71 Dan Dufour
ORG	— 61 John Scully, 71 Dan Dufour, 70 Ronnie Lee
ORT	— 66 Warren Bryant, 62 Brett Miller, 67 Eric Sanders
TE	— 80 Junior Miller, 88 Arthur Cox, 86 Ben Young, 87 Russ Mikeska*
WR	— 83 Floyd Hodge, 89 Willie Curran, 84 Alfred Jenkins*
QB	— 10 Steve Bartkowski, 15 Mike Moroski
H-B	— 33 Bo Robinson, 81 Billy Johnson, 49 Allama Matthews, 80 Junior Miller
FB	— 31 William Andrews, 42 Gerald Riggs, 21 Lynn Cain, 22 Richard Williams

DEFENSE

DLE	— 74 Mike Pitts, 79 Jeff Yeates
DLT	— 72 Andrew Provence, 69 Dan Benish, 63 Mike Zele*
DRT	— 65 Don Smith, 69 Dan Benish
DRE	— 75 Jeff Merrow, 74 Mike Pitts, 69 Dan Benish
LLB	— 59 John Rade, 51 Rich Dixon, 56 Al Richardson*, Lyman White*
MLB	— 54 Fulton Kuykendall, 52 John Harper
RLB	— 50 Buddy Curry, 58 David Frye, 55 Dave Levenick
LCB	— 23 Bobby Butler, 30 Steve Haworth, 43 Thomas Tutson
LS	— 26 James Britt, 36 Bob Glazebrook
RS	— 27 Tom Pridemore, 34 Blane Gaison
RCB	— 37 Kenny Johnson, 20 Earl Jones, 43 Thomas Tutson

SPECIAL TEAMS

K	— 18 Mike Luckhurst
P	— 1 Ralph Giacomarro
H	— 15 Mike Moroski, 1 Ralph Giacomarro
KR	— 42 Gerald Riggs, 22 Richard Williams
PR	— 81 Billy Johnson, 89 Willie Curran
LSN	— 71 Dan Dufour, 67 Eric Sanders

ATLANTA FALCONS

INDIVIDUAL RUSHERS

	Att	Yards	Avg	Long	TD
Andrews, William	331	1567	4.7	27	7
Riggs, Gerald	100	437	4.4	t40	8
Johnson, Billy	15	83	5.5	36	0
Cain, Lynn	19	63	3.3	10	1
Bartkowski, Steve	16	38	2.4	10	1
Giacomarro, Ralph	2	13	6.5	13	0
Moroski, Mike	2	12	6.0	7	0
Robinson, Bo	3	9	3.0	7	0
Williams, Richard	1	5	5.0	5	0
Miller, Junior	1	2	2.0	2	0
Bailey, Stacey	2	−5	−2.5	0	0

Leader based on most yards gained

INDIVIDUAL PASSING

	Att	Comp	% Comp	Yards	Avg Gain	TD	% TD	Long	Int	% Int	Rating Points
Bartkowski, Steve	432	274	63.4	3167	7.33	22	5.1	t76	5	1.2	97.6
Moroski, Mike	70	45	64.3	575	8.21	2	2.9	t50	4	5.7	75.6
Hodge, Floyd	2	1	50.0	28	14.00	0	0.0	28	1	50.0	
Giacomarro, Ralph	1	1	100.0	23	23.00	0	0.0	23	0	0.0	
Andrews, William	1	0	0.0	0	0.00	0	0.0	0	0	0.0	
Johnson, Billy	1	0	0.0	0	0.00	0	0.0	0	0	0.0	

INDIVIDUAL RECEIVERS

	No	Yards	Avg	Long	TD
Johnson, Billy	64	709	11.1	t47	4
Andrews, William	59	609	10.3	40	4
Bailey, Stacey	55	881	16.0	53	6
Jenkins, Alfred	38	487	12.8	26	1
Hodge, Floyd	25	280	11.2	t76	4
Riggs, Gerald	17	149	8.8	25	0
Miller, Junior	16	125	7.8	19	0
Jackson, Alfred	13	220	16.9	t54	3
Robinson, Bo	12	100	8.3	15	0
Cox, Arthur	9	83	9.2	19	1
Young, Benjamin	6	74	12.3	19	1
Matthews, Allama	3	37	12.3	23	0
Cain, Lynn	3	24	8.0	11	0
Curran, Willie	1	15	15.0	15	0

Leader based on most passes caught

INDIVIDUAL INTERCEPTORS

	No	Yards	Avg	Long	TD
Pridemore, Tom	4	56	14.0	25	0
Butler, Bobby	4	12	3.0	12	0
Glazebrook, Bob	3	30	10.0	25	0
Johnson, Kenny	2	57	28.5	t31	2
Richardson, Al	1	38	38.0	38	0
Jones, Earl	1	19	19.0	19	0

Leader based on most interceptions

INDIVIDUAL KICKOFF RETURNERS

	No	Yards	Avg	Long	TD
Williams, Richard	23	461	20.0	34	0
Riggs, Gerald	17	330	19.4	35	0
Johnson, Kenny	11	224	20.4	28	0
Cain, Lynn	11	200	18.2	24	0
Curran, Willie	2	26	13.0	16	0
Glazebrook, Bob	2	0	0.0	0	0
Butler, Bobby	1	17	17.0	17	0

Leader based on average return

INDIVIDUAL PUNTERS

	No	Yards	Long	Total Avg	Punts	TB	Blk	Opp Ret	Ret Yds	In 20	Net Avg
Giacomarro, Ralph	70	2823	57	40.3	71	8	1	34	179	18	35.0

INDIVIDUAL PUNT RETURNERS

	No	FC	Yards	Avg	Long	TD
Johnson, Billy	46	4	489	10.6	t71	1

INDIVIDUAL SCORERS

KICKERS	XP	XPA	FG	FGA	PTS
Luckhurst, Mick	43	45	17	22	94

NON-KICKERS	TD	TDR	TDP	TDM	PTS
Andrews, William	11	7	4	0	66
Riggs, Gerald	8	8	0	0	48
Bailey, Stacey	6	0	6	0	36
Johnson, Billy	5	0	4	1	30
Hodge, Floyd	4	0	4	0	24
Jackson, Alfred	3	0	3	0	18
Johnson, Kenny	2	0	0	2	12
Bartkowski, Steve	1	1	0	0	6
Cain, Lynn	1	1	0	0	6
Cox, Arthur	1	0	1	0	6
Gaison, Blane	1	0	0	1	6
Jenkins, Alfred	1	0	1	0	6
Rade, John	1	0	0	1	6
Young, Benjamin	1	0	1	0	6

t=Touchdown

CHICAGO BEARS

NFC Central Division

Corporate Headquarters and Tickets Address:
55 E. Jackson Blvd., Chicago, IL 60604
Halas Hall (Coaching Staff, Personnel, Public Relations): 250 N. Washington, Lake Forest, IL 60045
Telephone: (312) 663 5100 (Administrative),
(312) 663 5408 (Tickets),
(312) 295 6600 (Halas Hall)

CLUB OFFICIALS
Chairman of the Board, President, CEO: Edward W. McCaskey
Executive Vice President, General Manager: Jim Finks
Head Coach: Mike Ditka
Assistant Coaches: Jim Dooley, Dale Haupt, Ed Hughes, Jim LaRue, Ted Plumb, Johnny Roland, Buddy Ryan, Dick Stanfel
Assistant to General Manager: Bill McGrane
Director, Collegiate Scouting: Jim Parmer
Director, Pro Scouting: Bill Tobin
Stadium Operations, Admissions Director: George Arneson
Business Manager: Rudy Custer
Treasurer: Jerry Vainisi
Public Relations Director: Patrick McCaskey
Film Director: Mitch Friedman
Trainer: Fred Caito
Physical Coordinator: Clyde Emrich
Equipment Manager: Ray Earley

Stadium: Soldier Field (Capacity 65,793)
Playing Surface: AstroTurf
Stadium Address: 425 McFetridge Place, Chicago, IL 60605
Colors: Navy Blue, Orange & White
Summer Training Camp: Halas Hall, 250 N. Washington, Lake Forest, IL 60045

CHICAGO BEARS 1984 SCHEDULE

PRE-SEASON

Aug.	4	ST LOUIS CARDINALS	6:00
Aug.	11	GREEN BAY PACKERS at Milwaukee	7:00
Aug.	18	CINCINNATI BENGALS	6:00
Aug.	26	Buffalo Bills at Indianapolis	12:00

REGULAR SEASON

Sep.	2	TAMPA BAY BUCCANEERS	12:00
Sep.	9	DENVER BRONCOS	12:00
Sep.	16	at Green Bay Packers	12:00
Sep.	23	at Seattle Seahawks	1:00
Sep.	30	DALLAS COWBOYS	12:00
Oct.	7	NEW ORLEANS SAINTS	12:00
Oct.	14	at St Louis Cardinals	12:00
Oct.	21	at Tampa Bay Buccaneers	1:00
Oct.	28	MINNESOTA VIKINGS	12:00
Nov.	4	LOS ANGELES RAIDERS	12:00
Nov.	11	at Los Angeles Rams	1:00
Nov.	18	DETROIT LIONS	12:00
Nov.	25	at Minnesota Vikings	3:00
Dec.	3	at San Diego Chargers	6:00
Dec.	9	GREEN BAY PACKERS	12:00
Dec.	16	at Detroit Lions	1:00

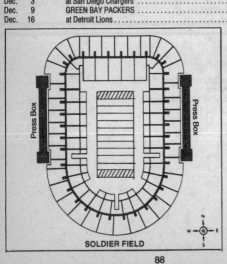

SOLDIER FIELD

CHICAGO BEARS END OF SEASON DEPTH CHART

OFFENSE

WR — 83 Willie Gault, 84 Brian Baschnagel
OLT — 74 Jimbo Covert, 72 John Janata
OLG — 65 Noah Jackson, 62 Mark Bortz, Tim Norman
C — 63 Jay Hilgenberg, 64 Rob Fada, 52 Dan Neal**
ORG — 79 Kurt Becker, 64 Rob Fada, Revie Sorey**
ORT — 78 Keith Van Horne, 71 Andy Frederick
TE — 87 Emery Moorehead, 81 Jay Saldi, 88 Pat Dunsmore
WR — 85 Dennis McKinnon, 82 Ken Margerum, 80 Rickey Watts*
QB — 9 Jim McMahon, 7 Bob Avellini, 8 Vince Evans**
RB — 34 Walter Payton, 29 Dennis Gentry, 31 Anthony Hutchison
RB — 26 Matt Suhey, 33 Calvin Thomas

DEFENSE

DLE — 73 Mike Hartenstine, 98 Tyrone Keys
DLT — 98 Tyrone Keys, 68 Jim Osborne
DRT — 76 Steve McMichael, 99 Dan Hampton***
DRE — 90 Al Harris, 95 Richard Dent, 99 Dan Hampton***
LLB — 55 Otis Wilson, 51 Kel Atkins, 57 Davie Simmons, 58 Jerry Muckensturm**
MLB — 50 Mike Singletary, 54 Brian Cabral
RLB — 59 Gary Campbell**, 90 Al Harris, 53 Dan Rains
LCB — 27 Mike Richardson, 44 Terry Schmidt
SS — 25 Todd Bell, 22 Dave Duerson, 20 Kevin Potter
FS — 45 Gary Fencik, 22 Dave Duerson, 24 Jeff Fisher*
RCB — 21 Leslie Frazier, 43 Walt Williams

SPECIAL TEAMS

K — 16 Bob Thomas
P — 15 Ray Stachowicz, 9 Jim McMahon, Bill Renner
H — 84 Brian Baschnagel, 7 Bob Avellini
KR — 83 Willie Gault, 31 Anthony Hutchison
PR — 85 Dennis McKinnon, 83 Willie Gault, 24 Jeff Fisher*
LSN — 63 Jay Hilgenberg

CHICAGO BEARS

INDIVIDUAL RUSHERS

	Att	Yards	Avg	Long	TD
Payton, Walter	314	1421	4.5	t49	6
Suhey, Matt	149	681	4.6	39	4
McMahon, Jim	55	307	5.6	32	2
Evans, Vince	22	142	6.5	27	1
Gentry, Dennis	16	65	4.1	17	0
Gault, Willie	4	31	7.8	22	0
Parsons, Bob	1	27	27.0	27	0
Thomas, Calvin	8	25	3.1	9	0
Hutchison, Anthony	6	13	2.2	5	1
Margerum, Ken	1	7	7.0	7	0
Moorehead, Emery	5	6	1.2	5	0
Baschnagel, Brian	2	2	1.0	2	0

Leader based on most yards gained

INDIVIDUAL PASSING

	Att	Comp	% Comp	Yards	Avg Gain	TD	% TD	Long	Int	% Int	Rating Points
McMahon, Jim	295	175	59.3	2184	7.40	12	4.1	t87	13	4.4	77.6
Evans, Vince	145	76	52.4	1108	7.64	5	3.4	t72	7	4.8	69.0
Payton, Walter	6	3	50.0	95	15.83	3	50.0	t56	2	33.3	
Suhey, Matt	1	1	100.0	74	74.00	1	100.0	t74	0	0.0	

INDIVIDUAL RECEIVERS

	No	Yards	Avg	Long	TD
Payton, Walter	53	607	11.5	t74	2
Moorehead, Emery	42	597	14.2	36	3
Gault, Willie	40	836	20.9	t87	8
Margerum, Ken	21	336	16.0	60	2
McKinnon, Dennis	20	326	16.3	t49	4
Saldi, Jay	12	119	9.9	16	0
Duinsmore, Pat	8	102	12.8	24	0
Baschnagel, Brian	5	70	14.0	24	0
Thomas, Calvin	2	13	6.5	7	0
Gentry, Dennis	2	8	4.0	6	0
McMahon, Jim	1	18	18.0	t18	1

Leader based on most passes caught

INDIVIDUAL INTERCEPTORS

	No	Yards	Avg	Long	TD
Frazier, Leslie	7	135	19.3	58	1
Schmidt, Terry	5	31	6.2	t32	1
Richardson, Mike	5	9	1.8	6	0
Fencik, Gary	2	34	17.0	20	0
Wilson, Otis	1	6	6:0	6	0

Leader based on most interceptions

INDIVIDUAL KICKOFF RETURNERS

	No	Yards	Avg	Long	TD
Hutchison, Anthony	17	259	15.2	28	0
Gault, Willie	13	276	21.2	38	0
Gentry, Dennis	7	130	18.6	28	0
Watts, Rickey	5	79	15.8	21	0
Duerson, Dave	3	66	22.0	24	0
Baschnagel, Brian	3	42	14.0	19	0
McKinnon, Dennis	2	42	21.0	25	0
Bell, Todd	2	18	9.0	18	0
Cabral, Brian	2	11	5.5	6	0
Rains, Dan	2	11	5.5	11	0
Richardson, Mike	1	17	17.0	17	0
Janata, John	1	2	2.0	2	0

Leader based on average return

INDIVIDUAL PUNTERS

	No	Yards	Long	Avg	Total Punts	TB	Blk	Opp Ret	Ret Yds	In 20	Net Avg
Parsons, Bob	79	2916	54	36.9	79	5	0	37	261	21	32.3
Stachowicz, Ray	12	447	48	37.3	14	0	2	7	61	0	27.6
McMahon, Jim	1	36	36	36.0	1	0	0	0	0	0	36.0

Leader based on gross average

INDIVIDUAL PUNT RETURNERS

	No	FC	Yards	Avg	Long	TD
McKinnon, Dennis	34	3	316	9.3	t59	1
Fisher, Jeff	13	3	71	5.5	11	0
Gault, Willie	9	1	60	6.7	12	0

Leader based on average return

INDIVIDUAL SCORERS

KICKERS	XP	XPA	FG	FGA	PTS
Thomas, Bob	35	38	14	25	77

NON-KICKERS	TD	TDR	TDP	TDM	PTS
Gault, Willie	8	0	8	0	48
Payton, Walter	8	6	2	0	48
McKinnon, Dennis	5	0	4	1	30
Suhey, Matt	5	4	1	0	30
McMahon, Jim	3	2	1	0	18
Moorehead, Emery	3	0	3	0	18
Margerum, Ken	2	0	2	0	12
Frazier, Leslie	1	0	0	1	6
Hartenstine, Mike	1	0	0	1	6
Hutchison, Anthony	1	1	0	0	6
Schmidt, Terry	1	0	0	1	6

t=Touchdown

DALLAS COWBOYS

NFC Eastern Division

Address: 6116 North Central Expressway, Dallas,
TX 75206
Telephone: (214) 369 8000

CLUB OFFICIALS
General Partner: H.R. 'Bum' Bright
President, General Manager: Texas E. Schramm
Head Coach: Tom Landry
Assistant Coaches: Ermal Allen, Neill Armstrong,
Al Lavan, Alan Lowry, Jim Myers (assistant head coach),
Dick Nolan, Gene Stallings, Jim Shofner, Ernie Stautner,
Jerry Tubbs, Bob Ward
Vice President, Personnel Development: Gil Brandt
Vice President, Treasurer: Don Wilson
Vice President, Administration: Joe Bailey
Director of Public Relations: Doug Todd
Business Manager: Dan Werner
Assistant Public Relations Director: Greg Aiello
Ticket Manager: Steve Orsini
Trainers: Don Cochren, Ken Locker
Equipment Manager: William T. (Buck) Buchanan
Cheerleaders Director: Suzanne Mitchell

Stadium: Texas Stadium (Capacity 65,101)
Playing Surface: Texas Turf
Stadium Address: Irving, TX 75062
Colors: Royal Blue, Metallic Silver Blue & White
Summer Training Camp: Campus of California Lutheran College, Conejo Hall,
3270 Campus Drive South, Thousand Oaks, CA 91360

DALLAS COWBOYS 1984 SCHEDULE

PRE-SEASON
Aug.	4	GREEN BAY PACKERS	8:00
Aug.	11	at San Diego Chargers	6:00
Aug.	16	PITTSBURGH STEELERS	8:00
Aug.	25	HOUSTON OILERS	8:00

REGULAR SEASON
Sep.	3	at Los Angeles Rams	6:00
Sep.	9	at New York Giants	1:00
Sep.	16	PHILADELPHIA EAGLES	3:00
Sep.	23	GREEN BAY PACKERS	3:00
Sep.	30	at Chicago Bears	12:00
Oct.	7	ST LOUIS CARDINALS	12:00
Oct.	14	at Washington Redskins	4:00
Oct.	21	NEW ORLEANS SAINTS	9:00
Oct.	28	INDIANAPOLIS COLTS	12:00
Nov.	4	NEW YORK GIANTS	12:00
Nov.	11	at St Louis Cardinals	12:00
Nov.	18	at Buffalo Bills	1:00
Nov.	22	NEW ENGLAND PATRIOTS	3:00
Dec.	2	at Philadelphia Eagles	1:00
Dec.	9	WASHINGTON REDSKINS	3:00
Dec.	17	at Miami Dolphins	9:00

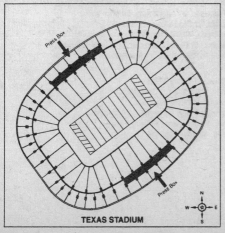

TEXAS STADIUM

DALLAS COWBOYS END OF SEASON DEPTH CHART

OFFENSE

WR	— 80 Tony Hill, 83 Doug Donley, 86 Butch Johnson**, Mike Renfro
OLT	— 67 Pat Donovan, 75 Phil Pozderac, 70 Howard Richards
OLG	— 68 Herbert Scott, 70 Howard Richards, 62 Brian Baldinger
C	— 64 Tom Rafferty, 63 Glen Titensor, 62 Brian Baldinger
ORG	— 65 Kurt Petersen, 70 Howard Richards, 62 Brian Baldinger
ORT	— 61 Jim Cooper, 75 Phil Pozderac, 66 Chris Schultz
TE	— 84 Doug Cosbie, 89 Billy Joe DuPree**, 82 Cleo Simmons
WR	— 88 Drew Pearson, 86 Butch Johnson**, 83 Doug Donley
QB	— 11 Danny White, 14 Gary Hogeboom, 18 Glenn Carano**
RB	— 33 Tony Dorsett, 30 Timmy Newsome, 31 Gary Allen, 23 James Jones*
RB	— 20 Ron Springs, 44 Robert Newhouse, 30 Timmy Newsome, 35 Chuck McSwain*

DEFENSE

DLE	— 72 Ed Jones, 76 Larry Bethea**, 77 Jim Jeffcoat, 92 Bryan Caldwell*
DLT	— 78 John Dutton, 60 Don Smerek, 71 Mark Tuinei
DRT	— 54 Randy White, 60 Don Smerek, 71 Mark Tuinei
DRE	— 79 Harvey Martin, 76 Larry Bethea**, 77 Jim Jeffcoat
LLB	— 58 Mike Hegman, 50 Jeff Rohrer, 57 Angelo King
MLB	— 53 Bob Breunig, 55 Bruce Huther**, 57 Angelo King, 52 Scott McLean*
RLB	— 51 Anthony Dickerson, 57 Angelo King, 59 Mike Walter
LCB	— 24 Everson Walls, 27 Ron Fellows, 25 Rod Hill
SS	— 47 Dextor Clinkscale, 40 Bill Bates, 26 Michael Downs
FS	— 26 Michael Downs, 47 Dextor Clinkscale, 32 Dennis Thurman
RCB	— 32 Dennis Thurman, 25 Rod Hill, 27 Ron Fellows

SPECIAL TEAMS

K	— 1 Rafael Septien, 11 Danny White
P	— 11 Danny White, 3 Jim Miller, 5 John Warren*
H	— 18 Glenn Carano**, 14 Gary Hogeboom
KR	— 27 Ron Fellows, 30 Timmy Newsome, 31 Gary Allen
PR	— 27 Ron Fellows, 31 Gary Allen, 83 Doug Donley
LSN	— 64 Tom Rafferty, 62 Brian Baldinger

DALLAS COWBOYS

INDIVIDUAL RUSHERS

	Att	Yards	Avg	Long	TD
Dorsett, Tony	289	1321	4.6	77	8
Springs, Ron	149	541	3.6	t19	7
Newsome, Tim	44	185	4.2	20	2
Newhouse, Robert	9	34	3.8	8	0
White, Danny	18	31	1.7	22	4
Pearson, Drew	2	13	6.5	10	0
Hill, Tony	1	2	2.0	2	0
Johnson, Butch	1	0	0.0	0	0
Hogeboom, Gary	6	−10	−1.7	−1	0
Leader based on most yards gained					

INDIVIDUAL PASSING

	Att	Comp	% Comp	Yards	Avg Gain	TD	% TD	Long	Int	% Int	Rating Points
White, Danny	533	334	62.7	3980	7.47	29	5.4	t80	23	4.3	85.6
Hogeboom, Gary	17	11	64.7	161	9.47	1	5.9	24	1	5.9	90.6
Springs, Ron	2	1	50.0	15	7.50	1	50.0	t15	0	0.0	
Dorsett, Tony	1	0	0.0	0	0.00	0	0.0	0	0	0.0	
Pearson, Drew	1	0	0.0	0	0.00	0	0.0	0	1	100.0	

INDIVIDUAL RECEIVERS

	No	Yards	Avg	Long	TD
Springs, Ron	73	589	8.1	t80	1
Hill, Tony	49	801	16.3	t75	7
Pearson, Drew	47	545	11.6	32	5
Cosbie, Doug	46	588	12.8	t61	6
Johnson, Butch	41	561	13.7	46	3
Dorsett, Tony	40	287	7.2	24	1
Donley, Doug	18	370	20.6	47	2
Newsome, Tim	18	250	13.9	t52	4
Dupree, Billy Joe	12	142	11.8	28	1
White, Danny	1	15	15.0	t15	1
Rafferty, Tom	1	8	8.0	8	0
Leader based on most passes caught					

INDIVIDUAL INTERCEPTORS

	No	Yards	Avg	Long	TD
Thurman, Dennis	6	49	8.2	34	0
Fellows, Ron	5	139	27.8	t58	1
Downs, Mike	4	80	20.0	28	0
Walls, Everson	4	70	17.5	37	0
Clinkscale, Dextor	2	68	34.0	t68	1
Hill, Rod	2	12	6.0	12	0
Bates, Bill	1	29	29.0	29	0
Jones, Ed	1	12	12.0	12	0
Dickerson, Anthony	1	8	8.0	8	0
Breunig, Bob	1	0	0.0	0	0
Leader based on most interceptions					

INDIVIDUAL KICKOFF RETURNERS

	No	Yards	Avg	Long	TD
Fellows, Ron	43	855	19.9	53	0
Hill, Rod	14	243	17.4	40	0
Allen, Gary	8	178	22.3	31	0
Cosbie, Doug	2	17	8.5	10	0
Newsome, Tim	1	28	28.0	28	0
McSwain, Chuck	1	17	17.0	17	0
Springs, Ron	1	13	13.0	13	0
Huther, Bruce	1	0	0.0	0	0

Leader based on average return

INDIVIDUAL PUNTERS

	No	Yards	Long	Avg	Total Punts	TB	Blk	Opp Ret	Ret Yds	In 20	Net Avg
White, Danny	38	1543	50	40.6	39	3	1	26	233	6	32.1
Warren, John	39	1551	54	39.8	39	1	0	24	283	7	32.0
Miller, Jim	5	178	43	35.6	5	0	0	3	72	1	21.2

Leader based on gross average

INDIVIDUAL PUNT RETURNERS

	No	FC	Yards	Avg	Long	TD
Hill, Rod	30	2	232	7.7	37	0
Allen, Gary	9	1	153	17.0	t68	1
Fellows, Ron	10	3	75	7.5	14	0
Donley, Doug	1	0	1	1.0	1	0
Newhouse, Robert	1	0	0	0.0	0	0

Leader based on average return

INDIVIDUAL SCORERS

KICKERS	XP	XPA	FG	FGA	PTS
Septien, Rafael	57	59	22	27	123

NON-KICKERS	TD	TDR	TDP	TDM	PTS
Dorsett, Tony	9	8	1	0	54
Springs, Ron	8	7	1	0	48
Hill, Tony	7	0	7	0	42
Cosbie, Doug	6	0	6	0	36
Newsome, Tim	6	2	4	0	36
Pearson, Drew	5	0	5	0	30
White, Danny	5	4	1	0	30
Johnson, Butch	3	0	3	0	18
Donley, Doug	2	0	2	0	12
Fellows, Ron	2	0	0	2	12
Allen, Gary	1	0	0	1	6
Clinkscale, Dextor	1	0	0	1	6
Downs, Mike	1	0	0	1	6
Dupree, Billy Joe	1	0	1	0	6
Hegman, Mike	1	0	0	1	6
Thurman, Dennis	1	0	0	1	6
Dickerson, Anthony	0	0	0	0	*2

*=Safety
t=Touchdown

DETROIT LIONS

NFC Central Division

Address: 1200 Featherstone Road, Box 4200, Pontiac, MI 48057
Telephone: (313) 335 4131 (Office), (313) 335 4151 (Tickets)

CLUB OFFICIALS
Owner and President: William Clay Ford
Executive Vice President and General Manager: Russ Thomas
Head Coach and Director of Football Operations: Monte Clark
Controller: Chuck Schmidt
Ticket Manager: Fred Otto
Public Relations Director: Don Kremer
Public Relations Assistant: Brian Muir
Assistant Ticket Manager: Tom Keating
Director of Player Personnel: Tim Rooney
Defensive Coordinator and Linebackers: Ed Beard
Special Assignments: Don Doll
Offensive Line: Fred Hoaglin
Offensive Backfield: Bill Johnson
Defensive Line: Ed Khayat
Special Teams: Joe Madden
Offensive Coordinator and Quarterbacks: Bill Nelsen
Defensive Backfield: Mel Phillips
Receivers: Larry Seiple
Strength and Conditioning: Gary Wade
Administrative Coordinator: Mike Working
Head Trainer: Kent Falb
Assistant Trainer: Joe Recknagel
Equipment Manager: Dan Jaroshewich
Assistant Equipment Manager: Mark Glenn
Area Scouts: Joe Bushofsky, Dirk Dierking, Ron Hughes, Jim Owens

Stadium: Pontiac Silverdome (Capacity 80,638)
Playing Surface: AstroTurf
Stadium Address: 1200 Featherstone Road, Box 4200, Pontiac, MI 48057
Colors: Honolulu Blue & Silver
Summer Training Camp: Oakland University, Rochester, MI 48063

DETROIT LIONS 1984 SCHEDULE

PRE-SEASON

Aug.	4	PHILADELPHIA EAGLES	7:00
Aug.	11	SEATTLE SEAHAWKS	7:00
Aug.	18	at Buffalo Bills	6:00
Aug.	24	at Cincinnati Bengals	7:00

REGULAR SEASON

Sep.	2	SAN FRANCISCO 49ers	1:00
Sep.	9	at Atlanta Falcons	1:00
Sep.	16	at Tampa Bay Buccaneers	4:00
Sep.	23	MINNESOTA VIKINGS	1:00
Sep.	30	at San Diego Chargers	1:00
Oct.	7	DENVER BRONCOS	1:00
Oct.	14	TAMPA BAY BUCCANEERS	1:00
Oct.	21	at Minnesota Vikings	12:00
Oct.	28	at Green Bay Packers	12:00
Nov.	4	PHILADELPHIA EAGLES	1:00
Nov.	11	at Washington Redskins	1:00
Nov.	18	at Chicago Bears	12:00
Nov.	22	GREEN BAY PACKERS	12:30
Dec.	2	at Seattle Seahawks	1:00
Dec.	10	LOS ANGELES RAIDERS	9:00
Dec.	16	CHICAGO BEARS	1:00

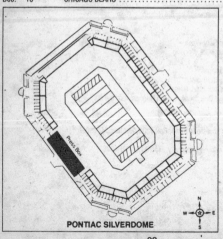

PONTIAC SILVERDOME

DETROIT LIONS END OF SEASON DEPTH CHART

OFFENSE

WR — 86 Mark Nichols, 87 Freddie Scott**, 83 Robbie Martin, 41 James Caver*
OLT — 72 Chris Dieterich, 71 Rich Strenger
OLG — 61 Homer Elias, 64 Larry Lee, 52 Steve Mott
C — 52 Steve Mott, 65 Amos Fowler, 55 Tom Turnure
ORG — 67 Don Greco, 65 Amos Fowler, 64 Larry Lee
ORT — 70 Keith Dorney, 71 Rich Strenger
TE — 80 Ulysses Norris, 84 Rob Rubick, 81 Reese McCall
WR — 89 Jeff Chadwick, 87 Freddie Scott**, 39 Leonard Thompson***
QB — 17 Eric Hipple, 16 Gary Danielson, 14 Mike Machurek
HB — 20 Billy Sims, 24 Dexter Bussey, 32 Rick Kane
FB — 30 James Jones, 38 Vince Thompson, 25 Horace King

DEFENSE

DLE — 62 Curtis Green, 66 Mike Cofer, 63 Martin Moss
DLT — 79 Bill Gay, 74 Mike Fanning**, 73 Mike Dawson
DRT — 78 Doug English, 74 Mike Fanning**
DRE — 66 Mike Cofer, 79 Bill Gay, 63 Martin Moss
LLB — 53 Garry Cobb, 54 Roosevelt Barnes, 51 James Harrell
MLB — 57 Ken Fantetti, 58 Steve Doig, 50 August Curley*
RLB — 59 Jimmy Williams, 54 Roosevelt Barnes, 51 James Harrell
LCB — 27 Bobby Watkins, 29 Bruce McNorton
LS — 33 William Graham, 21 Demetrious Johnson
RS — 35 Alvin Hall, 23 Maurice Harvey
RCB — 29 Bruce McNorton, 34 Danny Wagoner, 43 Al Latimer*

SPECIAL TEAMS

K — 3 Ed Murray
P — 11 Mike Black
H — 17 Eric Hipple, 16 Gary Danielson
KR — 35 Alvin Hall, 31 Ken Jenkins, 83 Robbie Martin
PR — 31 Ken Jenkins, 83 Robbie Martin
LSN — 55 Tom Turnure, 64 Larry Lee

DETROIT LIONS

INDIVIDUAL RUSHERS

	Att	Yards	Avg	Long	TD
Sims, Billy	220	1040	4.7	41	7
Jones, James	135	475	3.5	18	6
Bussey, Dexter	57	249	4.4	26	0
Hipple, Eric	41	171	4.2	27	3
Thompson, Vince	40	138	3.5	10	1
Thompson, Leonard	4	72	18.0	t40	1
Kane, Rick	4	19	4.8	9	0
Nichols, Mark	1	13	13.0	13	0
Danielson, Gary	6	8	1.3	8	0
King, Horace	3	6	2.0	4	0
Black, Mike	2	-10	-5.0	0	0

Leader based on most yards gained

INDIVIDUAL PASSING

	Att	Comp	% Comp	Yards	Avg Gain	TD	% TD	Long	Int	% Int	Rating Points
Hipple, Eric	387	204	52.7	2577	6.66	12	3.1	t80	18	4.7	64.7
Danielson, Gary	113	59	52.2	720	6.37	7	6.2	54	4	3.5	78.0
Jones, James	2	0	0.0	0	0.00	0	0.0	0	0	0.0	
Black, Mike	1	0	0.0	0	0.00	0	0.0	0	1	100.0	

INDIVIDUAL RECEIVERS

	No	Yards	Avg	Long	TD
Jones, James	46	467	10.2	46	1
Sims, Billy	42	419	10.0	54	0
Thompson, Leonard	41	752	18.3	t80	3
Chadwick, Jeff	40	617	15.4	45	4
Nichols, Mark	29	437	15.1	46	1
Norris, Ulysses	26	291	11.2	41	7
Rubick, Rob	10	81	8.1	15	1
King, Horace	9	76	8.4	14	0
Bussey, Dexter	8	49	6.1	t14	1
Scott, Fred	5	71	14.2	25	1
Thompson, Vince	4	16	4.0	8	0
Kane, Rick	2	15	7.5	9	0
McCall, Reese	1	6	6.0	6	0

Leader based on most passes caught

INDIVIDUAL INTERCEPTORS

	No	Yards	Avg	Long	TD
McNorton, Bruce	7	30	4.3	15	0
Watkins, Bobby	4	48	12.0	31	0
Cobb, Garry	4	19	4.8	13	0
Barnes, Roosevelt	2	70	35.0	70	0
Hall, Alvin	2	18	9.0	18	0
Fantetti, Ken	2	0	0.0	0	0
Latimer, Al	1	0	0.0	0	0

Leader based on most interceptions

INDIVIDUAL KICKOFF RETURNERS

	No	Yards	Avg	Long	TD
Hall, Alvin	23	492	21.4	32	0
Jenkins, Ken	22	459	20.9	30	0
Martin, Robbie	8	140	17.5	51	0
Caver, Jim	4	71	17.8	33	0
King, Horace	1	11	11.0	11	0
Lee, Edward	1	11	11.0	11	0
Curley, August	1	7	7.0	7	0
Norris, Ulysses	1	0	0.0	0	0

Leader based on average return

INDIVIDUAL PUNTERS

	No	Yards	Long	Avg	Total Punts	TB	Blk	Opp Ret	Ret Yds	In 20	Net Avg
Black, Mike	71	2911	60	41.0	72	9	1	39	302	17	33.7

INDIVIDUAL PUNT RETURNERS

	No	FC	Yards	Avg	Long	TD
Jenkins, Ken	23	1	230	10.0	43	0
Martin, Robbie	15	3	183	12.2	t81	1
Hall, Alvin	8	4	109	13.6	66	0
Latimer, Al	0	1	0	---	0	0

Leader based on average return

INDIVIDUAL SCORERS

KICKERS	XP	XPA	FG	FGA	PTS
Murray, Ed	38	38	25	32	113

NON-KICKERS	TD	TDR	TDP	TDM	PTS
Jones, James	7	6	1	0	42
Norris, Ulysses	7	0	7	0	42
Sims, Billy	7	7	0	0	42
Chadwick, Jeff	4	0	4	0	24
Thompson, Leonard	4	1	3	0	24
Hipple, Eric	3	3	0	0	18
Bussey, Dexter	1	0	1	0	6
Martin, Robbie	1	0	0	1	6
Nichols, Mark	1	0	1	0	6
Rubick, Rob	1	0	1	0	6
Scott, Fred	1	0	1	0	6
Thompson, Vince	1	1	0	0	6
English, Doug	0	0	0	0	*4
Fanning, Mike	0	0	0	0	*2

*=Safety
t=Touchdown

GREEN BAY PACKERS

NFC Central Division

Address: 1265 Lombardi Avenue, Green Bay, WI 54304
Telephone: (414) 494 2351

CLUB OFFICIALS
Chairman of the Board: Dominic Olejniczak
President: Hon. Robert J. Parins
Vice President: Tony Canadeo
Secretary: John Torinus
Assistant to the President: Bob Harlan
Assistant to the President: Tom Miller
Director of Public Relations: Lee Remmel
Executive Assistant: Phil Pionek
Head Coach: Forrest Gregg
Offense Coordinator: Bob Schnelker
Defense Coordinator: Hank Bullough
Receivers: Lew Carpenter
Strength and Conditioning Coordinator: Virgil Knight
Defensive Line Coach: Dick Modzelewski
Special Team: Herb Paterra
Secondary: Ken Riley
Offensive Backfield: George Sefcik
Offensive Line: Jerry Wampfler
Director, Player Personnel: Dick Corrick
Pro Personnel: Burt Gustafson
Scouting: Billy Atkins, Red Cochran, Lloyd Eaton, Dave Hanner, Baby Ray, Tom Tipps
Equipment Manager: Bob Noel
Head Trainer: Dom Gentile

Stadium: Lambeau Field (Capacity 56,189)
Playing Surface: Grass
Stadium Address: 1265 Lombardi Avenue, Green Bay, WI 54304
Stadium: Milwaukee County Stadium (Capacity 55,958)
Playing Surface: Grass
Stadium Address: Highway 1-94, Milwaukee, WI 53214
Colors: Dark Green, Gold & White
Summer Training Camp: St. Norbert College, DePere, WI 54115
(Practices at Lambeau Field, Green Bay)

GREEN BAY PACKERS 1984 SCHEDULE

PRE-SEASON

Aug.	4	at Dallas Cowboys	8:00
Aug.	11	CHICAGO BEARS at Milwaukee	7:00
Aug.	18	at Los Angeles Rams	7:00
Aug.	25	INDIANAPOLIS COLTS	7:00

REGULAR SEASON

Sep.	2	ST LOUIS CARDINALS	12:00
Sep.	9	at Los Angeles Raiders	1:00
Sep.	16	CHICAGO BEARS	12:00
Sep.	23	at Dallas Cowboys	3:00
Sep.	30	at Tampa Bay Buccaneers	4:00
Oct.	7	SAN DIEGO CHARGERS	3:00
Oct.	15	at Denver Broncos	7:00
Oct.	21	SEATTLE SEAHAWKS at Milwaukee	12:00
Oct.	28	DETROIT LIONS	12:00
Nov.	4	at New Orleans Saints	12:00
Nov.	11	MINNESOTA VIKINGS at Milwaukee	12:00
Nov.	18	LOS ANGELES RAMS at Milwaukee	12:00
Nov.	22	at Detroit Lions	12:30
Dec.	2	TAMPA BAY BUCCANEERS	12:00
Dec.	9	at Chicago Bears	12:00
Dec.	16	at Minnesota Vikings	12:00

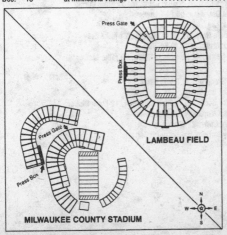

LAMBEAU FIELD

MILWAUKEE COUNTY STADIUM

GREEN BAY PACKERS END OF SEASON DEPTH CHART

OFFENSE

WR	—	80 James Lofton, 88 Ron Cassidy
OLT	—	67 Karl Swanke, 65 Ron Hallstrom
OLG	—	61 Dave Drechsler, 64 Syd Kitson
C	—	54 Larry McCarren, 58 Larry Rubens
ORG	—	64 Syd Kitson, 74 Tim Huffman, 69 Leotis Harris*
ORT	—	68 Greg Koch, 77 Charlie Getty**
TE	—	82 Paul Coffman, 81 Gary Lewis**
WR	—	83 John Jefferson, 85 Phillip Epps
QB	—	12 Lynn Dickey, 17 David Whitehurst, 19 Rich Campbell
HB	—	31 Gerry Ellis, 25 Harlan Huckleby, 20 Chet Winters, 40 Eddie Lee Ivery*
FB	—	39 Mike Meade, 33 Jessie Clark, 35 Del Rodgers*

DEFENSE

DLE	—	73 Byron Braggs, 79 Ron Spears, 72 Greg Boyd
NT	—	99 Charles Johnson, 91 Daryle Skaugstad, 63 Terry Jones*, 75 Rich Turner*, Myron Lapka
DRE	—	90 Ezra Johnson, 93 Robert Brown, 79 Ron Spears
LOLB	—	59 John Anderson, 51 Guy Prather
LILB	—	55 Randy Scott, 50 Rich Wingo, 57 Mike Curcio
RILB	—	52 George Cumby, 62 Jim Laughlin, 57 Mike Curcio
ROLB	—	53 Mike Douglass, 56 Cliff Lewis
LCB	—	22 Mark Lee, 38 Estus Hood
LS	—	24 Johnnie Gray, 37 Mark Murphy, 21 Mike Jolly
RS	—	37 Mark Murphy, 21 Mike Jolly
RCB	—	26 Tim Lewis, 44 Dwayne O'Steen, 29 Mike McCoy*

SPECIAL TEAMS

K	—	10 Jan Stenerud, 11 Eddie Garcia
P	—	28 Bucky Scribner
H	—	28 Bucky Scribner, 19 Rich Campbell, 12 Lynn Dickey
KR	—	25 Harlan Huckleby, 26 Tim Lewis
PR	—	85 Phillip Epps, 22 Mark Lee
LSN	—	58 Larry Rubens, 54 Larry McCarren

GREEN BAY PACKERS

INDIVIDUAL RUSHERS

	Att	Yards	Avg	Long	TD
Ellis, Gerry	141	696	4.9	71	4
Ivery, Eddie Lee	86	340	4.0	21	2
Clark, Jessie	71	328	4.6	42	0
Meade, Mike	55	201	3.7	15	1
Huckleby, Harlan	50	182	3.6	20	4
Lofton, James	9	36	4.0	13	0
Lewis, Gary	4	16	4.0	11	1
Dickey, Lynn	21	12	0.6	4	3
Whitehurst, David	2	−4	−2.0	0	0

Leader based on most yards gained

INDIVIDUAL PASSING

	Att	Comp	% Comp	Yards	Avg Gain	TD	% TD	Long	Int	% Int	Rating Points
Dickey, Lynn	484	289	59.7	4458	9.21	32	6.6	t75	29	6.0	87.3
Whitehurst, David	35	18	51.4	149	4.26	0	0.0	19	2	5.7	38.9
Ellis, Gerry	5	2	40.0	31	6.20	1	20.0	20	1	20.0	
Ivery, Eddie Lee	2	2	100.0	50	25.00	0	0.0	35	0	0.0	

INDIVIDUAL RECEIVERS

	No	Yards	Avg	Long	TD
Lofton, James	58	1300	22.4	t74	8
Jefferson, John	57	830	14.6	36	7
Coffman, Paul	54	814	15.1	74	11
Ellis, Gerry	52	603	11.6	56	2
Epps, Phillip	18	313	17.4	45	0
Clark, Jessie	18	279	15.5	t75	1
Ivery, Eddie Lee	16	139	8.7	17	1
Meade, Mike	16	110	6.9	t31	2
Lewis, Gary	11	204	18.5	49	1
Huckleby, Harlan	10	87	8.7	14	0
Kitson, Syd	1	9	9.0	9	0

Leader based on most passes caught

INDIVIDUAL INTERCEPTORS

	No	Yards	Avg	Long	TD
Lewis, Tim	5	111	22.2	46	0
Anderson, John	5	54	10.8	t27	1
Lee, Mark	4	23	5.8	15	0
Gray, Johnny	2	5	2.5	5	0
Laughlin, Jim	1	22	22.0	22	0
Scott, Randy	1	12	12.0	12	0
Jolly, Mike	1	0	0.0	0	0

Leader based on most interceptions

INDIVIDUAL KICKOFF RETURNERS

	No	Yards	Avg	Long	TD
Huckleby, Harlan	41	757	18.5	57	0
Lewis, Tim	20	358	17.9	30	0
Gray, Johnny	11	178	16.2	26	0
Winters, Chet	3	28	9.3	12	0
Ivery, Eddie Lee	1	17	17.0	17	0
Drechsler, Dave	1	1	1.0	1	0
Kitson, Syd	1	0	0.0	0	0
Lee, Mark	1	0	0.0	0	0

Leader based on average return

INDIVIDUAL PUNTERS

	No	Yards	Long	Avg	Total Punts	TB	Blk	Opp Ret	Ret Yds	In 20	Net Avg
Scribner, Bucky	69	2869	70	41.6	70	7	1	43	384	11	33.5

INDIVIDUAL PUNT RETURNERS

	No	FC	Yards	Avg	Long	TD
Epps, Phillip	36	13	324	9.0	t90	1
Gray, Johnny	2	0	9	4.5	5	0
Hood, Estus	1	0	0	0.0	0	0
Lewis, Cliff	1	0	0	0.0	0	0
Lee, Mark	1	0	−4	−4.0	−4	0

Leader based on average return

INDIVIDUAL SCORERS

KICKERS	XP	XPA	FG	FGA	PTS
Stenerud, Jan	52	52	21	26	115

NON-KICKERS	TD	TDR	TDP	TDM	PTS
Coffman, Paul	11	0	11	0	66
Lofton, James	8	0	8	0	48
Jefferson, John	7	0	7	0	42
Ellis, Gerry	6	4	2	0	36
Huckleby, Harlan	4	4	0	0	24
Dickey, Lynn	3	3	0	0	18
Ivery, Eddie Lee	3	2	1	0	18
Meade, Mike	3	1	2	0	18
Douglass, Mike	2	0	0	2	12
Lewis, Gary	2	1	1	0	12
Anderson, John	1	0	0	1	6
Clark, Jessie	1	0	1	0	6
Epps, Phillip	1	0	0	1	6
Boyd, Greg	0	0	0	0	*2

*=Safety
t=Touchdown

LOS ANGELES RAMS

NFC Western Division

Business Address: 2327 W. Lincoln Ave., Anaheim,
CA 92801
Ticket Office Anaheim Stadium, 1900 State College Blvd.,
Anaheim, CA 92806
Telephone: (714) 535 7267 or (213) 585 5400

CLUB OFFICIALS
President: Georgia Frontiere
Vice President, Finance: John Shaw
Administrator, Football Operations: Jack Faulkner
Director of Operations: Dick Beam
Director of Player Personnel: John Math
Director of Community Relations: Marshall Klein
Director of Public Relations: Pete Donovan
Head Coach: John Robinson
Assistant Coaches: Bob Baker, Marv Goux, Gil Haskell, Hudson Houck, Jimmy Raye, Steve Shafer,
Fritz Shurmur, Bruce Snyder, Fred Whittingham
Trainers: Gary Tuthill, George Menefee
Equipment Manager: Don Hewitt

Stadium: Anaheim Stadium (Capacity 69,007)
Playing Surface: Grass
Stadium Address: 1900 State College Blvd., Anaheim, CA 92806
Colors: Royal Blue, Gold, White
Summer Training Camp: Cal State-Fullerton, Fullerton, CA 92634

LOS ANGELES RAMS 1984 SCHEDULE

PRE-SEASON

Aug.	4	at San Diego Chargers	6:00
Aug.	13	CLEVELAND BROWNS	7:00
Aug.	18	GREEN BAY PACKERS	7:00
Aug.	23	SAN DIEGO CHARGERS	7:00

REGULAR SEASON

Sep.	3	DALLAS COWBOYS	6:00
Sep.	9	CLEVELAND BROWNS	1:00
Sep.	16	at Pittsburgh Steelers	4:00
Sep.	23	at Cincinnati Bengals	1:00
Sep.	30	NEW YORK GIANTS	1:00
Oct.	7	ATLANTA FALCONS	1:00
Oct.	14	at New Orleans Saints	12:00
Oct.	22	at Atlanta Falcons	9:00
Oct.	28	SAN FRANCISCO 49ers	1:00
Nov.	4	at St Louis Cardinals	3:00
Nov.	11	CHICAGO BEARS	1:00
Nov.	18	Green Bay Packers at Milwaukee	12:00
Nov.	25	at Tampa Bay Buccaneers	1:00
Dec.	2	NEW ORLEANS SAINTS	1:00
Dec.	9	HOUSTON OILERS	1:00
Dec.	14	at San Francisco 49ers	6:00

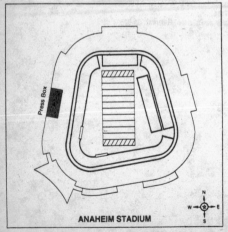

ANAHEIM STADIUM

LOS ANGELES RAMS END OF SEASON DEPTH CHART

OFFENSE

WR	— 88 Preston Dennard, 82 Otis Grant, 25 Gordon Jones*
OLT	— 62 Bill Bain, 73 Russ Bolinger, 75 Irv Pankey*
OLG	— 72 Kent Hill, 73 Russ Bolinger
C	— 56 Doug Smith, 64 Joe Shearin, 60 Dennis Harrah
ORG	— 60 Denis Harrah, 73 Russ Bolinger
ORT	— 78 Jackie Slater, 76 Gary Kowalski
TE	— 86 Mike Barber, 81 David Hill, 83 James McDonald
WR	— 84 George Farmer, 80 Henry Ellard, 87 Drew Hill*
QB	— 15 Vince Ferragamo, 9 Jeff Kemp, 4 Steve Fuller
HB	— 29 Eric Dickerson, 30 Barry Redden, 24 A.J. Jones, 31 Robert Alexander*
FB	— 44 Mike Guman, 81 David Hill, Dwayne Crutchfield

DEFENSE

DLE	— 85 Jack Youngblood, 77 Gary Jeter, 96 Doug Barnett
NT	— 69 Greg Meisner, 70 Charles DeJurnett, 67 Myron Lapka**
DRE	— 71 Reggie Doss, 77 Gary Jeter, 96 Doug Barnett
LOLB	— 58 Mel Owens, 51 David Lewis, 66 Eric Williams
LILB	— 50 Jim Collins, 53 Jim Youngblood**, 98 Mark Jerue
RILB	— 55 Carl Ekern, 54 Howard Carson**, 98 Mark Jerue
ROLB	— 52 George Andrews, 94 Mike Wilcher, 66 Eric Williams
LCB	— 26 Eric Harris, 20 Johnnie Johnson, 28 Mike Williams, 42 Kirk Collins**
SS	— 21 Nolan Cromwell, 37 Ivory Sully
FS	— 20 Johnnie Johnson, 22 Vince Newsome
RCB	— 47 LeRoy Irvin, 26 Eric Harris, 28 Mike Williams

SPECIAL TEAMS

K	— 1 Mike Lansford, 13 Chuck Nelson
P	— 6 John Misko
H	— 21 Nolan Cromwell, 9 Jeff Kemp
KR	— 80 Henry Ellard, 30 Barry Redden
PR	— 80 Henry Ellard, 47 LeRoy Irvin
LSN	— 63 Mike McDonald, 96 Doug Barnett

LOS ANGELES RAMS

INDIVIDUAL RUSHERS

	Att	Yards	Avg	Long	TD
Dickerson, Eric	390	1808	4.6	t85	18
Redden, Barry	75	372	5.0	t40	2
Guman, Mike	7	42	6.0	11	0
Alexander, Robert	7	28	4.0	15	0
Ferragamo, Vince	22	17	0.8	8	0
Ellard, Henry	3	7	2.3	12	0
Cromwell, Nolan	1	0	0.0	0	0
Kemp, Jeff	3	−2	−0.7	0	0
Farmer, George	1	−9	−9.0	−9	0
Grant, Otis	2	−10	−5.0	1	0

Leader based on most yards gained

INDIVIDUAL PASSING

	Att	Comp	% Comp	Yards	Avg Gain	TD	% TD	Long	Int	% Int	Rating Points
Ferragamo, Vince	464	274	59.1	3276	7.06	22	4.7	t61	23	5.0	75.9
Kemp, Jeff	25	12	48.0	135	5.40	1	4.0	21	0	0.0	77.9

INDIVIDUAL RECEIVERS

	No	Yards	Avg	Long	TD
Barber, Mike	55	657	11.9	t42	3
Dickerson, Eric	51	404	7.9	t37	2
Farmer, George	40	556	13.9	t46	5
Guman, Mike	34	347	10.2	60	4
Dennard, Preston	33	465	14.1	t61	5
Hill, David	28	280	10.0	34	2
Ellard, Henry	16	268	16.8	44	0
Grant, Otis	12	221	18.4	57	1
Jones, Gordon	11	172	15.6	46	0
Redden, Barry	4	30	7.5	9	0
Alexander, Robert	1	10	10.0	10	0
McDonald, James	1	1	1.0	t1	1

Leader based on most passes caught

INDIVIDUAL INTERCEPTORS

	No	Yards	Avg	Long	TD
Collins, Kirk	5	113	22.6	58	0
Johnson, Johnnie	4	115	28.8	t60	2
Harris, Eric	4	100	25.0	45	0
Irvin, LeRoy	4	42	10.5	22	0
Cromwell, Nolan	3	76	25.3	t43	1
Collins, Jim	2	46	23.0	29	0
Andrews, George	1	22	22.0	22	0
Ekern, Carl	1	1	1.0	1	0

Leader based on most interceptions

INDIVIDUAL KICKOFF RETURNERS

	No	Yards	Avg	Long	TD
Redden, Barry	19	358	18.8	43	0
Ellard, Henry	15	314	20.9	44	0
Alexander, Robert	13	222	17.1	30	0
Guman, Mike	2	30	15.0	21	0
Irvin, LeRoy	1	22	22.0	22	0
Barnett, Doug	1	0	0.0	0	0
Simmons, Jeff	1	0	0.0	0	0

Leader based on average return

INDIVIDUAL PUNTERS	No	Yards	Long	Avg	Total Punts	TB	Blk	Opp Ret	Ret Yds	In 20	Net Avg
Misko, John	82	3301	67	40.3	83	12	1	39	251	18	33.9

INDIVIDUAL PUNT RETURNERS

	No	FC	Yards	Avg	Long	TD
Ellard, Henry	16	4	217	13.6	t72	1
Irvin, LeRoy	25	3	212	8.5	20	0
Johnson, Johnnie	14	1	109	7.8	26	0

Leader based on average return

INDIVIDUAL SCORERS

KICKERS	XP	XPA	FG	FGA	PTS
Nelson, Chuck	33	37	5	11	48
Lansford, Mike	9	9	6	9	27

NON-KICKERS	TD	TDR	TDP	TDM	PTS
Dickerson, Eric	20	18	2	0	120
Dennard, Preston	5	0	5	0	30
Farmer, George	5	0	5	0	30
Guman, Mike	4	0	4	0	24
Barber, Mike	3	0	3	0	18
Hill, David	2	0	2	0	12
Johnson, Johnnie	2	0	0	2	12
Redden, Barry	2	2	0	0	12
Cromwell, Nolan	1	0	0	1	6
Ellard, Henry	1	0	0	1	6
Grant, Otis	1	0	1	0	6
McDonald, James	1	1	0	0	6
Youngblood, Jack	0	0	0	0	*2

*=Safety
t=Touchdown

MINNESOTA VIKINGS

NFC Central Division

Address: 9520 Viking Drive, Eden Prairie, MN 55344
Telephone: (612) 828 6500

CLUB OFFICIALS
President: Max Winter
Vice President, General Manager: Mike Lynn
Head Coach: Les Steckel
Assistant Coaches: Jerry Burns, Tom Cecchini,
Bob Holloway, Jed Hughes, Bus Mertes, John Michels,
Floyd Reese
Director of Administration: Harley Peterson
Director of Operations: Jeff Diamond
Ticket Manager: Harry Randolph
Director of Football Operations: Jerry Reichow
Director of Player Personnel: Frank Gilliam
Head Scout: Ralph Kohl
Assistant Head Scout: Don Deisch
Scout: John Carson
Director of Public Relations: Merrill Swanson
Assistant Public Relations Director: Kernal Buhler
Public Relations Assistant: Katie Hogan
Trainer: Fred Zamberletti
Equipment Manager: Dennis Ryan

Stadium: Hubert H. Humphrey Metrodome (Capacity 62,212)
Playing Surface: Super Turf
Stadium Address: 500 11th Avenue, So. Minneapolis, MN 55415
Colors: Purple, Gold & White
Summer Training Camp: Mankato State University, Mankato, MN 56001

MINNESOTA VIKINGS 1984 SCHEDULE

PRE-SEASON

Aug.	4	ATLANTA FALCONS	7:00
Aug.	11	MIAMI DOLPHINS	7:00
Aug.	18	PHILADELPHIA EAGLES	7:00
Aug.	24	at St Louis Cardinals	7:30

REGULAR SEASON

Sep.	2	SAN DIEGO CHARGERS	12:00
Sep.	9	at Philadelphia Eagles	1:00
Sep.	16	ATLANTA FALCONS	12:00
Sep.	23	at Detroit Lions	1:00
Sep.	30	SEATTLE SEAHAWKS	12:00
Oct.	7	at Tampa Bay Buccaneers	1:00
Oct.	14	at Los Angeles Raiders	1:00
Oct.	21	DETROIT LIONS	12:00
Oct.	28	at Chicago Bears	12:00
Nov.	4	TAMPA BAY BUCCANEERS	12:00
Nov.	11	Green Bay Packers at Milwaukee	12:00
Nov.	18	at Denver Broncos	2:00
Nov.	25	CHICAGO BEARS	3:00
Nov.	29	WASHINGTON REDSKINS	9:00
Dec.	8	at San Francisco 49ers	1:00
Dec.	16	GREEN BAY PACKERS	12:00

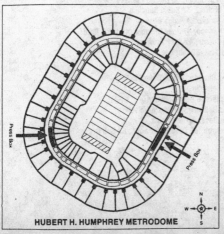

HUBERT H. HUMPHREY METRODOME

MINNESOTA VIKINGS END OF SEASON DEPTH CHART

OFFENSE

WR	— 84 Sam McCullum, 80 Terry LeCount, 88 Mardye McDole
OLT	— 78 Steve Riley, 68 Curtis Rouse
OLG	— 51 Jim Hough, 62 Brent Boyd
C	— 67 Dennis Swilley, 56 Dave Huffman**, 51 Jim Hough
ORG	— 61 Wes Hamilton, 62 Brent Boyd
ORT	— 76 Tim Irwin, 66 Terry Tausch
TE	— 44 Dave Casper, 82 Bob Bruer, 83 Steve Jordan, 81 Joe Senser***, 86 Mike Mularkey*
QB	— 12 Steve Dils, 4 Archie Manning, 11 Wade Wilson, 9 Tommy Kramer*
WR	— 85 Sammy White, 87 Leo Lewis, 89 Mike Jones
RB	— 32 Tony Galbreath, 22 Jarvis Redwine, 23 Ted Brown***
RB	— 20 Darrin Nelson, 34 Rickey Young, 33 Rick Bell

DEFENSE

DLE	— 79 Doug Martin, 75 Randy Holloway
NT	— 65 Charlie Johnson, 72 James White
DRE	— 73 Neil Elshire, 75 Randy Holloway, 77 Mark Mullaney*
LOLB	— 59 Matt Blair, 57 Robin Sendlein
LILB	— 55 Scott Studwell, 58 Walker Lee Ashley
RILB	— 52 Dennis Johnson, 50 Dennis Fowlkes
ROLB	— 54 Fred McNeill, 57 Robin Sendlein
LCB	— 29 John Swain, 21 Rufus Bess
LS	— 45 Tom Hannon, 47 Joey Browner, 49 Keith Nord*
RS	— 27 John Turner, 47 Joey Browner
RCB	— 37 Willie Teal, 39 Carl Lee

SPECIAL TEAMS

K	— 1 Benny Ricardo, 7 Rick Danmeier*
P	— 8 Greg Coleman
H	— 12 Steve Dils, 8 Greg Coleman
KR	— 22 Jarvis Redwine, 20 Darrin Nelson
PR	— 21 Rufus Bess, 87 Leo Lewis
LSN	— 51 Jim Hough, 56 Dave Huffman**, 82 Bob Bruer

MINNESOTA VIKINGS

INDIVIDUAL RUSHERS

	Att	Yards	Avg	Long	TD
Nelson, Darrin	154	642	4.2	t56	1
Brown, Ted	120	476	4.0	43	10
Galbreath, Tony	113	474	4.2	t52	4
Young, Rickey	39	90	2.3	9	2
Redwine, Jarvis	10	48	4.8	21	0
LeCount, Terry	2	42	21.0	40	0
Dils, Steve	16	28	1.8	8	0
Manning, Archie,Hou.-Minn.	3	12	4.0	11	0
Jones, Mike	1	9	9.0	9	0
White, Sammy	1	7	7.0	7	0
Kramer, Tommy	8	3	0.4	8	0
Lewis, Leo	1	2	2.0	2	0
Wilson, Wade	3	−3	−1.0	2	0
Coleman, Greg	1	−9	−9.0	−9	0

Leader based on most yards gained

INDIVIDUAL PASSING

	Att	Comp	% Comp	Yards	Avg Gain	TD	% TD	Long	Int	% Int	Rating Points
Dils, Steve	444	239	53.8	2840	6.40	11	2.5	68	16	3.6	66.8
Kramer, Tommy	82	55	67.1	550	6.71	3	3.7	49	4	4.9	77.8
Wilson, Wade	28	16	57.1	124	4.43	1	3.6	36	2	7.1	50.3
LeCount, Terry	1	0	0.0	0	0.00	0	0.0	0	0	0.0	

INDIVIDUAL RECEIVERS

	No	Yards	Avg	Long	TD
Nelson, Darrin	51	618	12.1	68	0
Galbreath, Tony	45	348	7.7	23	2
Brown, Ted	41	357	8.7	25	1
Bruer, Bob	31	315	10.2	26	2
White, Sammy	29	412	14.2	t43	4
LeCount, Terry	21	318	15.1	49	2
McCullum, Sam	21	314	15.0	t49	2
Young, Rickey	21	193	9.2	48	0
Casper, Dave, Hou.-Minn.	20	251	12.6	34	0
Jordan, Steve	15	212	14.1	28	2
Lewis, Leo	12	127	10.6	18	0
Jones, Mike	6	95	15.8	47	0
McDole, Mardye	3	29	9.7	10	0
Redwine, Jarvis	1	4	4.0	4	0

Leader based on most passes caught

INDIVIDUAL INTERCEPTORS

	No	Yards	Avg	Long	TD
Turner, John	6	37	6.2	14	0
Swain, John	6	12	2.0	11	0
Bess, Rufus	3	38	12.7	19	0
Teal, Willie	3	26	8.7	12	0
Browner, Joey	2	0	0.0	0	0
Lee, Carl	1	31	31.0	31	0

	No	Yards	Avg	Long	TD
White, James	1	22	22.0	22	0
Johnson, Charlie	1	2	2.0	2	0
Blair, Matt	1	0	0.0	0	0
Nord, Keith	1	0	0.0	0	0

Leader based on most interceptions

INDIVIDUAL KICKOFF RETURNERS

	No	Yards	Avg	Long	TD
Nelson, Darrin	18	445	24.7	50	0
Redwine, Jarvis	38	838	22.1	41	0
Huffman, Dave	3	42	14.0	15	0
Young, Rickey	3	27	9.0	15	0
Bess, Rufus	2	44	22.0	30	0
Jones, Mike	2	31	15.5	16	0
Lewis, Leo	1	25	25.0	25	0
Bell, Rick	1	14	14.0	14	0

Leader based on average return

INDIVIDUAL PUNTERS

	No	Yards	Long	Avg	Total Punts	TB	Blk	Opp Ret	Ret Yds	In 20	Net Avg
Coleman, Greg	91	3780	65	41.5	91	8	0	40	297	28	36.5

INDIVIDUAL PUNT RETURNERS

	No	FC	Yards	Avg	Long	TD
Bess, Rufus	21	10	158	7.5	17	0
Lewis, Leo	3	3	52	17.3	34	0
Bell, Rick	0	2	0	----	0	0

Leader based on average return

INDIVIDUAL SCORERS

KICKERS

	XP	XPA	FG	FGA	PTS
Ricardo, Benny	33	34	25	33	108

NON-KICKERS

	TD	TDR	TDP	TDM	PTS
Brown, Ted	11	10	1	0	66
Galbreath, Tony	6	4	2	0	36
White, Sammy	4	0	4	0	24
Bruer, Bob	2	0	2	0	12
Jordan, Steve	2	0	2	0	12
LeCount, Terry	2	0	2	0	12
McCullum, Sam	2	0	2	0	12
Young, Rickey	2	2	0	0	12
Huffman, Dave	1	0	0	1	6
Johnson, Charlie	1	0	0	1	6
Nelson, Darrin	1	1	0	0	6

t=*Touchdown*

NEW ORLEANS SAINTS

NFC Western Division

Address: 944 St Charles Ave., New Orleans, LA 70130
Telephone: (504) 525 0792

CLUB OFFICIALS
Owner: John W. Mecom, Jr.
President: Eddie Jones
Vice President, Administration: Fred Williams
Director of Football Operations: Pat Peppler
Head Coach, General Manager: O.A. (Bum) Phillips
Assistant Coaches: Andy Everest, King Hill, John Levra,
Carl Mauck, Lamar McHan, Russell Paternostro, Wade
Phillips, Harold Richardson, Joe Spencer, Lance Van
Zandt, John Paul Young, Willie Zapalac
Director of Scouting: Bob Whitman
Director of Public Relations: Greg Suit
Assistant Director of Public Relations: Rusty Kasmiersky
Public Relations Assistant: Sylvia Alfortish
Ticket Manager: Don Johnson
Controller: Bob Landry
Director of Marketing: Barra Birrcher
Administrative Assistant; Jack Cherry
Trainer: Dean Kleinschmidt
Equipment Manager: Dan Simmons

Stadium: Louisiana Superdome (Capacity 71,330)
Playing Surface: AstroTurf
Stadium Address: 1500 Poydras Street, New Orleans, LA 70112
Colors: Old Gold, Black & White
Summer Training Camp: Dodgertown, Vero Beach, FA 32960

NEW ORLEANS SAINTS 1984 SCHEDULE

PRE-SEASON

Aug.	4	at Kansas City Chiefs	7:30
Aug.	11	ATLANTA FALCONS	7:00
Aug.	18	at Houston Oilers	8:00
Aug.	25	WASHINGTON REDSKINS	12:00

REGULAR SEASON

Sep.	2	ATLANTA FALCONS	12:00
Sep.	9	TAMPA BAY BUCCANEERS	12:00
Sep.	16	at San Francisco 49ers	1:00
Sep.	23	ST LOUIS CARDINALS	12:00
Sep.	30	at Houston Oilers	3:00
Oct.	7	at Chicago Bears	12:00
Oct.	14	LOS ANGELES RAMS	12:00
Oct.	21	at Dallas Cowboys	9:00
Oct.	28	at Cleveland Browns	1:00
Nov.	4	GREEN BAY PACKERS	12:00
Nov.	11	at Atlanta Falcons	1:00
Nov.	19	PITTSBURGH STEELERS	8:00
Nov.	25	SAN FRANCISCO 49ers	3:00
Dec.	2	at Los Angeles Rams	1:00
Dec.	9	CINCINNATI BENGALS	12:00
Dec.	15	at New York Giants	12.30

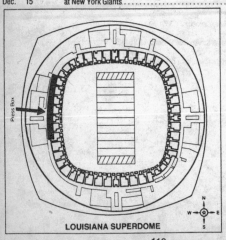

LOUISIANA SUPERDOME

NEW ORLEANS SAINTS END OF SEASON DEPTH CHART

OFFENSE

WR	— 88 Eugene Goodlow, 80 Lindsay Scott, 89 Tyrone Young
OLT	— 64 Dave Lafary, 72 Leon Gray
OLG	— 63 Brad Edelman, 60 Steve Korte
C	— 62 John Hill, 76 Jim Pietrzak
ORG	— 66 Louis Oubre, 78 Kelvin Clark
ORT	— 67 Stan Brock, 64 Dave Lafary
TE	— 85 Hoby Brenner, 82 John Tice, 87 Larry Hardy*
WR	— 86 Jeff Groth, 83 Kenny Duckett, 84 Rich Mauti
QB	— 16 Ken Stabler, 18 Dave Wilson, 19 Guido Merkens, Richard Todd
HB	— 38 George Rogers, 41 Jimmy Rogers
FB	— 46 Hokie Gajan, 30 Wayne Wilson, 47 Cliff Austin, 45 Tim Wilson***

DEFENSE

DLE	— 75 Bruce Clark, 73 Frank Warren, 98 Reggie Lewis
NT	— 74 Derland Moore, 93 Gary Lewis, 99 Tony Elliot***
DRE	— 94 Jim Wilks, 73 Frank Warren
LOLB	— 57 Rickey Jackson, 51 Whitney Paul, 59 Chris Martin*
LILB	— 52 Jim Kovach, 58 Glen Redd
RILB	— 56 Dennis Winston, 53 Scott Pelluer
ROLB	— 51 Whitney Paul, 55 Rob Nairne, 50 Ken Bordelon*
LCB	— 44 Dave Waymer, 27 Greg Stemrick
SS	— 20 Russell Gary, 32 Vernon Perry
FS	— 49 Frank Wattelet, 34 Bobby Johnson
RCB	— 25 Johnnie Poe, 27 Greg Stemrick, 29 Rodney Lewis*

SPECIAL TEAMS

K	— 7 Morten Anderson
P	— 14 Russell Erxleben
H	— 19 Guido Merkens
KR	— 30 Wayne Wilson, 83 Kenny Duckett, 41 Jimmy Rogers
PR	— 86 Jeff Groth, 84 Rich Mauti
LSN	— 76 Jim Pietrzak, 62 John Hill, 63 Brad Edelman

NEW ORLEANS SAINTS

INDIVIDUAL RUSHERS

	Att	Yards	Avg	Long	TD
Rogers, George	256	1144	4.5	t76	5
Wilson, Wayne	199	787	4.0	29	9
Gajan, Hokie	81	415	5.1	58	4
Rogers, Jimmy	26	80	3.1	13	0
Wilson, Tim	8	21	2.6	7	0
Austin, Cliff	4	16	4.0	5	0
Merkens, Guido	1	16	16.0	16	0
Groth, Jeff	1	15	15.0	15	0
Goodlow, Eugene	1	3	3.0	3	0
Wilson, Dave	5	3	0.6	5	1
Erxleben, Russell	2	−9	−4.5	1	0
Stabler, Ken	9	−14	−1.6	0	0
Duckett, Kenny	2	−16	−8.0	2	0

Leader based on most yards gained

INDIVIDUAL PASSING

	Att	Comp	% Comp	Yards	Avg Gain	TD	% TD	Long	Int	% Int	Rating Points
Stabler, Ken	311	176	56.6	1988	6.39	9	2.9	48	18	5.8	61.4
Wilson, Dave	112	66	58.9	770	6.88	5	4.5	42	7	6.3	68.7
Erxleben, Russell	1	1	100.0	24	24.00	0	0.0	24	0	0.0	
Gajan, Hokie	1	0	0.0	0	0.00	0	0.0	0	0	0.0	

INDIVIDUAL RECEIVERS

	No	Yards	Avg	Long	TD
Groth, Jeff	49	585	11.9	42	1
Brenner, Hoby	41	574	14.0	t38	3
Goodlow, Eugene	41	487	11.9	26	2
Scott, Lindsay	24	274	11.4	35	0
Wilson, Wayne	20	178	8.9	24	0
Duckett, Kenny	19	283	14.9	48	2
Gajan, Hokie	17	130	7.6	26	0
Rogers, George	12	69	5.8	22	0
Young, Tyrone	7	85	12.1	32	3
Tice, John	7	33	4.7	t12	1
Mauti, Rich	2	30	15.0	23	0
Hardy, Larry	2	29	14.5	22	0
Austin, Cliff	2	25	12.5	18	0

Leader based on most passes caught

INDIVIDUAL INTERCEPTORS

	No	Yards	Avg	Long	TD
Poe, Johnnie	7	146	20.9	t31	1
Gary, Russell	3	70	23.3	26	0
Winston, Dennis	3	21	7.0	15	0
Johnson, Bobby	2	80	40.0	t70	1
Wattelet, Frank	2	33	16.5	24	0
Paul, Witney	2	3	1.5	3	0
Lewis, Reggie	1	27	27.0	t27	1
Stemrick, Greg	1	26	26.0	26	0
Warren, Frank	1	6	6.0	6	0
Jackson, Rickey	1	0	0.0	0	0

Leader based on most interceptions

INDIVIDUAL KICKOFF RETURNERS

	No	Yards	Avg	Long	TD
Duckett, Kenny	33	719	21.8	61	0
Wilson, Wayne	9	239	26.6	52	0
Mauti, Rich	8	147	18.4	35	0
Austin, Cliff	7	112	16.0	27	0
Rogers, Jimmy	7	103	14.7	25	0
Brock, Stan	1	15	15.0	15	0
Wattelet, Frank	1	4	4.0	4	0

Leader based on average return

INDIVIDUAL PUNTERS

	No	Yards	Long	Avg	Total Punts	TB	Blk	Opp Ret	Ret Yds	In 20	Net Avg
Erxleben, Russell	74	3034	60	41.0	74	9	0	49	571	10	30.9
Merkens, Guido	4	144	45	36.0	4	1	0	2	2	0	30.5

Leader based on gross average

INDIVIDUAL PUNT RETURNERS

	No	FC	Yards	Avg	Long	TD
Groth, Jeff	39	15	275	7.1	30	0

INDIVIDUAL SCORERS

KICKERS	XP	XPA	FG	FGA	PTS
Andersen, Morten	37	38	18	23	91

NON-KICKERS	TD	TDR	TDP	TDM	PTS
Wilson, Wayne	11	9	2	0	66
Rogers, George	5	5	0	0	30
Gajan, Hokie	4	4	0	0	24
Brenner, Hoby	3	0	3	0	18
Young, Tyrone	3	0	3	0	18
Duckett, Kenny	2	0	2	0	12
Goodlow, Eugene	2	0	2	0	12
Clark, Kelvin	1	0	0	1	6
Groth, Jeff	1	0	1	0	6
Johnson, Bobby	1	0	1	0	6
Korte, Steve	1	0	0	1	6
Lewis, Reggie	1	0	0	1	6
Poe, Johnnie	1	0	0	1	6
Tice, John	1	0	1	0	6
Wilson, Dave	1	1	0	0	6

t=Touchdown

NEW YORK GIANTS

NFC Eastern Division

Address: Giants Stadium, East Rutherford, NJ 07073
Telephone: (201) 935 8111

CLUB OFFICIALS
President: Wellington T. Mara
Vice President, Treasurer: Timothy J. Mara
Vice President, Secretary: Raymond J. Walsh
Vice President, General Manager: George Young
Assistant General Manager: Harry Hulmes
Head Coach: Bill Parcells
Assistant Coaches: Bill Belichick, Tom Bresnahan, Romeo Crennel, Ron Erhardt, Len Fontes, Pat Hodgson, Lamar Leachman, Johnny Parker, Mike Pope, Steve Schnall
Controller: John Pasquali
Director of Player Personnel: Tom Boisture
Director of Pro Personnel: Ernie Adams
Director of Media Services: Ed Croke
Director of Promotions: Tom Power
Director of Special Projects: Victor Del Guercio
Box Office Treasurer: Jim Gleason
Trainers: Dave Barringer, John Dziegiel, John Johnson
Equipment Manager: Ed Wagner, Jr.

Stadium: Giants Stadium (Capacity 76,891)
Playing Surface: AstroTurf
Stadium Address: East Rutherford, NJ 07073
Colors: Blue, Red & White
Summer Training Camp: Pace University, Pleasantville, NY 10570

NEW YORK GIANTS 1984 SCHEDULE

PRE-SEASON

Aug.	3	at New England Patriots	7:30
Aug.	11	at Indianapolis Colts	7:00
Aug.	18	NEW YORK JETS	8:00
Aug.	25	PITTSBURGH STEELERS	8:00

REGULAR SEASON

Sep.	2	PHILADELPHIA EAGLES	1:00
Sep.	9	DALLAS COWBOYS	1:00
Sep.	16	at Washington Redskins	4:00
Sep.	23	TAMPA BAY BUCCANEERS	4:00
Sep.	30	at Los Angeles Rams	1:00
Oct.	8	SAN FRANCISCO 49ers	9:00
Oct.	14	at Atlanta Falcons	1:00
Oct.	21	at Philadelphia Eagles	1:00
Oct.	28	WASHINGTON REDSKINS	4:00
Nov.	4	at Dallas Cowboys	12:00
Nov.	11	at Tampa Bay Buccaneers	4:00
Nov.	18	ST LOUIS CARDINALS	1:00
Nov.	25	KANSAS CITY CHIEFS	1:00
Dec.	2	at New York Jets	1:00
Dec.	9	at St Louis Cardinals	12:00
Dec.	15	NEW ORLEANS SAINTS	12:30

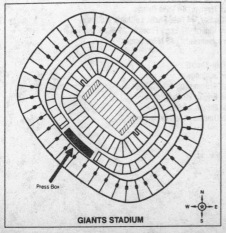

Press Box

GIANTS STADIUM

NEW YORK GIANTS END OF SEASON DEPTH CHART

OFFENSE

WR — 83 Earnest Gray, 87 Byron Williams, 89 Mike Miller
OLT — 60 Brad Benson, 65 John Tautolo
OLG — 67 Billy Ard, 73 Kevin Belcher
C — 61 Ernie Hughes, 66 Chris Foote**, Al Steinfeld, 59 Rich Umphrey*
ORG — 68 J.T. Turner, 73 Kevin Belcher
ORT — 72 Gordon King, 65 John Tautolo, Karl Nelson*
TE — 84 Zeke Mowatt, 81 Tom Mullady, 80 Malcolm Scott
WR — 88 Floyd Eddings, 85 John Mistler, 86 Johnny Perkins*
QB — 12 Scott Brunner, 17 Jeff Rutledge, 9 Tom Owen, 11 Phil Simms*
RB — 25 Butch Woolfolk, 20 Joe Morris, 45 Leon Bright
RB — 38 John Tuggle, 27 Larry Heater, 26 Rob Carpenter*

DEFENSE

DLE — 75 George Martin, 71 Casey Merrill, 76 Curtis McGriff*
NT — 78 Jerome Sally, 74 Charles Cook, 77 Bill Neill*, 64 Jim Burt*
DRE — 70 Leonard Marshall, 79 Dee Hardison, 78 Jerome Sally
LOLB — 10 Brad Van Pelt, 57 Byron Hunt
LILB — 55 Brian Kelley**, 51 Frank Marion, 58 Mike Whittington*
RILB — 53 Harry Carson, 51 Frank Marion, 52 Joe McLaughlin
ROLB — 56 Lawrence Taylor, 54 Andy Headen
LCB — 36 Mark Haynes, 46 Mike Dennis
SS — 29 Bill Currier, 44 Pete Shaw, LeCharls McDaniel
FS — 43 Terry Kinard, 37 Larry Flowers, 39 Mike Macock
RCB — 24 Terry Jackson**, 46 Mike Dennis

SPECIAL TEAMS

K — 6 Ali Haji-Sheikh
P — 13 Dave Jennings
H — 12 Scott Brunner, 85 John Mistler
KR — 45 Leon Bright, 20 Joe Morris
PR — 45 Leon Bright, 44 Pete Shaw
LSN — 59 Rich Umphrey*, 66 Chris Foote**

NEW YORK GIANTS

INDIVIDUAL RUSHERS

	Att	Yards	Avg	Long	TD
Woolfolk, Butch	246	857	3.5	22	4
Carpenter, Rob	170	624	3.7	37	4
Morris, Joe	35	145	4.1	16	0
Brunner, Scott	26	64	2.5	12	0
Tuggle, John	17	49	2.9	t7	1
Rutledge, Jeff	7	27	3.9	14	0
Campfield, Billy	2	21	10.5	13	0
Eddings, Floyd	1	3	3.0	3	0
Bright, Leon	1	2	2.0	2	0
Miller, Mike	1	2	2.0	2	0

Leader based on most yards gained

INDIVIDUAL PASSING

	Att	Comp	% Comp	Yards	Avg Gain	TD	% TD	Long	Int	% Int	Rating Points
Brunner, Scott	386	190	49.2	2516	6.52	9	2.3	62	22	5.7	54.3
Rutledge, Jeff	174	87	50.0	1208	6.94	3	1.7	54	8	4.6	59.3
Simms, Phil	13	7	53.8	130	10.00	0	0.0	36	1	7.7	56.6
Jennings, Dave	1	0	0.0	0	0.00	0	0.0	0	0	0.0	
Mistler, John	1	0	0.0	0	0.00	0	0.0	0	0	0.0	

INDIVIDUAL RECEIVERS

	No	Yards	Avg	Long	TD
Gray, Earnest	78	1139	14.6	62	5
Mistler, John	45	422	9.4	24	0
Woolfolk, Butch	28	368	13.1	44	0
Carpenter, Rob	26	258	9.9	38	2
Mowatt, Zeke	21	280	13.3	t46	1
Williams, Byron	20	346	17.3	t43	1
Scott, Malcolm	17	206	12.1	24	0
Eddings, Floyd	14	231	16.5	33	0
Mullady, Tom	13	184	14.2	35	1
Miller, Mike	7	170	24.3	54	0
Tuggle, John	3	50	16.7	27	0
Bright, Leon	2	33	16.5	19	0
Morris, Joe	2	1	0.5	t6	1
Campfield, Billy	1	12	12.0	12	0

Leader based on most passes caught

INDIVIDUAL INTERCEPTORS

	No	Yards	Avg	Long	TD
Jackson, Terry	6	20	3.3	17	0
Kinard, Terry	3	49	16.3	25	0
Haynes, Mark	3	18	6.0	23	0
Currier, Bill	2	37	18.5	t30	1
Taylor, Lawrence	2	10	5.0	10	0
Van Pelt, Brad	2	7	3.5	6	0
Flowers, Larry	1	19	19.0	19	0
Kelley, Brian	1	17	17.0	17	0
Dennis, Mike	1	0	0.0	0	0

Leader based on most interceptions

INDIVIDUAL KICKOFF RETURNERS

	No	Yards	Avg	Long	TD
Bright, Leon	21	475	22.6	36	0
Morris, Joe	14	255	18.2	26	0
Tuggle, John	9	156	17.3	28	0
Campfield, Billy	9	154	17.1	23	0
Pittman, Danny	6	107	17.8	24	0
Heater, Larry	5	71	14.2	26	0
Miller, Mike	2	31	15.5	26	0
Woolfolk, Butch	2	13	6.5	11	0
Dennis, Mike	1	54	54.0	54	0
Mayock, Mike	1	9	9.0	9	0
McLaughlin, Joe	1	8	8.0	8	0

Leader based on average return

INDIVIDUAL PUNTERS

	No	Yards	Long	Avg	Total Punts	TB	Blk	Opp Ret	Ret Yds	In 20	Net Avg
Jennings, Dave	84	3386	66	40.3	85	5	1	47	283	29	35.3

INDIVIDUAL PUNT RETURNERS

	No	FC	Yards	Avg	Long	TD
Shaw, Pete	29	4	234	8.1	27	0
Bright, Leon	17	0	117	6.9	20	0
Reece, Beasley	9	2	26	2.9	7	0
Pittman, Danny	0	1	0	---	0	0

Leader based on average return

INDIVIDUAL SCORERS

KICKERS

	XP	XPA	FG	FGA	PTS
Haji-Sheikh, Ali	22	23	35	42	127

NON-KICKERS

	TD	TDR	TDP	TDM	PTS
Carpenter, Bob	6	4	2	0	36
Gray, Earnest	5	0	5	0	30
Woolfolk, Butch	4	4	0	0	24
Currier, Bill	1	0	0	1	6
Jackson, Terry	1	0	0	1	6
Morris, Joe	1	0	1	0	6
Mowatt, Zeke	1	0	1	0	6
Mullady, Tom	1	0	1	0	6
Pittman, Danny	1	0	1	0	6
Tuggle, John	1	1	0	0	6
Williams, Byron	1	0	1	0	6
Marshall, Leonard	0	0	0	0	*2

*=Safety
t=Touchdown

PHILADELPHIA EAGLES

NFC Eastern Division

Address: Philadelphia Veterans Stadium, Broad Street and
Pattison Avenue, Philadelphia, PA 19148
Telephone: (215) 463 2500

CLUB OFFICIALS
General Partner: Leonard H. Tose
Vice President, Legal Counsel: Susan Fletcher
Head Coach: Marion Campbell
Assistant Coaches: John Becker, Fred Bruney, Chuck
Clausen, Frank Gansz, George Hill, Ken Iman, Billie
Matthews, Jerry Wampfler, Dick Wood
Coaching and Administrative Assistant: Harry Gamble
Director of Public Relations: Jim Gallagher
Public Relations Assistant: Chick McElrone
Administrative Director: Mimi Box
Sales and Marketing: Bob Caesar
Ticket Manager: Hugh Ortman
Director of Player Personnel: Lynn Stiles
Assistant Director of Player Personnel: Jackie Graves
Talent Scouts: Ken Blair, Jim Katcavage, Phil Neri
Trainer: Otho Davis
Equipment Manager: Rusty Sweeney

Stadium: Philadelphia Veterans Stadium (Capacity 72,204)
Playing Surface: AstroTurf
Stadium Address; Broad Street and Pattison Avenue, Philadelphia, PA 19148
Colors: Kelly Green, Silver & White
Summer Training Camp: West Chester State College, West Chester, PA 19380

PHILADELPHIA EAGLES 1984 SCHEDULE

PRE-SEASON

Aug.	4	at Detroit Lions	7:00
Aug.	11	at Pittsburgh Steelers	6:00
Aug.	18	at Minnesota Vikings	7:00
Aug.	23	CLEVELAND BROWNS	7:00

REGULAR SEASON

Sep.	2	at New York Giants	1:00
Sep.	9	MINNESOTA VIKINGS	1:00
Sep.	16	at Dallas Cowboys	3:00
Sep.	23	SAN FRANCISCO 49ers	1:00
Sep.	30	at Washington Redskins	4:00
Oct.	7	at Buffalo Bills	1:00
Oct.	14	INDIANAPOLIS COLTS	1:00
Oct.	21	NEW YORK GIANTS	1:00
Oct.	28	ST LOUIS CARDINALS	1:00
Nov.	4	at Detroit Lions	1:00
Nov.	11	at Miami Dolphins	1:00
Nov.	18	WASHINGTON REDSKINS	1:00
Nov.	25	at St Louis Cardinals	12:00
Dec.	2	DALLAS COWBOYS	1:00
Dec.	9	NEW ENGLAND PATRIOTS	1:00
Dec.	16	at Atlanta Falcons	4:00

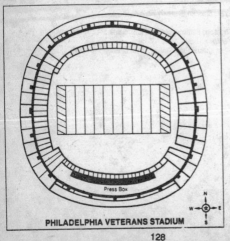

Press Box

PHILADELPHIA VETERANS STADIUM

PHILADELPHIA EAGLES END OF SEASON DEPTH CHART

OFFENSE

WR — 17 Harold Carmichael, 83 Tony Woodruff, 89 Glen Young
OLT — 75 Stan Walters**, 64 Dean Miraldi, 72 Jim Fritzsche, Tom Jelesky
OLG — 73 Steve Kenney, 72 Jim Fritzche, 62 Petey Perot*
C — 50 Guy Morriss**, 61 Mark Slater**, 67 Gerry Feehery*, Mark Dennard
ORG — 63 Ron Baker, 72 Jim Fritzsche
ORT — 76 Jerry Sisemore, 74 Leonard Mitchell, 72 Jim Fritzsche
TE — 87 Lawrence Sampleton, 84 Vyto Kab*, 88 John Spagnola*
WR — 82 Mike Quick, 89 Glen Young, 85 Mel Hoover
QB — 7 Ron Jaworski, 9 Joe Pisarcik, 6 Dan Pastorini**
HB — 26 Michael Haddix, 32 Michael Williams, 31 Wilbert Montgomery***, 35 Perry Harrington***
FB — 34 Hubert Oliver, 39 Major Everett

DEFENSE

DLE — 68 Dennis Harrison, 94 Byron Darby, 93 Thomas Strauthers
NT — 71 Ken Clarke, 96 Harvey Armstrong, 94 Byron Darby
DRE — 78 Carl Hairston**, 98 Greg Brown, 93 Thomas Strauthers
LOLB — 51 Reggie Wilkes, 52 Rich Kraynak, 53 Jody Schulz*
LILB — 56 Jerry Robinson, 57 Bill Cowher, 52 Rich Kraynak
RILB — 58 Anthony Griggs, 57 Bill Cowher, 52 Rich Kraynak, 55 Frank LeMaster**
ROLB — 59 Joel Williams, 52 Rich Kraynak, 54 Zack Valentine*
LCB — 43 Roynell Young, 22 Brenard Wilson, 25 Dennis DeVaughn
SS — 41 Randy Logan, 24 Ray Ellis, 21 John Sciarra**, 22 Brenard Wilson
FS — 48 Wes Hopkins, 22 Brenard Wilson, 21 John Sciarra**
RCB — 46 Herman Edwards, 29 Elbert Foules, 25 Dennis DeVaughn

SPECIAL TEAMS

K — 1 Tony Franklin**, 6 Dan Pastorini**
P — 5 Max Runager, 6 Dan Pastorini**
H — 6 Dan Pastorini**, 7 Ron Jaworski
KR — 89 Glen Young, 39 Major Everett, 24 Ray Ellis
PR — 21 John Sciarra**, 89 Glen Young
LSN — 61 Mark Slater**, 50 Guy Morriss**

PHILADELPHIA EAGLES

INDIVIDUAL RUSHERS

	Att	Yards	Avg	Long	TD
Oliver, Hubert	121	434	3.6	24	1
Williams, Mike	103	385	3.7	32	0
Haddix, Michael	91	220	2.4	11	2
Montgomery, Wilbert	29	139	4.8	32	0
Jaworski, Ron	25	129	5.2	29	1
Harrington, Perry	23	98	4.3	35	1
Everett, Major	5	7	1.4	7	0
Runager, Max	1	6	6.0	6	0
Pastorini, Dan	1	0	0.0	0	0
Pisarcik, Joe	3	−1	−0.3	0	0

Leader based on most yards gained

INDIVIDUAL PASSING

	Att	Comp	% Comp	Yards	Avg Gain	TD	% TD	Long	Int	% Int	Rating Points
Jaworski, Ron	446	235	52.7	3315	7.43	20	4.5	t83	18	4.0	75.1
Pisarcik, Joe	34	16	47.1	172	5.06	1	2.9	33	0	0.0	72.2
Carmichael, Harold	1	1	100.0	45	45.0	1	100.0	t45	0	0.0	
Pastorini, Dan	5	0	0.0	0	0.0	0	0.0	0	0	0.0	

INDIVIDUAL RECEIVERS

	No	Yards	Avg	Long	TD
Quick, Mike	69	1409	20.4	t83	13
Oliver, Hubert	49	421	8.6	25	2
Carmichael, Harold	38	515	13.6	35	3
Haddix, Michael	23	254	11.0	34	0
Kab, Vyto	18	195	10.8	25	1
Williams, Mike	17	142	8.4	29	0
Hoover, Mel	10	221	22.1	68	0
Montgomery, Wilbert	9	53	5.9	13	0
Woodruff, Tony	6	70	11.7	t29	2
Dixon, Al	4	54	13.5	22	0
Young, Glen	3	125	41.7	t71	1
Sampleton, Lawrence	2	28	14.0	19	0
Everett, Major	2	18	9.0	11	0
Harrington, Perry	1	19	19.0	19	0
Smith, Ron	1	8	8.0	8	0

Leader based on most passes caught

INDIVIDUAL INTERCEPTORS

	No	Yards	Avg	Long	TD
Griggs, Anthony	3	61	20.3	32	0
Ellis, Ray	1	18	18.0	18	0
Edwards, Herman	1	0	0.0	0	0
Foules, Elbert	1	0	0.0	0	0
Logan, Randy	1	0	0.0	0	0
Young, Roynell	1	0	0.0	0	0

Leader based on most interceptions

INDIVIDUAL KICKOFF RETURNERS

	No	Yards	Avg	Long	TD
Young, Glen	26	547	21.0	52	0
Everett, Major	14	275	19.6	46	0
Ellis, Ray	7	119	17.0	25	0
Harrington, Perry	4	79	19.8	26	0
Williams, Mike	3	59	19.7	25	0
Haddix, Michael	3	51	17.0	24	0
Fitzsche, Jim	2	17	8.5	15	0
Darby, Byron	2	3	1.5	3	0
Young, Roynell	1	18	18.0	18	0

Leader based on average return

INDIVIDUAL PUNTERS

	No	Yards	Long	Avg	Total Punts	TB	Blk	Opp Ret	Ret Yds	In 20	Net Avg
Runager, Max	59	2459	55	41.7	59	5	0	37	339	12	34.2
Skladany, Tom	27	1062	51	39.3	27	2	0	20	172	5	31.5

Leader based on gross average

INDIVIDUAL PUNT RETURNERS

	No	FC	Yards	Avg	Long	TD
Sciarra, John	22	3	115	5.2	14	0
Young, Glen	14	3	93	6.6	23	0
Hoover, Mel	7	4	44	6.3	13	0
Foules, Elbert	1	0	7	7.0	7	0
Logan, Randy	1	0	0	0.0	0	0

Leader based on average return

INDIVIDUAL SCORERS

KICKERS

	XP	XPA	FG	FGA	PTS
Franklin, Tony	24	27	15	26	69

NON-KICKERS

	TD	TDR	TDP	TDM	PTS
Quick, Mike	13	0	13	0	78
Carmichael, Harold	3	0	3	0	18
Oliver, Hubert	3	1	2	0	18
Haddix, Michael	2	2	0	0	12
Woodruff, Tony	2	0	2	0	12
Harrington, Perry	1	1	0	0	6
Jaworski, Ron	1	1	0	0	6
Kab, Vyto	1	0	1	0	6
Young, Glen	1	0	1	0	6

t=Touchdown

ST LOUIS CARDINALS

NFC Eastern Division

Address: Busch Stadium, Box 888, St Louis, MO 63188
Telephone: (314) 421 0777

CLUB OFFICIALS
Chairman of the Board, CEO: William V. Bidwill
President: Bing Devine
Vice President Administration: Curt Mosher
Director of Pro Personnel: Larry Wilson
Treasurer: Charley Schlegel
Head Coach: Jim Hanifan
Assistant Coaches: Chuck Banker, Tom Bettis,
Don Brown, Rod Dowhower, Rudy Feldman, Dick Jamieson,
Tom Lovat, Leon McLaughlin, Floyd Peters, Emmitt Thomas
Director of Player Personnel: George Boone
Media Coordinator: Greg Gladysiewski
Director of Community Relations: Adele Harris
Ticket Manager: Steve Walsh
Trainer: John Omohundro
Assistant Trainers: Jim Shearer, Ed Fleming
Equipment Manager: Bill Simmons
Assistant Equipment Manager: Mark Ahlemeier

Stadium: Busch Memorial Stadium (Capacity 51,392)
Playing Surface: AstroTurf
Stadium Address: 200 Stadium Plaza, St Louis, MO 63102
Colors; Cardinal Red, Black & White
Summer Training Camp; Eastern Illinois University, Charleston, IL 61920

ST LOUIS CARDINALS 1984 SCHEDULE

PRE-SEASON

Aug.	4	at Chicago Bears	6:00
Aug.	10	KANSAS CITY CHIEFS	7:30
Aug.	17	at Seattle Seahawks	7:30
Aug.	24	MINNESOTA VIKINGS	7:30

REGULAR SEASON

Sep.	2	at Green Bay Packers	12:00
Sep.	9	BUFFALO BILLS	12:00
Sep.	16	at Indianapolis Colts	1:00
Sep.	23	at New Orleans Saints	12:00
Sep.	30	MIAMI DOLPHINS	12:00
Oct.	7	at Dallas Cowboys	12:00
Oct.	14	CHICAGO BEARS	12:00
Oct.	21	WASHINGTON REDSKINS	12:00
Oct.	28	at Philadelphia Eagles	1:00
Nov.	4	LOS ANGELES RAMS	3:00
Nov.	11	DALLAS COWBOYS	12:00
Nov.	18	at New York Giants	1:00
Nov.	25	PHILADELPHIA EAGLES	12:00
Dec.	2	at New England Patriots	1:00
Dec.	9	NEW YORK GIANTS	12:00
Dec.	16	at Washington Redskins	1:00

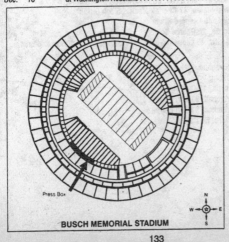

Press Box

N
W   E
S

BUSCH MEMORIAL STADIUM

ST LOUIS CARDINALS END OF SEASON DEPTH CHART

OFFENSE

WR — 81 Roy Green, Danny Pittman
OLT — 67 Luis Sharpe, 70 Art Plunkett
OLG — 68 Terry Stieve, 61 Dan Audick
C — 72 Dan Dierdorf**, 64 Randy Clark, 56 Carlos Scott
ORG — 71 Joe Bostic, 56 Carlos Scott
ORT — 63 Tootie Robbins, 70 Art Plunkett
TE — 80 Doug Marsh, 89 Greg LaFleur, 87 Eddie McGill***
WR — 83 Pat Tilley, 84 Mike Shumann, 82 Steve Bird
QB — 15 Neil Lomax, 17 Jim Hart**, 16 Rusty Lisch
HB — 32 Ottis Anderson, 30 Stump Mitchell, 39 Willard Harrell
FB — 40 Randy Love, 31 Earl Ferrell, 24 Wayne Morris*

DEFENSE

DLE — 60 Al Baker, 76 Stafford Mays
DLT — 65 David Galloway, 73 Mark Duda
DRT — 78 Elois Grooms, 69 Rush Brown**, 66 Ramsey Dardar*
DRE — 75 Curtis Greer, 76 Stafford Mays
LLB — 52 Charlie Baker, 58 Dave Ahrens, 53 Craig Shaffer*, Craig Puki*
MLB — 51 Kurt Allerman, 57 Chet Parlavecchio
RLB — 54 E.J. Junior, 59 Paul Davis, 55 Bill Whitaker, 50 Bob Harris*
LCB — 48 Lionel Washington, 47 Cedrick Mack, 35 Jeff Griffin*
SS — 38 Lee Nelson, 45 Leonard Smith
FS — 23 Benny Perrin, 26 George Schmitt
RCB — 44 Wayne Smith, 45 Leonard Smith, 46 Victor Heflin, 41 Vance Bedford*

SPECIAL TEAMS

K — 11 Neil O'Donoghue
P — 18 Carl Birdsong
H — 23 Benny Perrin, 18 Carl Birdsong
KR — 30 Stump Mitchell, 31 Earl Ferrell
PR — 30 Stump Mitchell, 31 Earl Ferrell
LSN — 64 Randy Clark, 56 Carlos Scott

ST LOUIS CARDINALS

INDIVIDUAL RUSHERS

	Att	Yards	Avg	Long	TD
Anderson, Ottis	296	1270	4.3	43	5
Mitchell, Stump	68	373	5.5	46	3
Morris, Wayne	75	257	3.4	17	2
Lomax, Neil	27	127	4.7	35	2
Love, Randy	35	103	2.9	16	2
Ferrell, Earl	7	53	7.6	21	1
Green, Roy	4	49	12.3	25	0
Harrell, Willard	4	13	3.3	8	0
Hart, Jim	5	12	2.4	13	0
Sharpe, Luis	1	11	11.0	11	0
Lisch, Rusty	2	9	4.5	5	0
Perrin, Benny	1	0	0.0	0	0

Leader based on most yards gained

INDIVIDUAL PASSING

	Att	Comp	% Comp	Yards	Avg Gain	TD	% TD	Long	Int	% Int	Rating Points
Lomax, Neil	354	209	59.0	2636	7.45	24	6.8	t71	11	3.1	92.0
Hart, Jim	91	50	54.9	592	6.51	4	4.4	t39	8	8.8	53.0
Lisch, Rusty	13	6	46.2	66	5.08	1	7.7	26	2	15.4	47.8
Birdsong, Carl	1	1	100.0	11	11.00	0	0.0	11	0	0.0	
Perrin, Benny	1	1	100.0	4	4.00	0	0.0	4	0	0.0	

INDIVIDUAL RECEIVERS

	No	Yards	Avg	Long	TD
Green, Roy	78	1227	15.7	t71	14
Anderson, Ottis	54	459	8.5	40	1
Tilley, Pat	44	690	15.7	t71	5
Marsh, Doug	32	421	13.2	38	8
Morris, Wayne	14	55	3.9	11	0
LaFleur, Greg	12	99	8.3	21	0
Shumann, Mike	11	154	14.0	33	0
Pittman, Danny, Giants-St L.	9	175	19.4	t40	1
Mitchell, Stump	7	54	7.7	17	0
Love, Randy	6	58	9.7	16	1
Harrell, Willard	3	25	8.3	13	0
Thompson, Kenny	2	31	15.5	22	0
McGill, Eddie	1	11	11.0	11	0
Ahrens, Dave	1	4	4.0	4	0

Leader based on most passes caught

INDIVIDUAL INTERCEPTORS

	No	Yards	Avg	Long	TD
Washington, Lionel	8	92	11.5	26	0
Perrin, Benny	4	50	12.5	30	0
Junior, E.J.	3	27	9.0	19	0
Mack, Cedric	3	25	8.3	13	0
Harris, Bob	3	10	3.3	10	.0
Baker, Al	2	24	12.0	19	0
Smith, Wayne	2	3	1.5	3	0
Galloway, David	1	17	17.0	17	0
Grooms, Elois	1	10	10.0	10	0
Nelson, Lee	1	8	8.0	8	0

Leader based on most interceptions

INDIVIDUAL KICKOFF RETURNERS

	No	Yards	Avg	Long	TD
Mitchell, Stump	36	778	21.6	66	0
Ferrell, Earl	13	257	19.8	28	0
Bird, Steve	9	194	21.6	33	0
Schmitt, George	4	41	10.3	19	0
Love, Randy	3	71	23.7	23	0
Harrell, Willard	3	62	20.7	26	0
Smith, Leonard	1	19	19.0	19	0
Green, Roy	1	14	14.0	14	0
Duda, Mark	1	12	12.0	12	0
Allerman, Kurt	1	11	11.0	11	0

Leader based on average return

INDIVIDUAL PUNTERS

	No	Yards	Long	Avg	Total Punts	TB	Blk	Opp Ret	Ret Yds	In 20	Net Avg
Birdsong, Carl	85	3529	59	41.5	85	7	0	47	307	14	36.3

INDIVIDUAL PUNT RETURNERS

	No	FC	Yards	Avg	Long	TD
Mitchell, Stump	38	1	337	8.9	34	0
Bird, Steve	14	2	76	5.4	16	0
Harrell, Willard	5	1	31	6.2	11	0
Ferrell, Earl	1	0	17	17.0	17	0

Leader based on average return

INDIVIDUAL SCORERS

KICKERS

	XP	XPA	FG	FGA	PTS
O'Donoghue, Neil	45	47	15	28	90

NON-KICKERS

	TD	TDR	TDP	TDM	PTS
Green, Roy	14	0	14	0	84
Marsh, Doug	8	0	8	0	48
Anderson, Ottis	6	5	1	0	36
Tilley, Pat	5	0	5	0	30
Love, Randy	3	2	1	0	18
Mitchell, Stump	3	3	0	0	18
Lomax, Neil	2	2	0	0	12
Morris, Wayne	2	2	0	0	12
Ferrell, Earl	1	1	0	0	6
Grooms, Elois	1	0	0	1	6
Nelson, Lee	1	0	0	1	6
Perrin, Benny	1	0	0	1	6
Galloway, David	0	0	0	0	*2

*=Safety
t=Touchdown

SAN FRANCISCO 49ers

NFC Western Division

Address: 711 Nevada St., Redwood City, CA 94061
Telephone: (415) 365 3420

CLUB OFFICIALS

Owner, Chairman of the Board: Edward J. DeBartolo, Jr.
President, Head Coach: Bill Walsh
General Manager: John McVay
Assistant Coaches: Jerry Attaway, Paul Hackett, Norb
Hecker, Sherman Lewis, Bobb McKittrick, Bill McPherson,
Ray Rhodes, George Seifert, Fred von Appen
Director of Marketing and Community Affairs: Ken Flowers
Director of Pro Scouting: Alan Webb
Director of College Scouting: Tony Razzano
Public Relations Director: George Heddleston
Public Relations Assistant: Jerry Walker
Business Manager: Keith Simon
Ticket Manager: Ken Dargel
Trainer: Lindsy McClean
Assistant Trainer: John Miller
Equipment Manager: Chico Norton
Equipment Assistant: Bronco Hinek

Stadium: Candlestick Park (Capacity 61,185)
Playing Surface: Grass
Stadium Address: San Francisco, CA 94124
Colors: Forty-Niner Gold & Scarlet
Summer Training Camp: Sierra Community College, Rocklin, CA 95677

SAN FRANCISCO 49ers 1984 SCHEDULE

PRE-SEASON

Aug.	4	LOS ANGELES RAIDERS	6:00
Aug.	11	at Denver Broncos	7:00
Aug.	18	at San Diego Chargers	6:00
Aug.	24	SEATTLE SEAHAWKS	6:00

REGULAR SEASON

Sep.	2	at Detroit Lions	1:00
Sep.	10	WASHINGTON REDSKINS	6:00
Sep.	16	NEW ORLEANS SAINTS	1:00
Sep.	23	at Philadelphia Eagles	1:00
Sep.	30	ATLANTA FALCONS	1:00
Oct.	8	at New York Giants	9:00
Oct.	14	PITTSBURGH STEELERS	1:00
Oct.	21	at Houston Oilers	3:00
Oct.	28	at Los Angeles Rams	1:00
Nov.	4	CINCINNATI BENGALS	1:00
Nov.	11	at Cleveland Browns	1:00
Nov.	18	TAMPA BAY BUCCANEERS	1:00
Nov.	25	at New Orleans Saints	3:00
Dec.	2	at Atlanta Falcons	1:00
Dec.	8	MINNESOTA VIKINGS	1:00
Dec.	14	LOS ANGELES RAMS	6:00

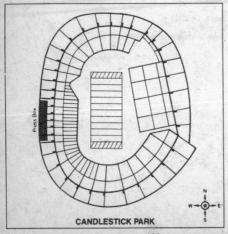

CANDLESTICK PARK

SAN FRANCISCO 49ERS END OF SEASON DEPTH CHART

OFFENSE

WR	—	85 Mike Wilson, 84 Darius Durham, 87 Dwight Clark*
OLT	—	77 Bubba Paris, 66 Allan Kennedy
OLG	—	68 John Ayers, 62 Walt Downing
C	—	56 Fred Quillan, 61 Jesse Sapolu, 62 Walt Downing
ORG	—	51 Randy Cross, 61 Jesse Sapolu, 62 Walt Downing
ORT	—	71 Keith Fahnhorst, 66 Allan Kennedy
TE	—	81 Russ Francis, 80 Eason Ramson**, 89 Earl Cooper
WR	—	88 Freddie Soloman, 83 Renaldo Nehemiah, 85 Mike Wilson
QB	—	16 Joe Montana, 7 Guy Benjamin, 6 Matt Cavanaugh
HB	—	26 Wendell Tyler, 25 Jeff Moore, 32 Carl Monroe
FB	—	33 Roger Craig, 30 Bill Ring, 89 Earl Cooper, 40 Vince Williams*

DEFENSE

DLE	—	65 Lawrence Pillers, 72 Jeff Stover, 75 John Harty*
NT	—	67 Pete Kugler**, 72 Jeff Stover, Bruce Lindstrom, Louie Kelcher, Manu Tuiasosopo
DRE	—	76 Dwaine Board, 79 Jim Stuckey, 74 Fred Dean
LOLB	—	59 Willie Harper**, 53 Milt McColl, 57 Dan Bunz
LILB	—	50 Riki Gray Ellison, 57 Dan Bunz, 63 Gary Moten, Frank LeMaster
RILB	—	64 Jack Reynolds, 52 Bobby Leopold**, 63 Gary Moten, 60 Blanchard Montgomery
ROLB	—	58 Keena Turner, 54 Ron Ferrari
LCB	—	42 Ronnie Lott, 47 Tim Collier, 44 Richie Blackmore
SS	—	27 Carlton Williamson, 28 Tom Holmoe, 24 Rick Gervais*
FS	—	22 Dwight Hicks, 28 Tom Holmoe
RCB	—	21 Eric Wright, 43 Dana McLemore, 44 Richie Blackmore

SPECIAL TEAMS

K	—	14 Ray Wersching
P	—	3 Tom Orosz
H	—	16 Joe Montana, 8 Matt Cavanaugh
KR	—	43 Dana McLemore, 30 Bill Ring
PR	—	43 Dana McLemore, 88 Freddie Solomon, 22 Dwight Hicks
LSN	—	51 Randy Cross, 56 Fred Quillan

SAN FRANCISCO 49ers

INDIVIDUAL RUSHERS

	Att	Yards	Avg	Long	TD
Tyler, Wendell	176	856	4.9	39	4
Craig, Roger	176	725	4.1	71	8
Montana, Joe	61	284	4.7	18	2
Ring, Bill	64	254	4.0	25	2
Moore, Jeff	15	43	2.9	14	1
Orosz, Tom	2	39	19.5	23	0
Monroe, Carl	10	23	2.3	5	0
Clark, Dwight	3	18	6.0	9	0
Cavanaugh, Matt	1	8	8.0	8	0
Ramson, Eason	1	3	3.0	3	0
Solomon, Freddie	1	3	3.0	3	0
Benjamin, Guy	1	1	1.0	1	0

Leader based on most yards gained

INDIVIDUAL PASSING

	Att	Comp	% Comp	Yards	Avg Gain	TD	% TD	Long	Int	% Int	Rating Points
Montana, Joe	515	332	64.5	3910	7.59	26	5.0	t77	12	2.3	94.6
Benjamin, Guy	12	7	58.3	111	9.25	1	8.3	t73	0	0.0	117.0
Clark, Dwight	1	0	0.0	0	0.00	0	0	0	0	0.0	

INDIVIDUAL RECEIVERS

	No	Yards	Avg	Long	TD
Clark, Dwight	70	840	12.0	t46	8
Craig, Roger	48	427	8.9	23	4
Tyler, Wendell	34	285	8.4	26	2
Francis, Russ	33	357	10.8	25	4
Solomon, Freddie	31	662	21.4	t77	4
Wilson, Mike	30	433	14.4	49	0
Ring, Bill	23	182	7.9	24	0
Moore, Jeff	19	206	10.8	34	0
Nehemiah, Renaldo	17	236	13.9	27	1
Ramson, Eason	17	125	7.4	16	1
Cooper, Earl	15	207	13.8	t73	3
Monroe, Carl	2	61	30.5	50	0

Leader based on most passes caught

INDIVIDUAL INTERCEPTORS

	No	Yards	Avg	Long	TD
Wright, Eric	7	164	23.4	t60	2
Williamson, Carlton	4	51	12.8	26	0
Lott, Ronnie	4	22	5.5	22	0
Collier, Tim	3	32	10.7	t32	1
Hicks, Dwight	2	102	51.0	t62	2
Leopold, Bobby	2	13	6.5	9	0
Harper, Willie	1	37	37.0	37	0
Pillers, Lawrence	1	16	16.0	16	0

Leader based on most interceptions

INDIVIDUAL KICKOFF RETURNERS

	No	Yards	Avg	Long	TD
McLemore, Dana	30	576	19.2	39	0
Monroe, Carl	8	152	19.0	32	0
Moore, Jeff	7	117	16.7	46	0
Ring, Bill	4	68	17.0	18	0
Cooper, Earl	3	45	15.0	20	0

Leader based on average return

INDIVIDUAL PUNTERS

	No	Yards	Long	Avg	Total Punts	TB	Blk	Opp Ret	Ret Yds	In 20	Net Avg
Orosz, Tom	65	2552	61	39.3	66	6	1	38	278	16	32.6

INDIVIDUAL PUNT RETURNERS

	No	FC	Yards	Avg	Long	TD
McLemore, Dana	31	6	331	10.7	t56	1
Solomon, Freddie	5	3	34	6.8	11	0

Leader based on average return

INDIVIDUAL SCORERS

KICKERS	XP	XPA	FG	FGA	PTS
Wersching, Ray	51	51	25	30	126

NON-KICKERS	TD	TDR	TDP	TDM	PTS
Craig, Roger	12	8	4	0	72
Clark, Dwight	8	0	8	0	48
Tyler, Wendell	6	4	2	0	36
Francis, Russ	4	0	4	0	24
Solomon, Freddie	4	0	4	0	24
Cooper, Earl	3	0	3	0	18
Hicks, Dwight	2	0	0	2	12
Montana, Joe	2	2	0	0	12
Ring, Bill	2	2	0	0	12
Wright, Eric	2	0	0	2	12
Collier, Tim	1	0	0	1	6
McLemore, Dana	1	0	0	1	6
Moore, Jeff	1	1	0	0	6
Nehemiah, Renaldo	1	0	1	0	6
Ramson, Eason	1	0	1	0	6

t=Touchdown

TAMPA BAY BUCCANEERS

NFC Central Division

Address: One Buccaneer Place, Tampa, FA 33607
Telephone: (813) 870 2700

CLUB OFFICIALS
Owner, President: Hugh F. Culverhouse
Vice President, Head Coach: John H. McKay
Vice President: Joy Culverhouse
Secretary, Treasurer: Ward Holland
Director of Administration: Herbert M. Gold
Assistant to the President: Phil Krueger
Director of Player Personnel: Ken Herock
Director of Public Relations: Rick Odioso
Director of Marketing, Advertising: Bob Passwaters
Assistant Director, Community Relations: Sandy Cottrell
Assistant Director, Media Relations: John Gerdes
Head Coach: John H. McKay
Assistant Head Coach, Defensive Coordinator and Secondary: Wayne Fontes
Defensive Linemen: Abe Gibron
Linebackers: Howard Tippett
Offensive Moderator: John Brunner
Quarterbacks: Boyd Dowler
Running Backs: Jim Gruden
Offensive Linemen: Kim Helton
Receivers: Chip Myers
Strength: Joe Diange
Pro Personnel Scout: Gary Horton
Director of Ticket Operations: Terry Wooten
Ticket Office Staff: Earl Russell, Jim Overton
Controller: Edward Easom
Trainer: Tom Oxley
Assistant Trainer: Scott Anderson
Equipment Manager: Frank Pupello

Stadium: Tampa Stadium (Capacity 74,273)
Playing Surface: Grass
Stadium Address: North Dale Mabry, Tampa, FA 33607
Colors: Florida Orange, White and Red Trim
Summer Training Camp: One Buccaneer Place, Tampa, FA 33607

TAMPA BAY BUCCANEERS 1984 SCHEDULE

PRE-SEASON
Jul.	28	SEATTLE SEAHAWKS at Canton, Ohio	3:00
Aug.	4	HOUSTON OILERS	8:00
Aug.	11	CINCINNATI BENGALS	8:00
Aug.	18	at Atlanta Falcons	8:00
Aug.	24	MIAMI DOLPHINS	8:00

REGULAR SEASON
Sep.	2	at Chicago Bears	12:00
Sep.	9	at New Orleans Saints	12:00
Sep.	16	DETROIT LIONS	4:00
Sep.	23	at New York Giants	4:00
Sep.	30	GREEN BAY PACKERS	4:00
Oct.	7	MINNESOTA VIKINGS	1:00
Oct.	14	at Detroit Lions	1:00
Oct.	21	CHICAGO BEARS	1:00
Oct.	28	at Kansas City Chiefs	12:00
Nov.	4	at Minnesota Vikings	12:00
Nov.	11	NEW YORK GIANTS	4:00
Nov.	18	at San Francisco 49ers	1:00
Nov.	25	LOS ANGELES RAMS	1:00
Dec.	2	at Green Bay Packers	12:00
Dec.	9	ATLANTA FALCONS	1:00
Dec.	16	NEW YORK JETS	1:00

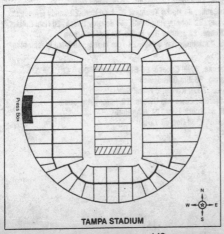

TAMPA STADIUM

TAMPA BAY BUCCANEERS END OF SEASON DEPTH CHART

OFFENSE

WR	— 83 Theo Bell, 87 Gerald Carter, 80 Rheugene Branton*
OLT	— 74 Gene Sanders, 75 Dave Reavis, 68 George Yarno**
OLG	— 68 George Yarno**, 77 Glenn Bujnoch, 72 Ray Snell, 60 Randy Grimes
C	— 60 Randy Grimes, 57 Jim Leonard**, 50 Steve Wilson***
ORG	— 62 Sean Farrell, 77 Glenn Bujnoch, 68 George Yarno**
ORT	— 70 Kelly Thomas, 74 Gene Sanders, 50 Steve Wilson***
TE	— 88 Jimmie Giles, 82 Jerry Bell, 86 Jim Obradovich, 85 Mark Witte
WR	— 89 Kevin House, 81 Andre Tyler, 87 Gerald Carter
QB	— 14 Jack Thompson, 11 Jerry Golsteyn, 7 Jeff Komlo, 8 Bob Hewko*
HB	— 26 James Owens, 28 Mel Carver, 44 Terdell Middleton**, 1 Michael Morton
FB	— 46 Adger Armstrong, 28 Mel Carver, 44 Terdell Middleton**, 32 James Wilder*, Scott Dierking

DEFENSE

DLE	— 66 Booker Reese, 78 John Cannon
NT	— 76 Dave Logan, 90 Brad White
DRE	— 63 Lee Roy Selmon, 78 John Cannon, 69 Hasson Arbubakkr, 90 Brad White
LOLB	— 51 Ed Judie, 56 Robert Thompson, 64 Quentin Lowry*, 59 Andy Hawkins**
LILB	— 58 Jeff Davis, 55 Danny Spradlin, 52 Scot Brantley, 56 Cecil Johnson*
RILB	— 52 Scot Brantley, 54 Richard Wood, 55 Danny Spradlin
ROLB	— 53 Hugh Green, 56 Robert Thompson, 64 Quentin Lowry*
LCB	— 23 Jeremiah Catille, 41 Norris Thomas, 21 John Holt, 29 Sandy LaBeaux*
SS	— 33 Mark Cotney, 22 Johnny Ray Smith, 43 Beesley Reece, 20 Neal Colzie*
FS	— 43 Beesley Reece, 22 Johnny Ray Smith, 34 Cedric Brown*
RCB	— 21 John Holt, 22 Johnny Ray Smith, 24 Tom Morris, 40 Mike Washington*

SPECIAL TEAMS

K	— David Warnke, 3 Bill Capece, 68 George Yarno**
P	— 5 Frank Garcia, 86 Jim Obradovich
H	— 81 Andre Tyler, 7 Jeff Komlo, 5 Frank Garcia
KR	— 1 Michael Morton, 26 James Owens, 22 Johnny Ray Smith
PR	— 83 Theo Bell, 81 Andre Tyler, 21 John Holt
LSN	— 57 Jim Leonard**, 68 George Yarno**

TAMPA BAY BUCCANEERS

INDIVIDUAL RUSHERS

	Att	Yards	Avg	Long	TD
Wilder, James	161	640	4.0	t75	4
Carver, Mel	114	348	3.1	16	0
Owens, James	96	266	2.8	15	5
Armstrong, Adger	7	30	4.3	7	0
Morton, Michael	13	28	2.2	5	0
Thompson, Jack	26	27	1.0	10	0
Komlo, Jeff	2	11	5.5	11	0
Middleton, Terdell	2	4	2.0	2	0
Golsteyn, Jerry	5	3	0.6	2	0
Carter, Gerald	1	0	0.0	0	0
House, Kevin	1	−4	−4.0	−4	0

Leader based on most yards gained

INDIVIDUAL PASSING

	Att	Comp	% Comp	Yards	Avg Gain	TD	% TD	Long	Int	% Int	Rating Points
Thompson, Jack	423	249	58.9	2906	6.87	18	4.3	80	21	5.0	73.3
Golsteyn, Jerry	97	47	48.5	535	5.52	0	0.0	52	2	2.1	56.9
Komlo, Jeff	8	4	50.0	49	6.13	0	0.0	17	1	12.5	

INDIVIDUAL RECEIVERS

	No	Yards	Avg	Long	TD
Wilder, James	57	380	6.7	31	2
Carter, Gerald	48	694	14.5	t56	2
House, Kevin	47	769	16.4	t74	5
Carver, Mel	32	262	8.2	20	1
Bell, Theo	25	410	16.4	52	2
Giles, Jimmie	25	349	14.0	80	1
Bell, Jerry	18	200	11.1	33	1
Armstrong, Adger	15	173	11.5	41	2
Owens, James	15	81	5.4	11	1
Obradovich, Jim	9	71	7.9	19	1
Tyler, Andre	6	77	12.8	21	0
Witte, Mark	2	15	7.5	10	0
Morton, Michael	1	9	9.0	9	0

Leader based on most passes caught

INDIVIDUAL INTERCEPTORS

	No	Yards	Avg	Long	TD
Reece, Beasley, Giants-T.B.	8	103	12.9	29	0
Brown, Cedric	4	78	19.5	36	0
Holt, John	3	43	14.3	25	0
Green, Hugh	2	54	27.0	t33	2
Washington, Mike	2	41	20.5	25	0
Reese, Booker	2	11	5.5	11	0
Cotney, Mark	2	1	0.5	1	0
Castille, Jeremiah	1	69	69.0	t69	1
Brantley, Scot	1	0	0.0	0	0

Leader based on most interceptions

INDIVIDUAL KICKOFF RETURNERS

	No	Yards	Avg	Long	TD
Morton, Michael	30	689	23.0	50	0
Owens, James	20	380	19.0	31	0
Smith, Johnny Ray	8	136	17.0	43	0
Spradlin, Danny	3	35	11.7	24	0
O'Steen, Dwayne	2	30	15.0	16	0
Carver, Mel	2	24	12.0	13	0
Armstrong, Adger	1	10	10.0	10	0
Middleton, Terdell	1	10	10.0	10	0
Obradovich, Jim	1	0	0.0	0	0

Leader based on average return

INDIVIDUAL PUNTERS

	No	Yards	Long	Avg	Total Punts	TB	Blk	Opp Ret	Ret Yds	In 20	Net Avg
Garcia, Frank	95	4008	64	42.2	96	12	1	59	603	15	33.0

INDIVIDUAL PUNT RETURNERS

	No	FC	Yards	Avg	Long	TD
Tyler, Andre	27	5	208	7.7	16	0
Bell, Theo	10	2	48	4.8	11	0
Holt, John	5	0	43	8.6	17	0

Leader based on average return

INDIVIDUAL SCORERS

KICKERS

	XP	XPA	FG	FGA	PTS
Capece, Bill	23	26	10	20	53
Warnke, David	1	2	0	1	1

NON-KICKERS

	TD	TDR	TDP	TDM	PTS
Owens, James	6	5	1	0	36
Wilder, James	6	4	2	0	36
House, Kevin	5	0	5	0	30
Armstrong, Adger	2	0	2	0	12
Bell, Theo	2	0	2	0	12
Carter, Gerald	2	0	2	0	12
Green, Hugh	2	0	0	2	12
Bell, Jerry	1	0	1	0	6
Carver, Mel	1	0	1	0	6
Castille, Jeremiah	1	0	0	1	6
Giles, Jimmie	1	0	1	0	6
Logan, Dave	1	0	0	1	6
Obradovich, Jim	1	0	1	0	6
Yarno, George	0	0	0	0	#1

# = Scored extra point
t=Touchdown

WASHINGTON REDSKINS

NFC Eastern Division

Address: 13832 Redskin Drive, Herndon, VA 22070
Mailing Address: P O Box 17247, Dulles Airport,
Washington DC 22047
Telephone: (703) 471 9100

CLUB OFFICIALS
Chairman of the Board; Chief Operating Executive:
Jack Kent Cooke
President: Edward Bennett Williams, Esq.
Executive Vice President: John Kent Cooke
Senior Vice President: Gerard T. Gabrys
Secretary and General Counsel: Lawrence Lucchino, Esq.
General Manager: Bobby Beathard
Assistant General Manager: Bobby Mitchell
Assistant General Manager: Charles Casserly
Head Coach: Joe Gibbs
Assistant Head Coach, Defense: Richie Petitbon
Assistant Head Coach, Offense: Joe Bugel
Defensive Coordinator: Larry Peccatiello
Offensive Backfield Coach: Don Breaux
Receivers Coach: Charley Taylor
Quarterbacks Coach: Jerry Rhome
Tight Ends, Offensive Scouting Reports: Warren Simmons
Defensive Line Coach: LaVern 'Torgy' Torgeson
Administrative Assistant, Defensive Scouting Reports: Bill Hickman
Special Teams Coach: Wayne Sevier
Strength Coach: Dan Riley
Assistant: John Dunn
Director of Player Personnel: Mike Allman
Director of Pro Scouting: Kirk Mee
Talent Scout: Billy Devaney
Public Relations Director: Charles M. Taylor
Ticket Manager: Sue Barton
Head Trainer: Lamar 'Bubba' Tyer
Assistant Trainers: Joe Kuczo, Keoki Kamau
Director of Stadium Operations: Joel Margolis
Equipment Manager: Jay Brunetti

Stadium: Robert F. Kennedy Memorial (Capacity 55,363)
Playing Surface: Grass
Stadium Address: 2001 East Capitol Street, Washington, DC 20003
Colors: Burgundy and Gold
Summer Training Camp: Dickinson College, Carlisle, PA 17013

WASHINGTON REDSKINS 1984 SCHEDULE

PRE-SEASON

Aug.	4	at Denver Broncos	7:00
Aug.	10	LOS ANGELES RAIDERS	8:00
Aug.	17	NEW ENGLAND PATRIOTS	8:00
Aug.	25	at New Orleans Saints	12:00

REGULAR SEASON

Sep.	2	MIAMI DOLPHINS	1:00
Sep.	10	at San Francisco 49ers	6:00
Sep.	16	NEW YORK GIANTS	4:00
Sep.	23	at New England Patriots	1:00
Sep.	30	PHILADELPHIA EAGLES	4:00
Oct.	7	at Indianapolis Colts	1:00
Oct.	14	DALLAS COWBOYS	4:00
Oct.	21	at St Louis Cardinals	12:00
Oct.	28	at New York Giants	4:00
Nov.	5	ATLANTA FALCONS	9:00
Nov.	11	DETROIT LIONS	1:00
Nov.	18	at Philadelphia Eagles	1:00
Nov.	25	BUFFALO BILLS	1:00
Nov.	29	at Minnesota Vikings	9:00
Dec.	9	at Dallas Cowboys	3:00
Dec.	16	ST LOUIS CARDINALS	1:00

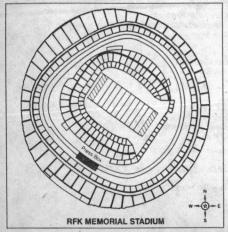

Press Box

RFK MEMORIAL STADIUM

WASHINGTON REDSKINS END OF SEASON DEPTH CHART

OFFENSE

WR	— 87 Charlie Brown, 80 Virgil Seay, 83 Mark McGrath, 21 Mike Nelms*
TE	— 88 Rick Walker, 86 Clint Didier, 84 Mike Williams
OLT	— 66 Joe Jacoby, 73 Mark May, 62 Don Laster*
OLG	— 68 Russ Grimm, 60 Roy Simmons, 67 Bruce Kimball
C	— 53 Jeff Bostic, 68 Russ Grimm
ORG	— 73 Mark May, 61 Ken Huff, 67 Bruce Kimball
ORT	— 74 George Starke, 73 Mark May
TE	— 85 Don Warren, 86 Clint Didier, 84 Mike Williams
WR	— 81 Art Monk, 89 Alvin Garrett, 83 Mark McGrath, 21 Mike Nelms*
QB	— 7 Joe Theismann, 8 Bob Holly, 12 Babe Laufenberg, Jim Hart
RB	— 44 John Riggins, 25 Joe Washington, 39 Otis Wonsley, 30 Nick Giaquinto, 26 Reggie Evans

DEFENSE

DLE	— 79 Todd Liebenstein, 78 Tony McGee, 71 Charles Mann
DLT	— 65 Dave Butz, 69 Perry Brooks
DRT	— 77 Darryl Grant, 69 Perry Brooks
DRE	— 72 Dexter Manley, 71 Charles Mann
LLB	— 55 Mel Kaufman, 51 Monte Coleman, 58 Stuart Anderson
MLB	— 52 Neal Olkewicz, 50 Larry Kubin, 54 Peter Cronan
RLB	— 57 Rich Milot, 51 Monte Coleman, 58 Stuart Anderson
LCB	— 28 Darrell Green, 41 Brian Carpenter
SS	— 48 Ken Coffey, 22 Curtis Jordan, 32 Vernon Dean
FS	— 29 Mark Murphy, 22 Curtis Jordan, 47 Greg Williams
RCB	— 24 Anthony Washington, 32 Vernon Dean

SPECIAL TEAMS

K	— 3 Mark Moseley
P	— 5 Jeff Hayes
H	— 7 Joe Theismann
KR	— 89 Alvin Garrett, 80 Virgil Seay, 26 Reggie Evans, 21 Mike Nelms*
PR	— 30 Nick Giaquinto, 80 Virgil Seay, 28 Darrell Green, 21 Mike Nelms*
LSN	— 53 Joe Bostic, 77 Darryl Grant, 67 Bruce Kimball

WASHINGTON REDSKINS

INDIVIDUAL RUSHERS

	Att	Yards	Avg	Long	TD
Riggins, John	375	1347	3.6	44	24
Washington, Joe	145	772	5.3	41	0
Theismann, Joe	37	234	6.3	22	1
Wonsley, Otis	25	88	3.5	9	0
Hayes, Jeff	2	63	31.5	48	0
Brown, Charlie	4	53	13.3	17	0
Giaquinto, Nick	14	53	3.8	11	1
Holly, Bob	4	13	3.3	13	0
Evans, Reggie	16	11	0.7	5	4
Walker, Rick	2	10	5.0	11	0
Garrett, Alvin	2	0	0.0	4	0
Monk, Art	3	−19	−6.3	2	0

Leader based on most yards gained

INDIVIDUAL PASSING

	Att	Comp	% Comp	Yards	Avg Gain	TD	% TD	Long	Int	% Int	Rating Points
Theismann, Joe	459	276	60.1	3714	8.09	29	6.3	84	11	2.4	97.0
Monk, Art	1	1	100.0	46	46.00	0	0.0	46	0	0.0	
Holly, Bob	1	1	100.0	5	5.00	0	0.0	5	0	0.0	
Riggins, John	1	0	0.0	0	0.00	0	0.0	0	0	0.0	
Washington, Joe	1	0	0.0	0	0.00	0	0.0	0	0	0.0	

INDIVIDUAL RECEIVERS

	No	Yards	Avg	Long	TD
Brown, Charlie	78	1225	15.7	t75	8
Monk, Art	47	746	15.9	t43	5
Washington, Joe	47	454	9.7	67	6
Giaquinto, Nick	27	372	13.8	35	0
Garrett, Alvin	25	332	13.3	84	0
Warren, Don	20	225	11.3	33	2
Walker, Rick	17	168	9.9	29	2
Didier, Clint	9	153	17.0	t40	4
Riggins, John	5	29	5.8	14	0
Seay, Virgil	2	55	27.5	t39	1
McGrath, Mark	1	6	6.0	6	0

Leader based on most passes caught

INDIVIDUAL INTERCEPTORS

	No	Yards	Avg	Long	TD
Murphy, Mark	9	127	14.1	48	0
Dean, Vernon	5	54	10.8	26	0
Coffey, Ken	4	62	15.5	29	0
Washington, A.	4	12	3.0	8	0
Kaufman, Mel	2	93	46.5	t70	1
Williams, Greg	2	25	12.5	25	0
Milot, Rich	2	20	10.0	20	0
Green, Darrell	2	7	3.5	7	0
Jordan, Curtis	1	20	20.0	20	0
Olkewicz, Neal	1	14	14.0	14	0
Carpenter, Brian	1	2	2.0	2	0
Manley, Dexter	1	1	1.0	1	0

Leader based on most interceptions

INDIVIDUAL KICKOFF RETURNERS

	No	Yards	Avg	Long	TD
Nelms, Mike	35	802	22.9	41	0
Evans, Reggie	10	141	14.1	28	0
Seay, Virgil	9	218	24.2	50	0
Garrett, Alvin	2	50	25.0	28	0
Wonsley, Otis	2	36	18.0	20	0
Cronan, Pete	1	17	17.0	17	0
Washington, Joe	1	16	16.0	16	0
Sawyer, John	1	15	15.0	15	0
Williams, Greg	1	6	6.0	6	0
Giaquinto, Nick	1	0	0.0	0	0

Fair Catches: Giaquinto
Leader based on average return

INDIVIDUAL PUNTERS

	No	Yards	Long	Avg	Total Punts	TB	Blk	Opp Ret	Ret Yds	In 20	Net Avg
Hayes, Jeff	72	2796	56	38.8	72	2	0	41	407	29	32.6

INDIVIDUAL PUNT RETURNERS

	No	FC	Yards	Avg	Long	TD
Nelms, Mike	38	0	289	7.6	35	0
Seay, Virgil	5	1	57	11.4	42	0
Green, Darrell	4	0	29	7.3	18	0
Giaquinto, Nick	2	4	12	6.0	12	0

Leader based on average return

INDIVIDUAL SCORERS

KICKERS	XP	XPA	FG	FGA	PTS
Moseley, Mark	62	63	33	47	161

NON-KICKERS	TD	TDR	TDP	TDM	PTS
Riggins, John	24	24	0	0	144
Brown, Charlie	8	0	8	0	48
Washington, Joe	6	0	6	0	36
Didier, Clint	5	0	4	1	30
Monk, Art	5	0	5	0	30
Evans, Reggie	4	4	0	0	24
Kaufman, Mel	2	0	0	2	12
Walker, Rick	2	0	2	0	12
Warren, Don	2	0	2	0	12
Dean, Vernon	1	0	0	1	6
Garrett, Alvin	1	0	1	0	6
Giaquinto, Nick	1	1	0	0	6
Seay, Virgil	1	0	1	0	6
Theismann, Joe	1	1	0	0	6
Mann, Charles	0	0	0	0	*2

*=Safety
t=Touchdown

ACTIVE COACHES' CAREER RECORDS

			Season				Postseason				Career			
		Yrs	W	L	T	%	W	L	T	%	W	L	T	%
Joe Gibbs	WASH.	3	30	11	0	.732	6	1	0	.857	36	12	0	.750
Don Shula	Balt.MIA.	21	213	80	6	.722	13	11	0	.542	226	91	6	.709
Tom Flores	RAIDERS	5	47	26	0	.644	8	1	0	.889	55	27	0	.671
Tom Landry	DALL.	24	214	119	6	.640	20	15	0	.571	234	134	6	.634
Chuck Noll	PITT.	15	133	81	1	.621	14	6	0	.700	147	87	1	.628
Chuck Knox	Rams.Buff.SEA.	11	100	58	1	.632	6	8	0	.429	106	66	1	.616
Don Coryell	St Lou.S.D.	11	95	57	1	.624	3	6	0	.333	98	63	1	.608
John Robinson	RAMS	1	9	7	0	.563	1	1	0	.500	10	8	0	.556
Bum Phillips	Hou.N.O.	9	71	60	0	.542	4	3	0	.571	75	63	0	.543
Forrest Gregg	Cle.Cinn.G.B.	7	50	48	0	.510	2	2	0	.500	52	50	0	.510
Sam Rutigliano	CLE.	6	46	43	0	.517	0	2	0	.000	46	45	0	.505
Ron Meyer	N.ENG.	2	13	12	0	.520	0	1	0	.000	13	13	0	.500
Dan Reeves	DEN.	3	21	20	0	.512	0	1	0	.000	21	21	0	.500
Kay Stephenson	BUFF.	1	8	8	0	.500	0	0	0	.000	8	8	0	.500
Bill Walsh	S.F.	5	34	39	0	.466	4	1	0	.800	38	40	0	.487
Monte Clark	S.Fran.DET.	7	47	56	0	.456	0	2	0	.000	47	58	0	.448
Mike Ditka	CHI.	2	11	14	0	.440	0	0	0	.000	11	14	0	.440
Jim Hanifan	St LOU.	4	25	31	1	.447	0	1	0	.000	25	32	1	.440
Dan Henning	ATL.	1	7	9	0	.438	0	0	0	.000	7	9	0	.438
Joe Walton	N.Y.J.	1	7	9	0	.438	0	0	0	.000	7	9	0	.438
John Mackovic	K.C.	1	6	10	0	.375	0	0	0	.000	6	10	0	.375
John McKay	T.B.	8	38	78	1	.329	1	3	0	.250	39	81	1	.326
Frank Kush	BALT.	2	7	17	1	.300	0	0	0	.000	7	17	1	.300
Marion Campbell	Atl.PHIL.	4	11	30	0	.268	0	0	0	.000	11	30	0	.268
Bill Parcells	N.Y.G.	1	3	12	1	.219	0	0	0	.000	3	12	1	.219
Hugh Campbell*	HOU.	–	–	–	–	–	–	–	–	–	–	–	–	–
Les Steckel*	MINN.	–	–	–	–	–	–	–	–	–	–	–	–	–
Sam Wyche*	CINN.	–	–	–	–	–	–	–	–	–	–	–	–	–

Current team in capitals
* First year as head coach

AMERICAN FOOTBALL CONFERENCE

INDIVIDUAL PLAYER
STATISTICS

AFC – INDIVIDUAL RUSHERS

	Att	Yards	Avg	Long	TD
Warner, Curt, Sea.	335	1449	4.3	60	13
Campbell, Earl, Hou.	322	1301	4.0	42	12
Pruitt, Mike, Clev.	293	1184	4.0	27	10
Cribbs, Joe, Buff.	263	1131	4.3	45	3
Dickey, Curtis, Balt.	254	1122	4.4	56	4
Collins, Anthony, N.E.	219	1049	4.8	t50	10
Allen, Marcus, Raiders	266	1014	3.8	19	9
Harris, Franco, Pitt.	279	1007	3.6	19	5
Muncie, Chuck, S.D.	235	886	3.8	t34	12
McMillan, Randy, Balt.	198	802	4.1	t39	5
Johnson, Pete, Cin.	210	763	3.6	t16	14
Winder, Sammy, Den.	196	757	3.9	52	3
Franklin, Andra, Mia.	224	746	3.3	18	8
Nathan, Tony, Mia.	151	685	4.5	40	3
McNeil, Freeman, Jets.	160	654	4.1	19	1
Pollard, Frank, Pitt.	135	608	4.5	32	4
Crutchfield, Dwayne, Jets-Hou.	140	578	4.1	17	3
Tatupu, Mosi, N.E.	106	578	5.5	55	4
Hawkins, Frank, Raiders	110	526	4.8	32	6
Alexander, Charles, Cin.	153	523	3.4	12	3
Brooks, James, S.D.	127	516	4.1	61	3
Jackson, Billy, K.C.	152	499	3.3	19	2
Green, Boyce, Clev.	104	497	4.8	29	3
Brown, Theotis, Sea.-K.C.	130	481	3.7	t49	8
Stoudt, Cliff, Pitt.	77	479	6.2	23	4
Abercrombie, Walter, Pitt.	112	446	4.0	t50	4
Pagel, Mike, Balt.	54	441	8.2	33	0
Weathers, Robert, N.E.	73	418	5.7	77	1
Overstreet, David, Mia.	85	392	4.6	44	1
van Eeghen, Mark, N.E.	95	358	3.8	11	2
Harper, Bruce, Jets	51	354	6.9	t78	1
Moriarty, Larry, Hou.	65	321	4.9	80	3
Hughes, David, Sea.	83	313	3.8	26	1
King, Kenny, Raiders	82	294	3.6	16	1
Moore, Booker, Buff.	60	275	4.6	21	0
Wilson, Stanley, Cin.	56	267	4.8	18	1
Poole, Nathan, Den.	81	246	3.0	19	4
Preston, Dave, Den.	57	222	3.9	28	1
Moore, Alvin, Balt.	57	205	3.6	13	1
Bennett, Woody, Mia.	49	197	4.0	25	2
Willhite, Gerald, Den.	43	188	4.4	t24	3
Leaks, Roosevelt, Buff	58	157	2.7	12	1
Kinnebrew, Larry, Cin.	39	156	4.0	17	3
Pruitt, Greg, Raiders	26	154	5.9	18	2
Anderson, Ken, Cin.	22	147	6.7	29	1
Craft, Donald, Hou.	55	147	2.7	8	0
Elway, John, Den.	28	146	5.2	23	1

	Att	Yards	Avg	Long	TD
Wilson, Marc, Raiders	13	122	9.4	23	0
Schonert, Turk, Cin.	29	117	4.0	15	2
Thomas, Jewerl, K.C.	44	115	2.6	11	0
Dierking, Scott, Jets	28	113	4.0	31	3
Grogan, Steve, N.E.	23	108	4.7	17	2
Todd, Richard, Jets	35	101	2.9	17	0
Walker, Dwight, Clev.	19	100	5.3	15	0
Doornink, Dan, Sea.	40	99	2.5	9	2
Parros, Rick, Den.	30	96	3.2	13	1
Smith, Sherman, S.D.	24	91	3.8	20	0
Ferguson, Joe, Buff.	20	88	4.4	19	0
Bryant, Cullen, Sea.	27	87	3.2	9	0
Hector, Johnny, Jets	16	85	5.3	42	0
Plunkett, Jim, Raiders	26	78	3.0	20	0
Woodley, David, Mia.	19	78	4.1	15	0
Barber, Marion, Jets	15	77	5.1	13	1
Tate, Rodney, Cin.	25	77	3.1	13	0
Williams, Newton, Balt.	28	77	2.8	13	0
Zorn, Jim, Sea.	30	71	2.4	t18	1
Kenney, Bill, K.C.	23	59	2.6	11	3
Sipe, Brian, Clev.	26	56	2.2	9	0
Krieg, Dave, Sea.	16	55	3.4	t10	2
Luck, Oliver, Hou.	17	55	3.2	17	0
Thomas, Ken, K.C.	15	55	3.7	28	0
Myles, Jesse, Den.	8	52	6.5	16	0
Augustyniak, Mike, Jets	18	50	2.8	6	2
Hawthorne, Greg, Pitt.	5	47	9.4	20	0
Marino, Dan, Mia.	28	45	1.6	15	2
Walls, Herkie, Hou.	5	44	8.8	14	0
Nielsen, Gifford, Hou.	8	43	5.4	20	0
Davis, Johnny, Clev.	13	42	3.2	16	0
Edwards, Stan, Hou.	16	40	2.5	9	0
Eason, Tony, N.E.	19	39	2.1	12	0
Jackson, Ernest, S.D.	11	39	3.5	6	0
Dixon, Zachary, Balt.-Sea.	9	32	3.6	7	0
Verser, David, Cin.	2	31	15.5	29	0
DeBerg, Steve, Den.	13	28	2.2	11	1
Hunter, Tony, Buff.	2	28	14.0	24	0
Ricks, Lawrence, K.C.	21	28	1.3	10	0
Weathers, Clarence, N.E.	1	28	28.0	28	0
Reed, Mark, Balt.	2	27	13.5	18	0
Chandler, Wes, S.D.	2	25	12.5	23	0
Kofler, Matt, Buff.	4	25	6.3	11	0
Lewis, Kenny, Jets	5	25	5.0	7	0
Ryan, Pat, Jets	4	23	5.8	25	0
Berns, Rick, Raiders	6	22	3.7	13	0
Martin, Mike, Cin.	2	21	10.5	15	0

	Att	Yards	Avg	Long	TD
Branch, Cliff, Raiders	1	20	20.0	20	0
Carson, Carlos, K.C.	2	20	10.0	18	0
Jones, Bobby, Clev.	1	19	19.0	19	0
Upchurch, Rick, Den.	6	19	3.2	9	0
Riddick, Robb, Buff.	4	18	4.5	12	0
Kubiak, Gary, Den.	4	17	4.3	8	1
McDonald, Paul, Clev.	3	17	5.7	10	0
Watson, Steve, Den.	3	17	5.7	10	0
Smith, Tim, Hou.	2	16	8.0	9	0
Harris, Tim, Pitt.	2	15	7.5	10	0
Kerrigan, Mike, N.E.	1	14	14.0	14	0
Morgan, Stanley, N.E.	1	13	13.0	13	0
Barnwell, Malcolm, Raiders	1	12	12.0	12	0
Hill, Eddie, Mia.	2	12	6.0	10	0
Johns, Paul, Sea.	2	12	6.0	26	0
Williams, Van, Buff.	3	11	3.7	5	0
Hadnot, James, K.C.	4	10	2.5	7	0
Jones, Lam, Jets	4	10	2.5	9	0
Clayton, Mark, Mia.	2	9	4.5	9	0
Holt, Harry, Clev.	3	8	2.7	4	0
Stark, Rohn, Balt.	1	8	8.0	8	0
Montgomery, Cleotha, Raiders	2	7	3.5	5	0
Odom, Henry, Pitt.	2	7	3.5	4	0
Prestridge, Luke, Den.	1	7	7.0	7	0
Allen, Gary, Hou.	1	5	5.0	5	0
Cappelletti, John, S.D.	1	5	5.0	5	0
Crosby, Ron, Jets	1	5	5.0	5	0
Jensen, Derrick, Raiders	1	5	5.0	5	0
Bradshaw, Terry, Pitt.	1	3	3.0	3	0
Dressel, Chris, Hou.	1	3	3.0	3	0
Franklin, Byron, Buff.	1	3	3.0	3	0
Renfro, Mike, Hou.	1	3	3.0	3	0
Adams, Willis, Clev.	1	2	2.0	2	0
Collinsworth, Cris, Cin.	2	2	1.0	8	0
Hall, Dino, Clev.	1	2	2.0	2	0
Hardy, Bruce, Mia.	1	2	2.0	2	0
Kreider, Steve, Cin.	1	2	2.0	2	0
Lane, Eric, Sea.	3	1	0.3	7	0
Scott, Willie, K.C.	1	1	1.0	1	0
Blackledge, Todd, K.C.	1	0	0.0	0	0
Brown, Curtis, Hou.	3	0	0.0	t1	1
Harris, Duriel, Mia.	1	0	0.0	0	0
Herrmann, Mark, Balt.	1	0	0.0	0	0
James, John, Hou.	1	0	0.0	0	0
Mathison, Bruce, S.D.	1	0	0.0	0	0
Willis, Chester, Raiders	5	0	0.0	4	0
Humm, David, Raiders	1	−1	−1.0	−1	0
Krauss, Barry, Balt.	1	−1	−1.0	−1	0
Christensen, Jeff, Cin.	1	−2	−2.0	−2	0
Sweeney, Calvin, Pitt.	1	−2	−2.0	−2	0
Belk, Rocky, Clev.	1	−5	−5.0	−5	0

	Att	Yards	Avg	Long	TD
Fouts, Dan, S.D.	12	−5	−0.4	3	1
Sievers, Eric, S.D.	1	−7	−7.0	−7	0
Wright, James, Den.	1	−11	−11.0	−11	0
Guy, Ray, Raiders	2	−13	−6.5	−3	0
Luther, Ed, S.D.	9	−14	−1.6	8	0
Strock, Don, Mia.	6	−16	−2.7	0	0

t = Touchdown
Leader based on most yards gained

AFC – TEAM RUSHING

	Att	Yards	Avg	Long	TD
Baltimore	601	2695	4.5	56	10
Pittsburgh	614	2610	4.3	t50	17
New England	538	2605	4.8	77	19
Los Angeles Raiders	542	2240	4.1	32	18
Miami	568	2150	3.8	44	16
Seattle	546	2119	3.9	60	19
Cincinnati	542	2104	3.9	29	24
New York Jets	474	2068	4.4	t78	11
Houston	502	1998	4.0	80	16
Cleveland	465	1922	4.1	29	13
Denver	471	1784	3.8	52	15
Buffalo	415	1736	4.2	45	4
San Diego	423	1536	3.6	61	16
Kansas City	387	1254	3.2	t49	13
Conference Total	7088	28821	----	80	211
Conference Average	506.3	2058.6	4.1	--	15.1

AFC – INDIVIDUAL PASSING

QUALIFIERS	Att	Comp	% Comp	Yards	Avg Gain	TD	% TD	Long	Int	% Int	Rating Points
Marino, Dan, Mia.	296	173	58.4	2210	7.47	20	6.8	t85	6	2.0	96.0
Krieg, Dave, Sea.	243	147	60.5	2139	8.80	18	7.4	t50	11	4.5	95.0
Fouts, Dan, S.D.	340	215	63.2	2975	8.75	20	5.9	t59	15	'4.4	92.5
Anderson, Ken, Cin.	297	198	66.7	2333	7.86	12	4.0	t80	13	4.4	85.6
Plunkett, Jim, Raiders	379	230	60.7	2935	7.74	20	5.3	t99	18	4.7	82.7
Grogan, Steve, N.E.	303	168	55.4	2411	7.96	15	5.0	t76	12	4.0	81.4
Kenney, Bill, K.C.	603	346	57.4	4348	7.21	24	4.0	53	18	3.0	80.8
DeBerg, Steve, Den.	215	119	55.3	1617	7.52	9	4.2	54	7	3.3	79.9
Sipe, Brian, Clev.	496	291	58.7	3566	7.19	26	5.2	t66	23	4.6	79.1
Todd, Richard, Jets	518	308	59.5	3478	6.71	18	3.5	t64	26	5.0	70.3
Ferguson, Joe, Buff.	508	281	55.3	2995	5.90	26	5.1	t43	25	4.9	69.3
Zorn, Jim, Sea.	205	103	50.2	1166	5.69	7	3.4	43	7	3.4	64.8
Pagel, Mike, Balt.	328	163	49.7	2353	7.17	12	3.7	t72	17	5.2	64.0
Luck, Oliver, Hou.	217	124	57.1	1375	6.34	8	3.7	66	13	6.0	63.4
Stoudt, Cliff, Pitt.	381	197	51.7	2553	6.70	12	3.1	52	21	5.5	60.6
Luther, Ed, S.D.	287	151	52.6	1875	6.53	7	2.4	46	17	5.9	56.6
Elway, John, Den.	259	123	47.5	1663	6.42	7	2.7	t49	14	5.4	54.9

NON-QUALIFIERS	Att	Comp	% Comp	Yards	Avg Gain	TD	% TD	Long	Int	% Int	Rating Points
Blackledge, Todd, K.C.	34	20	58.8	259	7.62	3	8.8	43	0	0.0	112.3
Strock, Don, Mia.	52	34	65.4	403	7.75	4	7.7	47	1	1.9	106.5
Wilson, Marc, Raiders	117	67	57.3	864	7.38	8	6.8	t50	6	5.1	82.0
Kofler, Matt, Buff.	61	35	57.4	440	7.21	4	6.6	t28	3	4.9	81.3
Kubiak, Gary, Den.	22	12	54.5	186	8.45	1	4.5	t78	1	4.5	79.0
Schonert, Turk, Cin.	156	92	59.0	1159	7.43	2	1.3	54	5	3.2	73.1
Ryan, Pat, Jets	40	21	52.5	259	6.48	2	5.0	36	2	5.0	68.6
Nielsen, Gifford, Hou.	175	90	51.4	1125	6.43	5	2.9	48	8	4.6	62.2
Woodley, David, Mia.	89	43	48.3	528	5.93	3	3.4	t64	4	4.5	59.6
Manning, Archie, Hou.	88	44	50.0	755	8.58	2	2.3	t47	8	9.1	49.2
Eason, Tony, N.E.	95	46	48.4	557	5.86	1	1.1	35	5	5.3	48.4
McDonald, Paul, Clev.	68	32	47.1	341	5.01	1	1.5	27	4	5.9	42.6
Malone, Mark, Pitt.	20	9	45.0	124	6.20	1	5.0	38	2	10.0	42.5
Herrmann, Mark, Balt.	36	18	50.0	256	7.11	0	0.0	35	3	8.3	38.7
Kerrigan, Mike, N.E.	14	6	42.9	72	5.14	0	0.0	19	1	7.1	29.5
Reed, Mark, Balt.	10	6	60.0	34	3.40	0	0.0	16	1	10.0	26.7
(Fewer than 10 attempts)											
Allen, Marcus, Raiders	7	4	57.1	111	15.86	3	42.9	t43	0	0.0	
Bradshaw, Terry, Pitt.	8	5	62.5	77	9.63	2	25.0	24	0	0.0	
Brown, Theotis, K.C.	1	1	100.0	11	11.00	0	0.0	11	0	0.0	
Bryant, Steve, Hou.	1	1	100.0	24	24.00	1	100.0	t24	0	0.0	
Buford, Maury, S.D.	1	0	0.0	0	0.00	0	0.0	0	0	0.0	
Carson, Carlos, K.C.	1	1	100.0	48	48.00	1	100.0	t48	0	0.0	
Chandler, Wes, S.D.	0	0	---	0	---	0	---	0	0	---	
Clayton, Mark, Mia.	1	1	100.0	48	48.00	1	100.0	t48	0	0.0	
Cribbs, Joe, Buff.	2	1	50.0	3	1.50	0	0.0	3	0	0.0	
Holohan, Pete, S.D.	1	0	0.00	0	0.00	0	0.0	0	0	0.0	

	Att	Comp	% Comp	Yards	Avg Gain	TD	% TD	Long	Int	% Int
James, John, Hou.	1	1	100.0	7	7.00	0	0.0	7	0	0.0
Kreider, Steve, Cin.	1	0	0.0	0	0.00	0	0.0	0	0	0.0
Largent, Steve, Sea.	1	1	100.0	11	11.00	0	0.0	11	0	0.0
Marshall, Henry, K.C.	0	0	---	0	---	0	---	0	0	---
Mathison, Bruce, S.D.	5	3	60.0	41	8.20	0	0.0	25	1	20.0
McNeil, Freeman, Jets	1	1	100.0	5	5.00	1	100.0	15	0	0.0
Nathan, Tony, Mia.	4	3	75.0	46	11.50	0	0.0	22	0	0.0
Pruitt, Greg, Raiders	1	0	0.0	0	0.00	0	0.0	0	0	0.0
Smith, Sherman, S.D.	1	0	0.0	0	0.00	0	0.0	0	0	0.0
Stark, Rohn, Balt.	1	0	0.0	0	0.00	0	0.0	0	0	0.0
Taylor, Jim Bob, Balt.	2	1	50.0	20	10.00	0	0.0	20	1	50.0
Thomas, Jewerl, K.C.	2	1	50.0	18	9.00	1	50.0	t18	1	50.0
Upchurch, Rick, Den.	2	0	0.0	0	0.00	0	0.0	0	0	0.0
Walker, Dwight, Clev.	3	1	33.3	25	8.33	0	0.0	25	1	33.3
Willhite, Gerald, Den.	1	0	0.0	0	0.00	0	0.0	0	0	0.0

t=Touchdown

AFC – TEAM PASSING

	Att	Comp	% Comp	Gross Yards	Tkd Lost	Net Yards	Avg Yds Att	Avg Yds Comp	TD	% TD	Long	Int	% Int
San Diego	635	369	58.1	4891	28	230	4661	7.70	13.25	27	4.3	159	33	5.2
Kansas City	641	369	57.6	4684	46	343	4341	7.31	12.69	29	4.5	53	19	3.0
Cleveland	567	324	57.1	3932	33	271	3661	6.93	12.14	27	4.8	t66	28	4.9
Los Angeles Raiders	504	301	59.7	3910	55	464	3446	7.76	12.99	31	6.2	199	24	4.8
New York Jets	559	330	59.0	3742	43	317	3425	6.69	11.34	21	3.8	t64	28	5.0
Cincinnati	454	290	63.9	3492	40	309	3183	7.69	12.04	14	3.1	180	18	4.0
Buffalo	571	317	55.5	3438	37	351	3087	6.02	10.85	30	5.3	143	28	4.9
Miami	442	254	57.5	3235	23	190	3045	7.32	12.74	28	6.3	t85	11	2.5
Denver	499	254	50.9	3466	55	439	3027	6.95	13.65	17	3.4	t78	22	4.4
Seattle	449	251	55.9	3316	47	343	2973	7.39	13.21	25	5.6	150	18	4.0
Houston	482	260	53.9	3286	49	384	2902	6.82	12.64	16	3.3	66	29	6.0
New England	412	220	53.4	3040	45	334	2706	7.38	13.82	16	3.9	t76	18	4.4
Pittsburgh	409	211	51.6	2754	52	350	2404	6.73	13.05	15	3.7	52	23	5.6
Baltimore	377	188	49.9	2663	47	340	2323	7.06	14.16	12	3.2	t72	22	5.8
Conference Total	7001	3938	—	49849	600	4665	45184	—	—	308	—	199	321	—
Conference Average	500.1	281.3	56.2	3560.6	42.9	333.2	3227.4	7.12	12.66	22.0	4.4	—	22.9	4.6

AFC – INDIVIDUAL RECEIVERS

	No	Yards	Avg	Long	TD
Christensen, Todd, Raiders	92	1247	13.6	45	12
Newsome, Ozzie, Clev.	89	970	10.9	t66	6
Winslow, Kellen, S.D.	88	1172	13.3	46	8
Smith, Tim, Hou.	83	1176	14.2	t47	6
Carson, Carlos, K.C.	80	1351	16.9	t50	7
Largent, Steve, Sea.	72	1074	14.9	t46	11
Allen, Marcus, Raiders	68	590	8.7	36	2
Collinsworth, Cris, Cin.	66	1130	17.1	63	5
Joiner, Charlie, S.D.	65	960	14.8	t33	3
Walker, Wesley, Jets	61	868	14.2	t64	7
Watson, Steve, Den.	59	1133	19.2	t78	5
Morgan, Stanley, N.E.	58	863	14.9	t50	2
Chandler, Wes, S.D.	58	845	14.6	t44	5
Cribbs, Joe, Buff.	57	524	9.2	t33	7
Nathan, Tony, Mia.	52	461	8.9	25	1
Duper, Mark, Mia.	51	1003	19.7	t85	10
Marshall, Henry, K.C.	50	788	15.8	52	6
Harper, Bruce, Jets	48	413	8.6	33	2
Brown, Theotis, Sea.	47	418	8.9	53	2
Jones, Lam, Jets	43	734	17.1	t50	4
Curtis, Issac, Cin.	42	571	13.6	t80	2
Kreider, Steve, Cin.	42	554	13.2	54	1
Ross, Dan, Cin.	42	483	11.5	30	3
Muncie, Chuck, S.D.	42	396	9.4	27	1
Warner, Curt, Sea.	42	325	7.7	28	1
Upchurch, Rick, Den.	40	639	16.0	40	2
Branch, Cliff, Raiders	39	696	17.8	t99	5
Sweeney, Calvin, Pitt.	39	577	14.8	42	5
Moore, Nat, Mia.	39	558	14.3	t66	6
Logan, Dave, Clev	37	627	16.9	34	2
Hancock, Anthony, K.C.	37	584	15.8	50	1
Young, Charle, Sea.	36	529	14.7	47	2
Jones, Bobby, Clev.	36	507	14.1	t32	4
Lewis, Frank, Buff.	36	486	13.5	t27	3
Hunter, Tony, Buff.	36	402	11.2	t40	3
Butler, Jerry, Buff.	36	385	10.7	25	3
Barnwell, Malcolm, Raiders	35	513	14.7	41	1
Cunningham, Bennie, Pitt	35	442	12.6	29	3
Johns, Paul, Sea.	34	486	14.3	t30	4
Harris, wfranco, Pitt.	34	278	8.2	t29	2
Moore, Booker, Buff.	34	199	5.9	21	1
Sievers, Eric, S.D.	33	452	13.7	28	3
Dierking, Scott, Jets	33	275	8.3	19	0
Barkum, Jerome, Jets	32	385	12.0	34	1
Dressel, Chris, Hou.	32	316	9.9	t35	4
Jackson, Billy, K.C.	32	243	7.6	29	0
Alexander, Charles, Cin.	32	187	5.8	14	0
Paige, Stephone, K.C.	30	528	17.6	43	6
Franklin, Byron, Buff.	30	452	15.1	t43	4
Henry, Bernard, Balt.	30	416	13.9	t40	4

	No	Yards	Avg	Long	TD
Pruitt, Mike, Clev.	30	157	5.2	21	2
Holt, Harry, Clev.	29	420	14.5	t48	3
Rose, Joe, Mia.	29	345	11.9	e7	3
Walker, Dwight, Clev.	29	273	9.4	35	1
Scott, Willie, K.C.	29	247	8.5	22	6
Porter, Tracy, Balt.	28	384	13.7	38	0
Thomas, Ken, K.C.	28	236	8.4	25	1
Collins, Anthony, N.E.	27	257	9.5	20	0
Abercrombie, Walter, Pitt.	26	391	15.0	t51	3
Shuler, Mickey, Jets	26	272	10.5	28	1
Bouza, Matt, Balt.	25	385	15.4	26	0
Sherwin, Tim, Balt.	25	358	14.3	30	0
Brammer, Mark, Buff.	25	215	8.6	21	2
Brooks, James, S.D.	25	215	8.6	36	0
Green, Boyce, Clev.	25	167	6.7	33	1
Dickey, Curtis, Balt.	24	483	20.1	t72	3
Ramsey, Derrick, N.E.	24	335	14.0	39	6
Doornink, Dan, Sea.	24	328	13.7	47	2
McMillan, Randy, Balt.	24	195	8.1	27	1
Johnson, Dan, Mia.	24	189	7.9	33	4
Renfro, Mike, Hou.	23	316	13.7	t38	2
Holohan, Pete, S.D.	23	272	11.8	35	2
Weathers, Robert, N.E.	23	212	9.2	19	0
Winder, Sammy, Den.	23	150	6.5	17	0
Hardy, Bruce, Mia.	22	202	9.2	25	0
McNeil, Freeman, Jets	21	172	8.2	21	3
Duckworth, Bobby, S.D.	20	422	21.1	t59	5
Adams, Willis, Clev.	20	374	18.7	59	2
Jones, Cedric, N.E.	20	323	16.2	30	1
Egloff, Ron, Den.	20	205	10.3	32	2
Poole, Nathan, Den.	20	184	9.2	23	0
Hawkins, Frank, Raiders	20	150	7.5	28	2
Weathers, Clarence, N.E.	19	379	19.9	t58	3
Hawthorne, Greg, Pitt.	19	300	15.8	52	0
Garrity, Gregg, Pitt.	19	279	14.7	38	1
Campbell, Earl, HXOU.	19	216	11.4	66	0
Crutchfield, Dwayne, Jets	19	133	7.0	15	0
Tate, Rodney, Cin.	18	142	7.9	25	0
Starring, Stephen, N.E.	17	389	22.9	t76	2
Tuttle, Perry, Buff.	17	261	15.4	38	3
Gaffney, Derrick, Jets	17	243	14.3	35	0
Preston, Dave, Den.	17	137	8.1	25	1
Bryant, Steve, Hou.	16	211	13.2	26	0
McCloskey, Mike, Hou.	16	137	8.6	20	1
Pollard, Frank, Pitt.	16	127	7.9	17	0
Harris, Duriel, Mia.	15	260	17.3	t64	0
Johnson, Pete, Cin.	15	129	8.6	18	0
Williams, Dokie, Raiders	14	259	18.5	t50	3
Holston, Michael, Hou.	14	205	14.6	43	0
Mosley, Mike, Buff.	14	180	12.9	35	3

	No	Yards	Avg	Long	TD
Willhite, Gerald, Den.	14	153	10.9	t26	1
King, Kenny, Raiders	14	149	10.6	t34	1
Muhammad, Calvin, Raiders	13	252	19.4	45	2
Feacher, Ricky, Clev.	13	217	16.7	t42	3
Wright, James, Den.	13	134	10.3	23	0
Beckman, Ed, K.C.	13	130	10.0	20	0
Walls, Herkie, Hou.	12	276	23.0	48	1
Walker, Byron, Sea.	12	248	20.7	t50	2
Thomas, Zack, Den.	12	182	15.2	44	0
Arnold, Walt, Hou.	12	137	11.4	37	1
Parros, Rick, Den.	12	126	10.5	t33	2
Wilson, Stanley, Cin.	12	107	8.9	19	1
Craft, Donald, Hou.	12	99	8.3	14	0
Dawkins, Julius, Buff.	11	123	11.2	t28	1
Butler, Raymond, Balt.	10	207	20.7	60	3
Sampson, Clinton, Den.	10	200	20.0	t49	3
Capers, Wayne, Pitt.	10	185	18.5	36	1
van Eeghen, Mark, N.E.	10	102	10.2	23	0
Hughes, David, Sea.	10	100	10.0	t33	1
Tatupu, Mosi, N.E.	10	97	9.7	17	1
Barnett, Buster, Buff.	10	94	9.4	14	0
Augustyniak, Mike, Jets	10	71	7.1	17	1
Thomas, Jewerl, K.C.	10	51	5.1	9	0
Dawson, Lin, N.E.	9	84	9.3	14	1
Edwards, Stan, Hou.	9	79	8.8	20	1
Jackson, Harold, Sea.	8	126	15.8	29	1
Stallworth, John, Pitt.	8	100	12.5	20	0
Leaks, Roosevelt, Buff.	8	74	9.3	12	0
Harris, M.L., Cin.	8	66	8.3	14	2
Overstreet, David, Mia.	8	55	6.9	20	0
Myles, Jesse, Den.	7	119	17.0	33	1
Smith, J.T., K.C.	7	85	12.1	18	0
Verser, David, Cin.	7	82	11.7	22	0
Metzelaars, Pete, Sea.	7	72	10.3	t17	1
Barber, Marion, Jets	7	48	6.9	12	1
Clayton, Mark, Mia.	6	114	19.0	39	1
Oatis, Victor, Balt.	6	93	15.5	25	0
Lewis, Kenny, Jets	6	62	10.3	23	0
Smith, Sherman, S.D.	6	51	8.5	21	0
Moore, Alvin, Balt.	6	38	6.3	16	0
Bennett, Woody, Mia.	6	35	5.8	9	0
Belk, Rocky, Clev.	5	141	28.2	t64	2
Hector, Johnny, Jets	5	61	12.2	t22	1
Beach, Pat, Balt.	5	56	11.2	16	1
Jackson, Ernest, S.D.	5	42	8.4	10	0
Davis, Johnny, Clev.	5	20	4.0	10	0
Odoms, Riley, Den.	4	62	15.5	21	0
Williams, Newton, Balt.	4	46	11.5	19	0
Hall, Dino, Clev.	4	33	8.3	18	0
Moriarty, Larry, Hou.	4	32	8.0	12	0
Riddick, Robb, Buff.	3	43	14.3	24	0

	No	Yards	Avg	Long	TD
Sawyer, John, Den.	3	42	14.0	17	0
Skansi, Paul, Pitt.	3	39	13.0	21	0
Hasselbeck, Don, N.E.-Raiders	3	24	8.0	t13	2
Bryant, Cullen, Sea.	3	8	2.7	3	0
Ricks, Lawrence, K.C.	3	5	1.7	7	0
Carr, Roger, S.D.	2	36	18.0	23	0
Rodgers, John, Pitt.	2	36	18.0	25	0
Montgomery, Cleotha, Raiders	2	29	14.5	15	0
Scales, Dwight, S.D.	2	28	14.0	14	0
Martin, Mike, Cin.	2	22	11.0	12	0
Hadnot, James, K.C.	2	18	9.0	16	0
Holman, Rodney, Cin.	2	15	7.5	10	0
Lane, Eric, Sea.	2	9	4.5	7	0
Kinnebrew, Larry, Cin.	2	4	2.0	2	0
Dieken, Doug, Clev.	1	14	14.0	t14	1
Stracka, Tim, Clev.	1	12	12.0	12	0
Krieg, Dave, Sea.	1	11	11.0	11	0
Kempf, Florian, Hou.	1	7	7.0	7	0
Vigorito, Tom, Mia.	1	7	7.0	7	0
Pruitt, Greg, Raiders	1	6	6.0	6	0
Woodley, David, Mia.	1	6	6.0	6	0
Harmon, Mike, Jets	1	4	4.0	4	0
Dixon, Zachary, Balt.	1	2	2.0	2	0
Jensen, Derrick, Raiders	1	2	2.0	t2	1
Coombs, Tom, Jets	1	1	1.0	1	0
Kenney, Bill, K.C.	1	0	0.0	0	0
Williams, Brooks, N.E.	1	0	0.0	0	0
Grogan, Steve, N.E.	1	−8	−8.0	−8	0

t=Touchdown
Leader based on most passes caught

AFC – TOP 25 PASS RECEIVERS BY YARDS

	Yards	No	Avg	Long	TD
Carson, Carlos, K.C.	1351	80	16.9	t50	7
Christensen, Todd, Raiders	1247	92	13.6	45	12
Smith, Tim, Hou.	1176	83	14.2	t47	6
Winslow, Kellen, S.D.	1172	88	13.3	46	8
Watson, Steve, Den.	1133	59	19.2	t78	5
Collinsworth, Cris, Cin.	1130	66	17.1	63	5
Largent, Steve, Sea.	1074	72	14.9	t46	11
Duper, Mark, Mia.	1003	51	19.7	t85	10
Newsome, Ozzie, Clev.	970	89	10.9	t66	6
Joiner, Charlie, S.D.	960	65	14.8	t33	3
Walker, Wesley, Jets	868	61	14.2	t64	7
Morgan, Stanley, N.E.	863	58	14.9	t50	2
Chandler, Wes, S.D.	845	58	14.6	t44	5
Marshall, Henry, K.C.	788	50	15.8	52	6
Jones, Lam, Jets	734	43	17.1	t50	4
Branch, Cliff, Raiders	696	39	17.8	t99	5
Upchurch, Rick, Den.	639	40	16.0	40	2
Logan, Dave, Clev.	627	37	16.9	34	2
Allen, Marcus, Raiders	590	68	8.7	36	2
Hancock, Anthony, K.C.	584	37	15.8	50	1
Sweeney, Calvin, Pitt.	577	39	14.8	42	5
Curtis, Issac, Cin.	571	42	13.6	t80	2
Moore, Nat, Mia.	558	39	14.3	t66	6
Kreider, Steve, Cin.	554	42	13.2	54	1
Young, Charle, Sea.	529	36	14.7	47	2

AFC – INDIVIDUAL INTERCEPTORS

	No	Yards	Avg	Long	TD
Riley, Ken, Cin.	8	89	11.1	t42	2
McElroy, Vann, Raiders	8	68	8.5	28	0
Easley, Ken, Sea.	7	106	15.1	48	0
Cherry, Deron, K.C.	7	100	14.3	41	0
Mehl, Lance, Jets	7	57	8.1	t34	1
Walters, Danny, S.D.	7	55	7.9	33	0
Sanford, Rick, N.E.	7	24	3.4	16	0
Brown, Dave, Sea.	6	83	13.8	37	0
Judson, William, Mia.	6	60	10.0	29	0
Green, Gary, K.C.	6	59	9.8	25	0
Wright, Louis, Den.	6	50	8.3	34	0
Horton, Ray, Cin.	5	121	24.2	t55	1
James, Roland, N.E.	5	99	19.8	46	0
Wilson, Steve, Den.	5	91	18.2	36	0
Tullis, Willie, Hou.	5	65	13.0	44	0
Small, Gerald, Mia.	5	60	12.0	28	0
Woods, Rick, Pitt.	5	53	10.6	31	0
Foley, Steve, Den.	5	28	5.6	16	0
Shell, Donnie, Pitt.	5	18	3.6	18	0
Harden, Mike, Den.	4	127	31.8	48	0
Roquemore, Durwood, K.C.	4	117	29.3	t42	1
Martin, Rod, Raiders	4	81	20.3	t40	2
Blackwood, Lyle, Mia.	4	77	19.3	45	0
Cousineau, Tom, Clev.	4	47	11.8	15	0
Burruss, Lloyd, K.C.	4	46	11.5	27	0
Lewis, Albert, K.C.	4	42	10.5	34	0
Simpson, Keith, Sea.	4	39	9.8	14	0
Smith, Dennis, Den.	4	39	9.8	23	0
Hatchett, Derrick, Balt.	4	36	9.0	25	0
Blount, Mel, Pitt.	4	32	8.0	21	0
Holmes, Johnny, Jets	3	107	35.7	t43	1
Smith, Lucious, K.C.	3	99	33.0	t58	1
Banks, Chip, Clev.	3	95	31.7	t65	1
Woodruff, Dwayne, Pitt.	3	85	28.3	47	0
Johnson, Ron, Pitt.	3	84	28.0	t34	1
Ray, Darrol, Jets	3	77	25.7	42	0
Lynn, Johnny, Jets	3	70	23.3	t42	1
Whitwell, Mike, Clev.	3	67	22.3	28	0
Merriweather, Mark, Pitt.	3	55	18.3	t31	1
Dixon, Hanford, Clev.	3	41	13.7	35	0
Freeman, Steve, Buff.	3	40	13.3	29	0
Glasgow, Nesby, Balt.	3	35	11.7	18	0
Kemp, Bobby, Cin.	3	26	8.7	26	0
Williams, Chris, Buff.	3	6	2.0	4	0
Blackwood, Glenn, Mia.	3	0	0.0	0	0
Anderson, Kim, Balt.	2	81	40.5	t71	1
Kozlowski, Mike, Mia.	2	73	36.5	t38	2
Hayes, Lester, Raiders	2	49	24.5	28	0
Young, Andre, S.D.	2	49	24.5	t40	1

	No	Yards	Avg	Long	TD
Breeden, Louis, Cin.	2	47	23.5	39	0
Bokamper, Kim, Mia.	2	43	21.5	t24	1
Sanford, Lucius, Buff.	2	39	19.5	20	0
Kay, Bill, Hou.	2	31	15.5	27	0
Romes, Charles, Buff.	2	27	13.5	27	0
Griffin, Ray, Cin.	2	24	12.0	24	0
Jackson, Robert, Cin.	2	21	10.5	15	0
Keating, Chris, Buff.	2	20	10.0	17	0
Bracelin, Greg, Balt.	2	19	9.5	19	0
Delaney, Jeff, Balt.	2	16	8.0	11	0
Harris, John, Sea.	2	15	7.5	10	0
Fox, Tim, S.D.	2	14	7.0	14	0
Burroughs, Jim, Balt.	2	8	4.0	8	0
Jackson, Bobby, Jets	2	8	4.0	8	0
Schroy, Ken, Jets	2	6	3.0	4	0
Marion, Fred, N.E.	2	4	2.0	4	0
Bostic, Keith, Hou.	2	0	0.0	0	0
Burrell, Clinton, Clev.	2	0	0.0	0	0
Johnson, Lawrence, Clev.	2	0	0.0	0	0
Scott, Clarence, Clev.	2	0	0.0	0	0
Lambert, Jack, Pitt.	2	-1	-0.5	0	0
Green, Jacob, Sea.	1	73	73.0	t73	1
Clayton, Harvey, Pitt.	1	70	70.0	t70	1
Griffin, James, Cin.	1	41	41.0	t41	1
Randle, Tate, Balt.	1	41	41.0	41	0
Blackmon, Don, N.E.	1	39	39.0	39	0
Williams, Kendall, Balt.	1	32	32.0	18	0
Maxwell, Vernon, Balt.	1	31	31.0	31	0
Washington, Sam, Pitt.	1	25	25.0	25	0
Kennedy, Mike, Buff.	1	22	22.0	t22	1
Perry, Rod, Clev.	1	21	21.0	21	0
Bryant, Trent, K.C.	1	19	19.0	19	0
King, Linden, S.D.	1	19	19.0	19	0
Moyer, Paul, Sea.	1	19	19.0	t19	1
Reinfeldt, Mike, Hou.	1	19	19.0	19	0
Gross, Al, Clev.	1	18	18.0	18	0
Robinson, Shelton, Sea.	1	18	18.0	18	0
Buttle, Greg, Jets	1	17	17.0	17	0
Brown, Steve, Hou.	1	16	16.0	16	0
Cooks, Johnie, Balt.	1	15	15.0	15	0
Jackson, Roger, Den.	1	15	15.0	15	0
Rhone, Earnest, Mia.	1	15	15.0	15	0
Hinkle, Bryan, Pitt.	1	14	14.0	t14	1
Millen, Matt, Raiders	1	14	14.0	14	0
Preston, Ray, S.D.	1	13	13.0	13	0
Watts, Ted, Raiders	1	13	13.0	13	0
Davis, James, Raiders	1	10	10.0	10	0
Lankford, Paul, Mia.	1	10	10.0	10	0
Scholtz, Bruce, Sea.	1	8	8.0	8	0
Golic, Bob, Clev.	1	7	7.0	t7	1
Walker, Fulton, Mia.	1	7	7.0	7	0

	No	Yards	Avg	Long	TD
Nelson, Steve, N.E.	1	6	6.0	6	0
Gradishar, Randy, Den.	1	5	5.0	5	0
Bingham, Gregg, Hou.	1	4	4.0	4	0
Davis, Mike, Raiders	1	3	3.0	3	0
Green, Mike, S.D.	1	3	3.0	3	0
McGrew, Larry, N.E.	1	3	3.0	3	0
Justin, Kerry, Sea.	1	2	2.0	2	0
Abraham, Robert, Hou.	1	0	0.0	0	0
Anderson, Larry, Balt.	1	0	0.0	0	0
Brown, Mark, Mia.	1	0	0.0	0	0
Butler, Keith, Sea.	1	0	0.0	0	0
Byrd, Gill, S.D.	1	0	0.0	0	0
Crable, Bob, Jets	1	0	0.0	0	0
Haynes, Mike, Raiders	1	0	0.0	0	0
Jackson, Tom, Den.	1	0	0.0	0	0
McKenney, Odis, Raiders	1	0	0.0	0	0
McPherson, Miles, S.D.	1	0	0.0	0	0
Potter, Steve, K.C.	1	0	0.0	0	0
Riley, Avon, Hou.	1	0	0.0	0	0
Williams, Eugene, Sea.	1	0	0.0	0	0
Weishuhn, Clayton, N.E.	0	27	----	t27	1

t=Touchdown
Leader based on most interceptions

AFC – TEAM INTERCEPTIONS

	No	Yards	Avg	Long	TD
Kansas City	30	482	16.1	t58	2
Pittsburgh	28	435	15.5	t70	4
Denver	27	355	13.1	48	0
Miami	26	345	13.3	45	3
Seattle	26	363	14.0	t73	2
Cincinnati	23	369	16.0	t55	4
Cleveland	22	296	13.5	t65	2
New York Jets	22	342	15.5	t43	3
Baltimore	20	314	15.7	t71	1
Los Angeles Raiders	20	238	11.9	t40	2
New England	17	202	11.9	46	1
San Diego	16	153	9.6	t40	1
Houston	14	135	9.6	44	0
Buffalo	13	154	11.8	29	1
Conference Total	304	4183	----	t73	26
Conference Average	21.7	298.8	13.8	----	1.9

AFC – INDIVIDUAL PUNTERS

	No	Yards	Long	Avg	Total Punts	TB	Blk	Opp Ret	Ret Yds	In 20	Net Avg
Stark, Rohn, Balt	91	4124	68	45.3	91	9	0	55	642	20	36.3
Camarillo, Rich, N.E.	81	3615	70	44.6	81	11	0	48	392	25	37.1
Buford, Maury, S.D.	63	2763	60	43.9	63	8	0	35	299	13	36.6
Roby, Reggie, Mia.	74	3189	64	43.1	75	11	1	32	229	26	36.5
Guy, Ray, Raiders	78	3336	67	42.8	78	10	0	35	334	17	35.9
Colquitt, Craig, Pitt.	80	3352	58	41.9	80	7	0	44	418	20	34.9
McInally, Pat, Cin.	67	2804	60	41.9	69	9	2	41	310	13	33.5
Prestridge, Luke, Den.	87	3620	60	41.6	87	7	0	55	524	19	34.0
Gossett, Jeff, Clev.	70	2854	60	40.8	70	8	0	30	309	17	34.1
Arnold, Jim, K.C.	93	3710	64	39.9	93	6	0	54	559	21	32.6
Ramsey, Chuck, Jets	81	3218	56	39.7	82	5	1	47	367	17	33.5
Cater, Greg, Buff.	89	3533	60	39.7	89	7	0	42	403	24	33.6
James, John, Hou.	79	3136	53	39.7	80	8	1	47	354	12	32.8
West, Jeff, Sea.	79	3118	56	39.5	79	10	0	36	185	25	34.6

Leader based on gross average, minimum 40 punts

AFC – TEAM PUNTING

	Total Punts	Yards	Long	Avg	TB	Blk	Opp Ret	Ret Yds	In 20	Net Avg
Baltimore	91	4124	68	45.3	9	0	55	642	20	36.3
New England	81	3615	70	44.6	11	0	48	392	25	37.1
San Diego	63	2763	60	43.9	8	0	35	299	13	36.6
Los Angeles Raiders	78	3336	67	42.8	10	0	35	334	17	35.9
Miami	75	3189	64	42.5	11	1	32	229	26	36.5
Pittsburgh	80	3352	58	41.9	7	0	44	418	20	34.9
Denver	87	3620	60	41.6	7	0	55	524	19	34.0
Cleveland	70	2854	60	40.8	8	0	30	309	17	34.1
Cincinnati	69	2804	60	40.6	9	2	41	310	13	33.5
Kansas City	93	3710	64	39.9	6	0	54	559	21	32.6
Buffalo	89	3533	60	39.7	7	0	42	403	24	33.6
Seattle	79	3118	56	39.5	10	0	36	185	25	34.6
New York Jets	82	3218	56	39.2	5	1	47	367	17	33.5
Houston	80	3136	53	39.2	8	1	47	354	12	32.8
Conference Total	1117	46372	70	—	116	5	601	5325	269	—
Conference Average	79.8	3312.3		41.5	8.3	0.4	42.9	380.4	19.2	34.7

AFC – INDIVIDUAL PUNT RETURNERS

	No	FC	Yards	Avg	Long	TD
Springs, Kirk, Jets	23	4	287	12.5	t76	1
Pruitt, Greg, Raiders	58	18	666	11.5	t97	1
Johns, Paul, Sea.	28	5	316	11.3	t75	1
Thomas, Zack, Den.	33	9	368	11.2	t70	1
Smith, Ricky, N.E.	38	12	398	10.5	55	0
Martin, Mike, Cin.	23	3	227	9.9	19	0
Clayton, Mark, Mia.	41	11	392	9.6	t60	1
Skansi, Paul, Pitt	43	9	363	8.4	57	0
Smith, J.T., K.C.	26	5	210	8.1	19	0
Roaches, Carl, Hou.	20	9	159	8.0	23	0
Brooks, James, S.D.	18	4	137	7.6	30	0
Hall, Dino, Clev.	39	12	284	7.3	19	0
Simmons, John, Cin.	25	2	173	6.9	43	0
Anderson, Larry, Balt.	20	4	138	6.9	20	0
Riddick, Robb, Buff.	42	5	241	5.7	24	0
(Non-Qualifiers)						
Porter, Ricky, Balt.	14	5	104	7.4	50	0
Hancock, Anthony, K.C.	14	9	81	5.8	18	0
Harmon, Mike, Jets	12	8	109	9.1	21	0
Williams, Kendall, Balt.	9	4	43	4.8	13	0
Walker, Fulton, Mia.	8	0	86	10.8	23	0
Chandler, Wes, S.D.	8	6	26	3.3	11	0
Woods, Rick, Pitt.	5	0	46	9.2	13	0
Upchurch, Rick, Den.	4	1	52	13.0	17	0
Fortune, Hosea, S.D.	4	0	16	4.0	9	0
Weathers, Clarence, N.E.	4	0	1	0.3	3	0
Walker, Dwight, Clev.	3	0	26	8.7	13	0
Johnson, Gregg, Sea.	3	1	17	5.7	10	0
Harris, Tim, Pitt.	3	0	12	4.0	8	0
Scales, Dwight, S.D.	2	0	34	17.0	30	0
Harris, John, Sea.	2	0	27	13.5	14	0
Mullen, Davlin, Jets	2	3	13	6.5	9	0
Kozlowski, Mike, Mia.	2	10	12	6.0	11	0
Vigorito, Tom, Mia.	1	0	62	62.0	62	0
Heflin, Vince, Mia.	1	0	19	19.0	19	0
Schroy, Ken, Jets	1	0	11	11.0	11	0
Blackwood, Glenn, Mia.	1	2	10	10.0	10	0
Horton, Ray, Cin.	1	1	10	10.0	10	0
Glasgow, Nesby, Balt.	1	1	9	9.0	9	0
Easley, Ken, Sea.	1	0	6	6.0	6	0
Hurley, Bill, Buff.	1	0	0	0.0	0	0
Laird, Bruce, S.D.	1	0	0	0.0	0	0
Lee, Keith, N.E.	1	0	0	0.0	0	0
Sanford, Rick, N.E.	1	2	0	0.0	0	0
Sowell, Robert, Mia.	1	0	0	0.0	0	0
Williams, Van, Buff.	1	0	0	0.0	0	0
Wright, Louis, Den.	1	0	0	0.0	0	0

t=Touchdown

Leader based on average return, minimum 16 returns

AFC -- TEAM PUNT RETURNS

	No	FC	Yards	Avg	Long	TD
Los Angeles Raiders	58	18	666	11.5	t97	1
Denver	38	10	420	11.1	t70	1
New York Jets	38	15	420	11.1	t76	1
Seattle	34	6	366	10.8	t75	1
Miami	55	23	581	10.6	62	1
New England	44	14	399	9.1	55	0
Cincinnati	49	6	410	8.4	43	0
Pittsburgh	51	9	421	8.3	57	0
Houston	20	9	159	8.0	23	0
Cleveland	42	12	310	7.4	19	0
Kansas City	40	14	291	7.3	19	0
Baltimore	44	14	294	6.7	50	0
San Diego	33	10	213	6.5	30	0
Buffalo	44	5	241	5.5	24	0
Conference Total	590	165	5191	----	t97	5
Conference Average	42.1	11.8	370.8	8.8	---	0.4

AFC – INDIVIDUAL KICKOFF RETURNERS

	No	Yards	Avg	Long	TD
Walker, Fulton, Mia.	36	962	26.7	78	0
Brown, Steve, Hou.	31	795	25.6	t93	1
Williams, Kendall, Balt.	20	490	24.5	90	0
Dixon, Zachary, Balt.-Sea.	51	1171	23.0	t94	1
Springs, Kirk, Jets	16	364	22.8	64	0
Williams, Van, Buff.	22	494	22.5	60	0
Brown, Preston, Jets	29	645	22.2	46	0
Montgomery, Cleotha, Raiders	21	464	22.1	48	0
Smith, Ricky, N.E.	42	916	21.8	53	0
Walker, Dwight, Clev.	29	627	21.6	38	0
Green, Boyce, Clev.	17	350	20.6	30	0
Thomas, Zack, Den.	28	573	20.5	42	0
Riddick, Robb, Buff.	28	568	20.3	49	0
Wilson, Steve, Den.	24	485	20.2	32	0
Pruitt, Greg, Raiders	31	604	19.5	42	0
Odom, Henry, Pitt.	39	756	19.4	35	0
Brooks, James, S.D.	32	607	19.0	34	0
Porter, Ricky, Balt.	18	340	18.9	28	0
Roaches, Carl, Hou.	34	641	18.9	t97	1
Hancock, Anthony, K.C.	29	515	17.8	33	0
Anderson, Larry, Balt.	18	309	17.2	26	0
Harris, Tim, Pitt.	18	289	16.1	32	0
(Non-Qualifiers)					
Laird, Bruce, S.D.	15	342	22.8	41	0
Brown, Theotis, K.C.	15	301	20.1	46	0
Simmons, John, Cin.	14	317	22.6	36	0
Hector, Johnny, Jets	14	274	19.6	45	0
Verser, David, Cin.	13	253	19.5	29	0
Tate, Rodney, Cin.	13	218	16.8	23	0
Hughes, David, Sea.	12	282	23.5	35	0
Hall, Dino, Clev.	11	237	21.5	28	0
Jackson, Ernest, S.D.	11	201	18.3	32	0
Mosley, Mike, Buff.	9	236	26.2	33	0
Walls, Herkie, Hou.	9	110	12.2	25	0
Wilson, Stanley, Cin.	7	161	23.0	32	0
Horton, Ray, Cin.	5	128	25.6	49	0
Williams, Dokie, Raiders	5	88	17.6	19	0
McPherson, Miles, S.D.	5	77	15.4	19	0
Jones, Cedric, N.E.	4	63	15.8	23	0
Lane, Eric, Sea.	4	58	14.5	18	0
Kozlowski, Mike, Mia.	4	50	12.5	23	0
Dressel, Chris, Hou.	4	40	10.0	13	0
Lee, Keith, N.E.	4	40	10.0	19	0
Weathers, Robert, N.E.	3	68	22.7	29	0
McAlister, Ken, Sea.	3	59	19.7	22	0
Weathers, Clarence, N.E.	3	58	19.3	33	0
Mullen, Davlin, Jets	3	57	19.0	26	0
Williams, Ben, Buff.	3	56	18.7	23	0
Jodat, Jim, S.D.	3	45	15.0	18	0

	No	Yards	Avg	Long	TD
Young, Andre, S.D.	3	41	13.7	19	0
Roquemore, Durwood, K.C.	3	36	12.0	13	0
Nathan, Tony, Mia.	3	15	5.0	12	0
Cherry, Deron, K.C.	2	54	27.0	31	0
Moore, Alvin, Balt.	2	40	20.0	23	0
Ferguson, Vagas, Clev.	2	36	18.0	27	0
Smith, Sherman, S.D.	2	32	16.0	21	0
Nicolas, Scott, Clev.	2	29	14.5	15	0
Tice, Mike, Sea.	2	28	14.0	19	0
Moriarty, Larry, Hou.	2	25	12.5	16	0
Millen, Matt, Raiders	2	19	9.5	10	0
Talley, Darryl, Buff.	2	9	4.5	5	0
Studdard, Dave, Den.	2	8	4.0	8	0
Heflin, Vince, Mia.	1	27	27.0	27	0
Clayton, Mark, Mia.	1	25	25.0	25	0
Martin, Mike, Cin.	1	1.0	19	0	
Harper, Bruce, Jets	1	16	16.0	16	0
Scales, Dwight, S.D.	1	16	16.0	16	0
Tullis, Willie, Hou.	1	16	16.0	16	0
Bingham, Craig, Pitt.	1	15	15.0	15	0
Carson, Carlos, K.C.	1	12	12.0	12	0
Hunt, Daryl, Hou.	1	12	12.0	12	0
McCloskey, Mike, Hou.	1	11	11.0	11	0
Golden, Tim, N.E.	1	10	10.0	10	0
Smith, Billy Ray, S.D.	1	10	10.0	10	0
Barber, Marion, Jets	1	9	9.0	9	0
Harden, Mike, Den.	1	9	9.0	9	0
Davis, Johnny, Clev.	1	8	8.0	8	0
McElroy, Reggie, Jets	1	7	7.0	7	0
Bennett, Woody, Mia.	1	6	6.0	6	0
Kohrs, Bob, Pitt.	1	6	6.0	6	0
Sievers, Eric, S.D.	1	6	6.0	6	0
Thomas, Ken, K.C.	1	6	6.0	6	0
Smith, J.T., K.C.	1	5	5.0	5	0
Contz, Bill, Clev.	1	3	3.0	3	0
Shuler, Mickey, Jets	1	3	3.0	3	0
Jackson, Tom, Den.	1	2	2.0	2	0
Dinkel, Tom, Cin.	1	1	1.0	1	0
Beach, Pat, Balt.	1	0	0.0	0	0
Brown, Mark, Mia.	1	0	0.0	0	0
Daniels, Calvin, K.C.	1	0	0.0	0	0
Jensen, Derrick, Raiders	1	0	0.0	0	0
Lindstrom, Dave, K.C.	1	0	0.0	0	0
Martin, Rod, Raiders	1	0	0.0	0	0
Metzelaars, Pete, Sea.	1	0	0.0	0	0
Bouza, Matt, Balt.	1	−4	−4.0	−4	0
Riley, Avon, Hou.	0	26	----	26	0
Donnalleyk, Rick, Pitt.	0	2	----	2	0
Burruss, Lloyd, K.C.	0	0	----	0	0

Fair Catches: Burruss, K.C.   Jones, N.E.

Leader based on average return, minimum 16 returns   t = *Touchdown*

AFC—TEAM KICKOFF RETURNS

	No	Yards	Avg	Long	TD
Miami	47	1085	23.1	78	0
Seattle	71	1575	22.2	t94	1
Buffalo	64	1363	21.3	60	0
New York Jets	66	1375	20.8	64	0
Cleveland	63	1290	20.5	38	0
Cincinnati	54	1097	20.3	49	0
New England	57	1155	20.3	53	0
Houston	83	1676	20.2	t97	2
Baltimore	62	1198	19.3	90	0
Los Angeles Raiders	61	1175	19.3	48	0
Denver	56	1077	19.2	42	0
San Diego	74	1377	18.6	41	0
Pittsburgh	59	1068	18.1	35	0
Kansas City	54	929	17.2	46	0
Conference Total	871	17440	----	t97	3
Conference Average	62.2	1245.7	20.0	--	0.2

AFC – INDIVIDUAL SCORERS

KICKERS	XP	XPA	FG	FGA	PTS
Anderson, Gary, Pitt.	38	39	27	31	119
Lowery, Nick, K.C.	44	45	24	30	116
Bahr, Chris, Raiders	51	53	21	27	114
Allegre, Raul, Balt.	22	24	30	35	112
Johnson, Norm, Sea	49	50	18	25	103
Bahr, Matt, Clev.	38	40	21	24	101
von Schamann, Uwe, Mia.	45	48	18	27	99
Karlis, Rich, Den.	33	34	21	25	96
Benirschke, Rolf, S.D.	43	45	15	24	88
Breech, Jim, Cin.	39	41	16	23	87
Kempf, Florian, Hou.	33	34	17	21	84
Leahy, Pat, Jets	36	37	16	24	84
Danelo, Joe, Buff.	33	34	10	20	63
Steinfort, Fred, Buff.-N.E.	17	18	7	21	38
Smith, John, N.E.	12	15	3	6	21
Cox, Steve, Clev.	0	0	1	1	3
Zendejas, Joaquin, N.E.	3	4	0	1	3

NON-KICKERS	TD	TDR	TDP	TDM	PTS
Johnson, Pete, Cin.	14	14	0	0	84
Warner, Curt, Sea.	14	13	1	0	84
Muncie, Chuck, S.D.	13	12	1	0	78
Allen, Marcus, Raiders	12	9	2	1	72
Campbell, Earl, Hou.	12	12	0	0	72
Christensen, Todd, Raiders	12	0	12	0	72
Pruitt, Mike, Clev.	12	10	2	0	72
Largent, Steve, Sea.	11	0	11	0	66
Brown, Theotis, K.C.	10	8	2	0	60
Collins, Anthony, N.E.	10	10	0	0	60
Cribbs, Joe, Buff.	10	3	7	0	60
Duper, Mark, Mia.	10	0	10	0	60
Franklin, Andra, Mia.	8	8	0	0	48
Hawkins, Frank, Raiders	8	6	2	0	48
Winslow, Kellen, S.D.	8	0	8	0	48
Abercrombie, Walter, Pitt.	7	4	3	0	42
Carson, Carlos, K.C.	7	0	7	0	42
Dickey, Curtis, Balt.	7	4	3	0	42
Harris, Franco, Pitt.	7	5	2	0	42
Walker, Wesley, Jets	7	0	7	0	42
Marshall, Henry, K.C.	6	0	6	0	36
McMillan Randy, Balt.	6	5	1	0	36
Moore, Nat, Mia.	6	0	6	0	36
Newsome, Ozzie, Clev.	6	0	6	0	36
Paige, Stephone, K.C.	6	0	6	0	36
Ramsey, Derrick, N.E.	6	0	6	0	36
Scott, Willie, K.C.	6	0	6	0	36
Smith, Tim, Hou.	6	0	6	0	36
Branch, Cliff, Raiders	5	0	5	0	30
Chandler, Wes, S.D.	5	0	5	0	30

	TD	TDR	TDP	TDM	PTS
Collinsworth, Cris, Cin.	5	0	5	0	30
Duckworth, Bobby, S.D.	5	0	5	0	30
Johns, Paul, Sea.	5	0	4	1	30
Sweeney, Calvin, Pitt.	5	0	5	0	30
Tatupu, Mosi, N.E.	5	4	1	0	30
Watson, Steve, Den.	5	0	5	0	30
Doornink, Dan, Sea.	4	2	2	0	24
Dressel, Chris, Hou.	4	0	4	0	24
Franklin, Byron, Buff.	4	0	4	0	24
Green, Boyce, Clev.	4	3	1	0	24
Henry, Bernard, Balt.	4	0	4	0	24
Johnson, Dan, Mia.	4	0	4	0	24
Jones, Bobby, Clev.	4	0	4	0	24
Jones, Lam, Jets	4	0	4	0	24
McNeil, Freeman, Jets	4	1	3	0	24
Nathan, Tony, Mia.	4	3	1	0	24
Pollard, Frank, Pitt.	4	4	0	0	24
Poole, Nathan, Den.	4	4	0	0	24
Stoudt, Cliff, Pitt.	4	4	0	0	24
Willhite, Gerald, Den.	4	3	1	0	24
Alexander, Charles, Cin.	3	3	0	0	18
Augustyniak, Mike, Jets	3	2	1	0	18
Brooks, James, S.D.	3	3	0	0	18
Butler, Jerry, Buff.	3	0	3	0	18
Butler, Raymond, Balt.	3	0	3	0	18
Crutchfield, Dwayne, Jets	3	3	0	0	18
Cunningham, Bennie, Pitt.	3	0	3	0	18
Dierking, Scott, Jets	3	3	0	0	18
Feacher, Ricky, Clev.	3	0	3	0	18
Harper, Bruce, Jets	3	1	2	0	18
Holt, Harry, Clev.	3	0	3	0	18
Hunter, Tony, Buff.	3	0	3	0	18
Joiner, Charlie, S.D.	3	0	3	0	18
Kenney, Bill, K.C.	3	3	0	0	18
Kinnebrew, Larry, Cin.	3	3	0	0	18
Lewis, Frank, Buff.	3	0	3	0	18
Moriarty, Larry, Hou.	3	3	0	0	18
Mosley, Mike, Buff.	3	0	3	0	18
Overstreet, David, Mia.	3	1	2	0	18
Parros, Rick, Den.	3	1	2	0	18
Pruitt, Greg, Raiders	3	2	0	1	18
Rose, Joe, Mia.	3	0	3	0	18
Ross, Dan, Cin.	3	0	3	0	18
Sampson, Clinton, Den.	3	0	3	0	18
Sievers, Eric, S.D.	3	0	3	0	18
Tuttle, Perry, Buff.	3	0	3	0	18
Weathers, Clarence, N.E.	3	0	3	0	18
Williams, Dokie, Raiders	3	0	3	0	18
Winder, Sammy, Den.	3	3	0	0	18

	TD	TDR	TDP	TDM	PTS
Adams, Willis, Clev.	2	0	2	0	12
Barber, Marion, Jets	2	1	1	0	12
Belk, Rocky, Clev.	2	0	2	0	12
Bennett, Woody, Mia.	2	2	0	0	12
Brammer, Mark, Buff.	2	0	2	0	12
Clayton, Mark, Mia.	2	0	1	1	12
Curtis, Issac, Cin.	2	0	2	0	12
Egloff, Ron, Den.	2	0	2	0	12
Grogan, Steve, N.E.	2	2	0	0	12
Harris, M.L., Cin.	2	0	2	0	12
Hasselbeck, Don, Raiders	2	0	2	0	12
Holmes, Johnny, Jets	2	0	0	2	12
Holohan, Pete, S.D.	2	0	2	0	12
Hughes, David, Sea.	2	1	1	0	12
Jackson, Billy, K.C.	2	2	0	0	12
King, Kenny, Raiders	2	1	1	0	12
Kozlowski, Mike, Mia.	2	0	0	2	12
Krieg, Dave, Sea.	2	2	0	0	12
Logan, Dave, Clev.	2	0	2	0	12
Marino, Dan, Mia.	2	2	0	0	12
Martin, Rod, Raiders	2	0	0	2	12
Morgan, Stanley, N.E.	2	0	2	0	12
Muhammad, Calvin, Raiders	2	0	2	0	12
Preston, Dave, Den.	2	1	1	0	12
Renfro, Mike, Hou.	2	0	0	0	12
Riley, Ken, Cin.	2	0	0	2	12
Robinson, Shelton, Sea.	2	0	0	2	12
Schonert, Turk, Cin.	2	2	0	0	12
Starring, Stephen, N.E.	2	0	2	0	12
Upchurch, Rick, Den.	2	0	2	0	12
Walker, Byron, Sea.	2	0	2	0	12
Wilson, Stanley, Cin.	2	1	1	0	12
Young, Charle, Sea.	2	0	2	0	12
van Eeghen, Mark, N.E.	2	2	0	0	12
Townsend, Greg, Raiders	1	0	0	1	*8
Anderson, Ken, Cin.	1	1	0	0	6
Anderson, Kim, Balt.	1	0	0	1	6
Anderson, Larry, Balt.	1	0	0	1	6
Arnold, Walt, Hou.	1	0	1	0	6
Banks, Chip, Clev.	1	0	0	1	6
Barkum, Jerome, Jets	1	0	1	0	6
Barnwell, Malcolm, Raiders	1	0	1	0	6
Beach, Pat, Balt.	1	0	1	0	6
Best, Greg, Pitt.	1	0	0	1	6
Blount, Mel, Pitt.	1	0	0	1	6
Bokamper, Kim, Mia.	1	0	0	1	6
Brown, Curtis, Hou.	1	1	0	0	6
Brown, Steve, Hou.	1	0	0	1	6
Capers, Wayne, Pitt.	1	0	1	0	6
Chavous, Barney, Den.	1	0	0	1	6
Clayton, Harvey, Pitt.	1	0	0	1	6

	TD	TDR	TDP	TDM	PTS
Cooks, Johnie, Balt.	1	0	0	1	6
Dawkins, Julius, Buff.	1	0	1	0	6
Dawson, Lin, N.E.	1	0	1	0	6
DeBerg, Steve, Den.	1	1	0	0	6
Dieken, Doug, Clev.	1	0	1	0	6
Dixon, Zachary, Sea.	1	0	0	1	6
Edwards, Stan, Hou.	1	0	1	0	6
Elway, John, Den.	1	1	0	0	6
Fouts, Dan, S.D.	1	1	0	0	6
Garrity, Greg, Pitt.	1	0	1	0	6
Gastineau, Mark, Jets	1	0	0	1	6
Golic, Bob, Clev.	1	0	0	1	6
Green, Jacob, Sea.	1	0	0	1	6
Griffin, James, Cin.	1	0	0	1	6
Hancock, Anthony, K.C.	1	0	1	0	6
Harris, Duriel, Mia.	1	0	1	0	6
Hector, Johnny, Jets	1	0	1	0	6
Hinkle, Bryan, Pitt.	1	0	0	1	6
Horton, Ray, Cin.	1	0	0	1	6
Jackson, Charles, K.C.	1	0	0	1	6
Jackson, Harold, Sea.	1	0	1	0	6
Jensen, Derrick, Raiders	1	0	1	0	6
Johnson, Ron, Pitt.	1	0	0	1	6
Jones, Cedric, N.E.	1	0	1	0	6
Kennedy, Mike, Buff.	1	0	0	1	6
Kilson, David, Buff.	1	0	0	1	6
Kreider, Steve, Cin.	1	0	1	0	6
Kubiak, Gary, Den.	1	1	0	0	6
Leaks, Roosevelt, Buff.	1	1	0	0	6
Lynn, Johnny, Jets	1	0	0	1	6
McCloskey, Mike, Hou.	1	0	1	0	6
Mehl, Lance, Jets	1	0	0	1	6
Merriweather, Mark, Pitt.	1	0	0	1	6
Metzelaars, Pete, Sea.	1	0	1	0	6
Moore, Alvin, Balt.	1	1	0	0	6
Moore, Booker, Buff.	1	0	1	0	6
Moyer, Paul, Sea.	1	0	0	1	6
Myles, Jesse, Den.	1	0	1	0	6
Nelson, Derrie, S.D.	1	0	0	1	6
Roaches, Carl, Hou.	1	0	0	1	6
Roquemore, Durwood, K.C.	1	0	0	1	6
Shuler, Mickey, Jets	1	0	1	0	6
Smith, Lucious, K.C.	1	0	0	1	6
Springs, Kirk, Jets	1	0	0	1	6
Thomas, Ken, K.C.	1	0	1	0	6
Thomas, Zack, Den.	1	0	0	1	6
Walker, Dwight, Clev.	1	0	1	0	6
Walls, Herkie, Hou.	1	0	1	0	6
Weathers, Robert, N.E.	1	1	0	0	6
Weishuhn, Clayton, N.E.	1	0	0	1	6
Williams, Reggie, Cin.	1	0	0	1	6

	TD	TDR	TDP	TDM	PTS
Woods, Rick, Pitt.	1	0	0	1	6
Young, Andre, S.D.	1	0	0	1	6
Zorn, Jim, Sea.	1	1	0	0	6
Alzado, Lyle, Raiders	0	0	0	0	★2
Charles, Mike, Mia.	0	0	0	0	★2
Jones, Rulon, Den.	0	0	0	0	★2
Kohrs, Bob, Pitt.	0	0	0	0	★2
Thompson, Donnell, Balt.	0	0	0	0	★2
Browner, Ross, Cin.	0	0	0	0	#1
Ryan, Pat, Jets	0	0	0	0	#1

★=Safety
#=Scored extra point

AFC – TEAM SCORING

	TD	TDR	TDP	TDM	XP	XPA	FG	FGA	SAF	POINTS
Los Angeles Raiders	54	18	31	5	51	54	21	27	2	442
Seattle	50	19	25	6	49	50	18	25	0	403
Miami	48	16	28	4	45	48	18	27	1	389
Kansas City	45	13	29	3	44	45	24	30	0	386
San Diego	45	16	27	2	43	45	15	24	0	358
Cleveland	42	13	27	2	38	40	22	25	0	356
Pittsburgh	39	17	15	7	38	39	27	31	1	355
Cincinnati	43	24	14	5	40	43	16	23	0	346
New York Jets	38	11	21	6	37	38	16	24	0	313
Denver	34	15	17	2	33	34	21	25	1	302
Houston	34	16	16	2	33	34	17	21	0	288
Buffalo	36	4	30	2	34	36	11	26	0	283
New England	36	19	16	1	31	36	9	22	0	274
Baltimore	25	10	12	3	22	24	30	35	1	264
Conference Total	569	211	308	50	538	566	265	365	6	4759
Conference Average	40.6	15.1	22.0	3.6	38.4	40.4	18.9	26.1	0.4	339.9

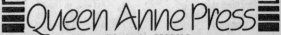

AFC — TEAM-BY-TEAM SUMMARY 1983

OFFENSE	Balt.	Buff.	Cin.	Clev.	Den.
Rushes	601	415	542	465	471
Net Yds. Gained	2695	1736	2104	1922	1784
Avg. Gain	4.5	4.2	3.9	4.1	3.8
Avg. Yds. per Game	168.4	108.5	131.5	120.1	111.5
Passes Attempted	377	571	454	567	499
Completed	188	317	290	324	254
% Completed	49.9	55.5	63.9	57.1	50.9
Total Yds. Gained	2663	3438	3492	3932	3466
Times Sacked	47	37	40	33	55
Yds. Lost	340	351	309	271	439
Net Yds. Gained	2323	3087	3183	3661	3027
Avg. Yds. per Game	145.2	192.9	198.9	228.8	189.2
Net Yds. per Pass Play	5.48	5.08	6.44	6.10	5.46
Yds. Gained per Comp.	14.16	10.85	12.04	12.14	13.65
Combined Net Yds. Gained	5018	4823	5287	5583	4811
% Total Yds., Rushing	53.71	35.99	39.80	34.43	37.08
% Total Yds., Passing	46.29	64.01	60.20	65.57	62.92
Avg. Yds. per Game	313.6	301.4	330.4	348.9	300.7
Had Intercepted	22	28	18	28	22
Yds. Opp. Returned	117	330	298	508	281
Ret. by Opp. for TD	0	2	2	3	3
Punts	91	89	69	70	87
Yds. Punted	4124	3533	2804	2854	3620
Avg. Yds. per Punt	45.3	39.7	40.6	40.8	41.6
Punt Returns	44	44	49	42	38
Yds. Returned	294	241	410	310	420
Avg. Yds. per Return	6.7	5.5	8.4	7.4	11.1
Returned for TD	0	0	0	0	1
Kickoff Returns	62	64	54	63	56
Yds. Returned	1198	1363	1097	1290	1077
Avg. Yds. per Return	19.3	21.3	20.3	20.5	19.2
Returned for TD	0	0	0	0	0
Total Points Scored	264	283	346	356	302
Total TDs	25	36	43	42	34
TDs Rushing	10	4	24	13	15
TDs Passing	12	30	14	27	17
TDs on Ret. and Rec.	3	2	5	2	2
Extra Points	22	34	40	38	33
Safeties	1	0	0	0	1
Field Goals Made	30	11	16	22	21
Field Goals Attempted	35	26	23	25	25
% Successful	85.7	42.3	69.6	88.0	84.0

Hou.	K.C.	Raid.	Mia.	N.E.	N.Y.J.	Pitt.	S.D.	Sea.
502	387	542	568	538	474	614	423	546
1998	1254	2240	2150	2605	2068	2610	1536	2119
4.0	3.2	4.1	3.8	4.8	4.4	4.3	3.6	3.9
124.9	78.4	140.0	134.4	162.8	129.3	163.1	96.0	132.4
482	641	504	442	412	559	409	635	449
260	369	301	254	220	330	211	369	251
53.9	57.6	59.7	57.5	53.3	59.0	51.6	58.1	55.9
3286	4684	3910	3235	3040	3742	2754	4891	3316
49	46	55	23	45	43	52	28	47
384	343	464	190	334	317	350	230	343
2902	4341	3446	3045	2706	3425	2404	4661	2973
181.4	271.3	215.4	190.3	169.1	214.1	150.3	291.3	185.8
5.47	6.32	6.16	6.55	5.92	5.69	5.21	7.03	5.99
12.64	12.69	12.99	12.74	13.82	11.34	13.05	13.25	13.21
4900	5595	5686	5195	5311	5493	5014	6197	5092
40.78	22.41	39.40	41.39	49.05	37.65	52.05	24.79	41.61
59.22	77.59	60.60	58.61	50.95	62.35	47.95	75.21	58.39
306.3	349.7	355.4	324.7	331.9	343.3	313.4	387.3	318.3
29	19	24	11	18	28	23	33	18
392	323	381	203	361	372	252	377	279
2	2	0	1	1	3	2	2	1
80	93	78	75	81	82	80	63	79
3136	3710	3336	3189	3615	3218	3352	2763	3118
39.2	39.9	42.8	42.5	44.6	39.2	41.9	43.9	39.5
20	40	58	55	44	38	51	33	34
159	291	666	581	399	420	421	213	366
8.0	7.3	11.5	10.6	9.1	11.1	8.3	6.5	10.8
0	0	1	1	0	1	0	0	1
83	54	61	47	57	66	59	74	71
1676	929	1175	1085	1155	1375	1068	1377	1575
20.2	17.2	19.3	23.1	20.3	20.8	18.1	18.6	22.2
2	0	0	0	0	0	0	0	1
288	386	442	389	274	313	355	358	403
34	45	54	48	36	38	39	45	50
16	13	18	16	19	11	17	16	19
16	29	31	28	16	21	15	27	25
2	3	5	4	1	6	7	2	6
33	44	51	45	31	37	38	43	49
0	0	2	1	0	0	1	0	0
17	24	21	18	9	16	27	15	18
21	30	27	27	22	24	31	24	25
81.0	80.0	77.8	66.7	40.9	66.7	87.1	62.5	72.0

AFC — TEAM-BY-TEAM SUMMARY 1983

DEFENSE

	Balt.	Buff.	Cin.	Clev.	Den.
Rushes	516	566	430	528	509
Net Yds. Gained	2118	2503	1499	2065	1938
Avg. Gain	4.1	4.4	3.5	3.9	3.8
Avg. Yds. per Game	132.4	156.4	93.7	129.1	121.1
Passes Attempted	488	480	502	469	552
Completed	281	286	288	280	307
% Completed	57.6	59.6	57.4	59.7	55.6
Total Yds. Gained	3832	3553	3163	3316	3988
Times Sacked	41	32	41	32	38
Yds. Lost	310	247	335	239	317
Net Yds. Gained	3522	3306	2828	3077	3671
Avg. Yds. per Game	220.1	206.6	176.8	192.3	229.4
Net Yds. per Pass Play	6.66	6.46	5.21	6.14	6.22
Yds. Gained per Comp	13.64	12.42	10.98	11.84	12.99
Combined Net Yds. Gained	5640	5809	4327	5142	5609
% Total Yds., Rushing	37.55	43.09	34.64	40.16	34.55
% Total Yds., Passing	62.45	56.91	65.36	59.84	65.45
Avg. Yds. per Game	352.5	363.1	270.4	321.4	350.6
Intercepted by	20	13	23	22	27
Yds. Returned by	314	154	369	296	355
Returned for TD	1	1	4	2	0
Punts	80	78	76	73	77
Yds. Punted	3329	3344	3211	2954	3406
Avg. Yds. per Punt	41.6	42.9	42.3	40.5	44.2
Punt Returns	55	42	41	30	55
Yds. Returned	642	403	310	309	524
Avg. Yds. per Return	11.7	9.6	7.6	10.3	9.5
Returned for TD	1	0	0	0	0
Kickoff Returns	61	53	68	61	46
Yds. Returned	1138	949	1298	1155	824
Avg. Yds. per Return	18.7	17.9	19.1	18.9	17.9
Returned for TD	0	0	0	1	0
Total Points Scored	354	351	302	342	327
Total TDs	45	39	36	42	36
TDs Rushing	13	14	16	15	14
TDs Passing	31	22	17	22	18
TDs on Ret. and Rec.	1	3	3	5	4
Extra Points	42	39	35	40	34
Safeties	0	0	0	1	1
Field Goals Made	14	26	17	16	25
Field Goals Attempted	23	39	22	22	33
% Successful	60.9	66.7	77.3	72.7	75.8

Hou.	K.C.	Raid.	Mia.	N.E.	N.Y.J.	Pitt.	S.D.	Sea.
576	554	436	460	549	547	509	552	511
2787	2275	1586	2037	2281	2378	1833	2173	2198
4.8	4.1	3.6	4.4	4.2	4.3	3.6	3.9	4.3
174.2	142.2	99.1	127.3	142.6	148.6	114.6	135.8	137.4
424	500	531	480	514	463	447	544	521
252	261	282	277	277	269	238	330	311
59.4	52.2	53.1	57.7	53.9	58.1	53.2	60.7	59.7
3095	3361	3646	3365	3565	3301	3260	4051	4182
31	35	57	49	39	48	50	31	43
250	250	484	363	270	378	361	269	351
2845	3111	3162	3002	3295	2923	2899	3782	3831
177.8	194.4	197.6	187.6	205.9	182.7	181.2	236.4	239.4
6.25	5.81	5.38	5.67	5.96	5.72	5.83	6.58	6.79
12.28	12.88	12.93	12.15	12.87	12.27	13.70	12.28	13.45
5632	5386	4748	5039	5576	5301	4732	5955	6029
49.49	42.24	33.40	40.42	40.91	44.86	38.74	36.49	36.46
50.51	57.76	66.60	59.58	59.09	55.14	61.26	63.51	63.54
352.0	336.6	296.8	314.9	348.5	331.3	295.8	372.2	376.8
14	30	20	26	17	22	28	16	26
135	482	238	345	202	342	435	153	363
0	2	2	3	1	3	4	1	2
65	85	100	90	78	85	88	70	68
2567	3500	4060	3674	3273	3491	3615	2780	2754
39.5	41.2	40.6	40.8	42.0	41.1	41.1	39.7	40.5
47	54	35	32	48	47	44	35	36
354	559	334	229	392	367	418	299	185
7.5	10.4	9.5	7.2	8.2	7.8	9.5	8.5	5.1
0	1	2	0	0	1	1	0	0
61	75	68	54	55	50	65	70	59
1280	1528	1227	1024	1082	1063	1507	1426	952
21.0	20.4	18.0	19.0	19.7	21.3	23.2	20.4	16.1
0	0	0	0	0	0	1	0	0
460	367	338	250	289	331	303	462	397
54	44	40	32	31	39	37	57	48
23	18	13	11	9	13	14	26	14
26	21	20	19	19	22	19	28	33
5	5	7	2	3	4	4	3	1
49	43	39	31	29	35	36	54	43
0	0	1	0	1	1	0	0	3
29	20	19	9	24	20	15	22	20
36	26	25	15	31	28	20	29	26
80.6	76.9	76.0	60.0	77.4	71.4	75.0	75.9	76.9

NATIONAL FOOTBALL CONFERENCE

INDIVIDUAL PLAYER STATISTICS

NFC – INDIVIDUAL RUSHERS

	Att	Yards	Avg	Long	TD
Dickerson, Eric, Rams	390	1808	4.6	t85	18
Andrews, William, Atl.	331	1567	4.7	27	7
Payton, Walter, Chi.	314	1421	4.5	t49	6
Riggins, John, Wash.	375	1347	3.6	44	24
Dorsett, Tony, Dall.	289	1321	4.6	77	8
Anderson, Ottis, St.L.	296	1270	4.3	43	5
Rogers, George, N.O.	256	1144	4.5	t76	5
Sims, Billy, Det.	220	1040	4.7	41	7
Woolfolk, Butch, Giants	246	857	3.5	22	4
Tyler, Wendell, S.F.	176	856	4.9	39	4
Wilson, Wayne, N.O.	199	787	4.0	29	9
Washington, Joe, Wash.	145	772	5.3	41	0
Craig, Roger, S.F.	176	725	4.1	71	4
Ellis, Gerry, G.B.	141	696	4.9	71	4
Suhey, Matt, Chi.	149	681	4.6	39	4
Nelson, Darrin, Minn.	154	642	4.2	t56	1
Wilder, James, T.B.	161	640	4.0	t75	4
Carpenter, Rob, Giants	170	624	3.7	37	4
Springs, Ron, Dall.	149	541	3.6	t19	7
Brown, Ted, Minn.	120	476	4.0	43	10
Jones, James, Det.	135	475	3.5	18	6
Galbreath, Tony, Minn.	113	474	4.2	t52	4
Riggs, Gerald, Atl.	100	437	4.4	t40	8
Oliver, Hubert, Phil.	121	434	3.6	24	1
Gajan, Hokie, N.O.	81	415	5.1	58	4
Williams, Mike, Phil.	103	385	3.7	32	0
Mitchell, Stump, St.L.	68	373	5.5	46	3
Redden, Barry, Rams	75	372	5.0	t40	2
Carver, Mel, T.B.	114	348	3.1	16	0
Ivery, Eddie Lee, G.B.	86	340	4.0	21	2
Clark, Jessie, G.B.	71	328	4.6	42	0
McMahon, Jim, Chi.	55	307	5.6	32	2
Montana, Joe, S.F.	61	284	4.7	18	2
Owens, James, T.B.	96	266	2.8	15	5
Morris, Wayne, St.L.	75	257	3.4	17	2
Ring, Bill, S.F.	64	254	4.0	25	2
Bussey, Dexter, Det.	57	249	4.4	26	0
Theismann, Joe, Wash.	37	234	6.3	22	1
Haddix, Michael, Phil.	91	220	2.4	11	2
Meade, Mike, G.B.	55	201	3.7	15	1
Newsome, Tim, Dall.	44	185	4.2	20	2
Huckleby, Harlan, G.B.	50	182	3.6	20	4
Hipple, Eric, Det.	41	171	4.2	27	3
Morris, Joe, Giants	35	145	4.1	16	0
Evans, Vince, Chi.	22	142	6.5	27	1
Montgomery, Wilbert, Phil.	29	139	4.8	32	0
Thompson, Vince, Det.	40	138	3.5	10	1
Jaworski, Ron, Phil.	25	129	5.2	29	1

	Att	Yards	Avg	Long	TD
Lomax, Neil, St L.	27	127	4.7	35	2
Love, Randy, St L.	35	103	2.9	16	2
Harrington, Perry, Phil.	23	98	4.3	35	1
Young, Rickey, Minn.	39	90	2.3	9	2
Wonsley, Otis, Wash.	25	88	3.5	9	0
Johnson, Billy, Atl.	15	83	5.5	36	0
Rogers, Jimmy, N.O.	26	80	3.1	13	0
Thompson, Leonard, Det.	4	72	18.0	t40	1
Gentry, Dennis, Chi.	16	65	4.1	17	0
Brunner, Scott, Giants	26	64	2.5	12	0
Cain, Lynn, Atl.	19	63	3.3	10	1
Hayes, Jeff, Wash.	2	63	31.5	48	0
Brown, Charlie, Wash.	4	53	13.3	17	0
Ferrell, Earl, St L.	7	53	7.6	21	1
Giaquinto, Nick, Wash.	14	53	3.8	11	1
Green, Roy, St L.	4	49	12.3	25	0
Tuggle, John, Giants	17	49	2.9	t7	1
Redwine, Jarvis, Minn.	10	48	4.8	21	0
Moore, Jeff, S.F.	15	43	2.9	14	1
Guman, Mike, Rams	7	42	6.0	11	0
LeCount, Terry, Minn.	2	42	21.0	40	0
Orosz, Tom, S.F.	2	39	19.5	23	0
Bartkowski, Steve, Atl.	16	38	2.4	10	1
Lofton, James, G.B.	9	36	4.0	13	0
Newhouse, Robert, Dall.	9	34	3.8	8	0
Gault, Willie, Chi.	4	31	7.8	22	0
White, Danny, Dall.	18	31	1.7	22	4
Armstrong, Adger, T.B.	7	30	4.3	7	0
Alexander, Robert, Rams	7	28	4.0	15	0
Dils, Steve, Minn.	16	28	1.8	8	0
Morton, Michael, T.B.	13	28	2.2	5	0
Parsons, Bob, Chi.	1	27	27.0	27	0
Rutledge, Jeff, Giants	7	27	3.9	14	0
Thompson, Jack, T.B.	26	27	1.0	10	0
Thomas, Calvin, Chi.	8	25	3.1	9	0
Monroe, Carl, S.F.	10	23	2.3	5	0
Campfield, Billy, Giants	2	21	10.5	13	0
Wilson, Tim, N.O.	8	21	2.6	7	0
Kane, Rick, Det.	4	19	4.8	9	0
Clark, Dwight, S.F.	3	18	6.0	9	0
Ferragamo, Vince, Rams	22	17	0.8	8	0
Austin, Cliff, N.O.	4	16	4.0	5	0
Lewis, Gary, G.B.	4	16	4.0	11	1
Merkens, Guido, N.O.	1	16	16.0	16	0
Groth, Jeff, N.O.	1	15	15.0	15	0
Giacomarro, Ralph, Atl.	2	13	6.5	13	0
Harrell, Willard, St L.	4	13	3.3	8	0
Holly, Bob, Wash.	4	13	3.3	13	0
Hutchison, Anthony, Chi.	6	13	2.2	5	1

	Att	Yards	Avg	Long	TD
Nichols, Mark, Det.	1	13	13.0	13	0
Pearson, Drew, Dall.	2	13	6.5	10	0
Dickey, Lynn, G.B.	21	12	0.6	4	3
Hart, Jim, St L.	5	12	2.4	13	0
Manning, Archie, Hou.-Minn.	3	12	4.0	11	0
Moroski, Mike, Atl.	2	12	6.0	7	0
Evans, Reggie, Wash.	16	11	0.7	5	4
Komlo, Jeff, T.B.	2	11	5.5	11	0
Sharpe, Luis, St L.	1	11	11.0	11	0
Walker, Rick, Wash.	2	10	5.0	11	0
Jones, Mike, Minn.	1	9	9.0	9	0
Lisch, Rusty, St L.	2	9	4.5	5	0
Robinson, Bo, Atl.	3	9	3.0	7	0
Cavanaugh, Matt, S.F.	1	8	8.0	8	0
Danielson, Gary, Det.	6	8	1.3	8	0
Ellard, Henry, Rams	3	7	2.3	12	0
Everett, Major, Phil.	5	7	1.4	7	0
Margerum, Ken, Chi.	1	7	7.0	7	0
White, Sammy, Minn.	1	7	7.0	7	0
King, Horace, Det.	3	6	2.0	4	0
Moorehead, Emery, Chi.	5	6	1.2	5	0
Runager, Max, Phil.	1	6	6.0	6	0
Williams, Richard, Atl.	1	5	5.0	5	0
Middleton, Terdell, T.B.	2	4	2.0	2	0
Eddings, Floyd, Giants	1	3	3.0	3	0
Golsteyn, Jerry, T.B.	5	3	0.6	2	0
Goodlow, Eugene, N.O.	1	3	3.0	3	0
Kramer, Tommy, Minn.	8	3	0.4	8	0
Ramson, Eason, S.F.	1	3	3.0	3	0
Solomon, Freddie, S.F.	1	3	3.0	3	0
Wilson, Dave, N.O.	5	3	0.6	5	1
Baschnagel, Brian, Chi.	2	2	1.0	2	0
Bright, Leon, Giants	1	2	2.0	2	0
Hill, Tony, Dall.	1	2	2.0	2	0
Lewis, Leo, Minn.	1	2	2.0	2	0
Miller, Junior, Atl.	1	2	2.0	2	0
Miller, Mike, Giants	1	2	2.0	2	0
Benjamin, Guy, S.F.	1	1	1.0	1	0
Carter, Gerald, T.B.	1	0	0.0	0	0
Cromwell, Nolan, Rams	1	0	0.0	0	0
Garrett, Alvin, Wash.	2	0	0.0	4	0
Johnson, Butch, Dall.	1	0	0.0	0	0
Pastorini, Dan, Phil.	1	0	0.0	0	0
Perrin, Benny, St L.	1	0	0.0	0	0
Pisarcik, Joe, Phil.	3	-1	-0.3	0	0
Kemp, Jeff, Rams	3	-2	-0.7	0	0
Wilson, Wade, Minn.	3	-3	-1.0	2	0
House, Kevin, T.B.	1	-4	-4.0	-4	0
Whitehurst, David, G.B.	2	-4	-2.0	0	0

	Att	Yards	Avg	Long	TD
Bailey, Stacey, Atl.	2	−5	−2.5	0	0
Coleman, Greg, Minn.	1	−9	−9.0	−9	0
Erxleben, Russell, N.O.	2	−9	−4.5	1	0
Farmer, George, Rams	1	−9	−9.0	−9	0
Black, Mike, Det.	2	−10	−5.0	0	0
Grant, Otis, Rams	2	−10	−5.0	1	0
Hogeboom, Gary, Dall.	6	−10	−1.7	−1	0
Stabler, Ken, N.O.	9	−14	−1.6	0	0
Duckett, Kenny, N.O.	2	−16	−8.0	2	0
Monk, Art, Wash.	3	−19	−6.3	2	0

t=Touchdown
Leader based on most yards gained

NFC – TEAM RUSHING

	Att	Yards	Avg	Long	TD
Chicago	583	2727	4.7	t49	14
Washington	629	2625	4.2	48	30
New Orleans	595	2461	4.1	t76	19
St Louis	525	2277	4.3	46	15
San Francisco	511	2257	4.4	71	17
Los Angeles Rams	511	2253	4.4	t85	20
Atlanta	492	2224	4.5	t40	17
Detroit	513	2181	4.3	41	18
Dallas	519	2117	4.1	77	21
Minnesota	470	1808	3.8	t56	17
Green Bay	439	1807	4.1	71	15
New York Giants	506	1794	3.5	37	9
Philadelphia	402	1417	3.5	35	5
Tampa Bay	428	1353	3.2	t75	9
Conference Total	7123	29301	—	t85	226
Conference Average	508.8	2092.9	4.1	—	16.1

NFC – INDIVIDUAL PASSING

QUALIFIERS	Att	Comp	% Comp	Yards	Avg Gain	TD	% TD	Long	Int	% Int	Rating Points
Bartkowski, Steve, Atl.	432	274	63.4	3167	7.33	22	5.1	t76	5	1.2	97.6
Theismann, Joe, Wash.	459	276	60.1	3714	8.09	29	6.3	84	11	2.4	97.0
Montana, Joe, S.F.	515	332	64.5	3910	7.59	26	5.0	t77	12	2.3	94.6
Lomax, Neil, St L.	354	209	59.0	2636	7.45	24	6.8	t71	11	3.1	92.0
Dickey, Lynn, G.B.	484	289	59.7	4458	9.21	32	6.6	t75	29	6.0	87.3
White, Danny, Dall.	533	334	62.7	3980	7.47	29	5.4	t80	23	4.3	85.6
McMahon, Jim, Chi.	295	175	59.3	2184	7.40	12	4.1	t87	13	4.4	77.6
Ferragamo, Vince, Rams	464	274	59.1	3276	7.06	22	4.7	t61	23	5.0	75.9
Jaworski, Ron, Phil.	446	235	52.7	3315	7.43	20	4.5	t83	18	4.0	75.1
Thompson, Jack, T.B.	423	249	58.9	2906	6.87	18	4.3	80	21	5.0	73.3
Dils, Steve, Minn.	444	239	53.8	2840	6.40	11	2.5	68	16	3.6	66.8
Hipple, Eric, Det.	387	204	52.7	2577	6.66	12	3.1	t80	18	4.7	64.7
Stabler, Ken, N.O.	311	176	56.6	1988	6.39	9	2.9	48	18	5.8	61.4
Brunner, Scott, Giants	386	190	49.2	2516	6.52	9	2.3	62	22	5.7	54.3

NON-QUALIFIERS	Att	Comp	% Comp	Yards	Avg Gain	TD	% TD	Long	Int	% Int	Rating Points
Benjamin, Guy, S.F.	12	7	58.3	111	9.25	1	8.3	t73	0	0.0	117.0
Hogeboom, Gary, Dall.	17	11	64.7	161	9.47	1	5.9	24	1	5.9	90.6
Danielson, Gary, Det.	113	59	52.2	720	6.37	7	6.2	54	4	3.5	78.0
Kemp, Jeff, Rams	25	12	48.0	135	5.40	1	4.0	21	0	0.0	77.9
Kramer, Tommy, Minn.	82	55	67.1	550	6.71	3	3.7	49	4	4.9	77.8
Moroski, Mike, Atl.	70	45	64.3	575	8.21	2	2.9	t50	4	5.7	75.6
Pisarcik, Joe, Phil.	34	16	47.1	172	5.06	1	2.9	33	0	0.0	72.2
Evans, Vince, Chi.	145	76	52.4	1108	7.64	5	3.4	t72	7	4.8	69.0
Wilson, Dave, N.O.	112	66	58.9	770	6.88	5	4.5	42	7	6.3	68.7
Rutledge, Jeff, Giants	174	87	50.0	1208	6.94	3	1.7	54	8	4.6	59.3
Golsteyn, Jerry, T.B.	97	47	48.5	535	5.52	0	0.0	52	2	2.1	56.9
Simms, Phil, Giants	13	7	53.8	130	10.00	0	0.0	36	1	7.7	56.6
Hart, Jim, St L.	91	50	54.9	592	6.51	4	4.4	t39	8	8.8	53.0
Wilson, Wade, Minn.	28	16	57.1	124	4.43	1	3.6	36	2	7.1	50.3
Lisch, Rusty, St L.	13	6	46.2	66	5.08	1	7.7	26	2	15.4	47.8
Whitehurst, David, G.B.	35	18	51.4	149	4.26	0	0.0	19	2	5.7	38.9
(Fewer than 10 attempts)											
Andrews, William, Atl.	1	0	0.0	0	0.00	0	0.0	0	0	0.0	0.0
Birdsong, Carl, St L.	1	1	100.0	11	11.00	0	0.0	11	0	0.0	0.0
Black, Mike, Det.	1	0	0.0	0	0.00	0	0.0	0	1	100.0	0.0
Carmichael, Harold, Phil.	1	1	100.0	45	45.00	1	100.0	t45	0	0.0	0.0
Clark, Dwight, S.F.	1	0	0.0	0	0.00	0	0.0	0	0	0.0	0.0
Dorsett, Tony, Dall.	1	0	0.0	0	0.00	0	0.0	0	0	0.0	0.0
Ellis, Gerry, G.B.	5	2	40.0	31	6.20	1	20.0	20	1	20.0	0.0
Erxleben, Russell, N.O.	1	1	100.0	24	24.00	0	0.0	24	0	0.0	0.0
Gajan, Hokie, N.O.	1	0	0.0	0	0.00	0	0.0	0	0	0.0	0.0
Giacomarro, Ralph, Atl.	1	1	100.0	23	23.00	0	0.0	23	0	0.0	0.0
Hodge, Floyd, Atl.	2	1	50.0	28	14.00	0	0.0	28	1	50.0	0.0
Holly, Bob, Wash.	1	1	100.0	5	5.00	0	0.0	5	0	0.0	0.0
Ivery, Eddie Lee, G.B.	2	2	100.0	50	25.00	0	0.0	35	0	0.0	0.0

	Att	Comp	% Comp	Yards	Avg Gain	TD	% TD	Long	Int	% Int
Jennings, Dave, Giants	1	0	0.0	0	0.00	0	0.0	0	0	0.0
Johnson, Billy, Atl.	1	0	0.0	0	0.00	0	0.0	0	0	0.0
Jones, James, Det.	2	0	0.0	0	0.00	0	0.0	0	0	0.0
Komlo, Jeff, T.B.	8	4	50.0	49	6.13	0	0.0	17	1	12.5
LeCount, Terry, Minn.	1	0	0.0	0	0.00	0	0.0	0	0	0.0
Mistler, John, Giants	1	0	0.0	0	0.00	0	0.0	0	0	0.0
Monk, Art, Wash.	1	1	100.0	46	46.00	0	0.0	46	0	0.0
Pastorini, Dan, Phil.	5	0	0.0	0	0.00	0	0.0	0	0	0.0
Payton, Walter, Chi.	6	3	50.0	95	15.83	3	50.0	t56	2	33.3
Pearson, Drew, Dall.	1	0	0.0	0	0.00	0	0.0	0	1	100.0
Perrin, Benny, St. L.	1	1	100.0	4	4.00	0	0.0	4	0	0.0
Riggins, John, Wash.	1	0	0.0	0	0.00	0	0.0	0	0	0.0
Springs, Ron, Dall.	2	1	50.0	15	7.50	1	50.0	t15	0	0.0
Suhey, Matt, Chi.	1	1	100.0	74	74.00	1	100.0	t74	0	0.0
Washington, Joe, Wash.	1	0	0.0	0	0.00	0	0.0	0	0	0.0

t=Touchdown

NFC – TEAM PASSING

	Att	Comp	% Comp	Gross Yards	Tkd	Yards Lost	Net Yards	Avg Yds Att	Avg Yds Comp	TD	% TD	Long	Int	% Int
Green Bay	526	311	59.1	4688	42	323	4365	8.91	15.07	33	6.3	t75	32	6.1
Dallas	554	346	62.5	4156	37	314	3842	7.50	12.01	31	5.6	t80	25	4.5
San Francisco	528	339	64.2	4021	33	224	3797	7.62	11.86	27	5.1	t77	12	2.3
Washington	463	278	60.0	3765	35	251	3514	8.13	13.54	29	6.3	84	11	2.4
New York Giants	575	284	49.4	3854	49	363	3491	6.70	13.57	12	2.1	62	31	5.4
Atlanta	507	321	63.3	3793	55	389	3404	7.48	11.82	24	4.7	t76	10	2.0
Los Angeles Rams	489	286	58.5	3411	23	190	3221	6.98	11.93	23	4.7	t61	23	4.7
Minnesota	555	310	55.9	3514	43	303	3211	6.33	11.34	15	2.7	68	22	4.0
Tampa Bay	528	300	56.8	3490	49	366	3124	6.61	11.63	18	3.4	80	24	4.5
Philadelphia	486	252	51.9	3532	57	415	3117	7.27	14.02	22	4.5	t83	18	3.7
Chicago	447	255	57.0	3461	53	358	3103	7 74	13.57	21	4.7	t87	22	4.9
Detroit	503	263	52.3	3297	45	342	2955	6.55	12.54	19	3.8	t80	23	4.6
St Louis	460	267	58.0	3309	59	441	2868	7 19	12.39	29	6.3	t71	21	4.6
New Orleans	425	243	57.2	2782	35	305	2477	6.55	11 45	14	3.3	48	25	5.9
Conference Total	7046	4055	—	51073	615	4584	46489	—	—	317	—		187	299	—
Conference Average	503 3	289 6	57 6	3648.1	43 9	327 4	3320.6	7.25	12 60	22.6	4.5	—	21 4	4.2

Leader based on net yards

NFC – INDIVIDUAL RECEIVERS

	No	Yards	Avg	Long	TD
Green, Roy, St L.	78	1227	15.7	t71	14
Brown, Charlie, Wash.	78	1225	15.7	t75	8
Gray, Earnest, Giants	78	1139	14.6	62	5
Springs, Ron, Dall.	73	589	8.1	t80	1
Clark, Dwight, S.F.	70	840	12.0	t46	8
Quick, Mike, Phil.	69	1409	20.4	t83	13
Johnson, Billy, Atl.	64	709	11.1	t47	4
Andrews, William, Atl.	59	609	10.3	40	4
Lofton, James, G.B.	58	1300	22.4	t74	8
Jefferson, John, G.B.	57	830	14.6	36	7
Wilder, James, T.B.	57	380	6.7	31	2
Bailey, Stacey, Atl.	55	881	16.0	53	6
Barber, Mike, Rams	55	657	11.9	t42	3
Coffman, Paul, G.B.	54	814	15.1	74	11
Anderson, Ottis, St L.	54	459	8.5	40	1
Payton, Walter, Chi.	53	607	11.5	t74	2
Ellis, Gerry, G.B.	52	603	11.6	56	2
Nelson, Darrin, Minn.	51	618	12.1	68	0
Dickerson, Eric, Rams	51	404	7.9	t37	2
Hill, Tony, Dall.	49	801	16.3	t75	7
Groth, Jeff, N.O.	49	585	11.9	42	1
Suhey, Matt, Chi.	49	429	8.8	52	1
Oliver, Hubert, Phil.	49	421	8.6	25	2
Carter, Gerald, T.B.	48	694	14.5	t56	2
Craig, Roger, S.F.	48	427	8.9	23	4
House, Kevin, T.B.	47	769	16.4	t74	5
Monk, Art, Wash.	47	746	15.9	t43	5
Pearson, Drew, Dall.	47	545	11.6	32	5
Washington, Joe, Wash.	47	454	9.7	67	6
Cosbie, Doug, Dall.	46	588	12.8	t61	6
Jones, James, Det.	46	467	10.2	46	1
Mistler, John, Giants	45	422	9.4	24	0
Galbreath, Tony, Minn.	45	348	7.7	23	2
Tilley, Pat, St L.	44	690	15.7	t71	5
Moorehead, Emery, Chi.	42	597	14.2	36	3
Sims, Billy, Det.	42	419	10.0	54	0
Thompson, Leonard, Det.	41	752	18.3	t80	3
Brenner, Hoby, N.O.	41	574	14.0	t38	3
Johnson, Butch, Dall.	41	561	13.7	46	3
Goodlow, Eugene, N.O.	41	487	11.9	26	2
Brown, Ted, Minn.	41	357	8.7	25	1
Gault, Willie, Chi.	40	836	20.9	t87	8
Chadwick, Jeff, Det.	40	617	15.4	45	4
Farmer, George, Rams	40	556	13.9	t46	5
Dorsett, Tony, Dall.	40	287	7.2	24	1
Carmichael, Harold, Phil.	38	515	13.6	35	3
Jenkins, Alfred, Atl.	38	487	12.8	26	1

	No	Yards	Avg	Long	TD
Guman, Mike, Rams	34	347	10.2	60	4
Tyler, Wendell, S.F.	34	285	8.4	26	2
Dennard, Preston, Rams	33	465	14.1	t61	5
Francis, Russ, S.F.	33	357	10.8	25	4
Marsh, Doug, St L.	32	421	13.2	38	8
Carver, Mel, T.B.	32	262	8.2	20	1
Solomon, Freddie, S.F.	31	662	21.4	t77	4
Bruer, Bob, Minn.	31	315	10.2	26	2
Wilson, Mike, S.F.	30	433	14.4	49	0
Nichols, Mark, Det.	29	437	15.1	46	1
White, Sammy, Minn.	29	412	14.2	t43	4
Woolfolk, Butch, Giants	28	368	13.1	44	0
Hill, David, Rams	28	280	10.0	34	2
Giaquinto, Nick, Wash.	27	372	13.8	35	0
Norris, Ulysses, Det.	26	291	11.2	41	7
Carpenter, Rob, Giants	26	258	9.9	38	2
Bell, Theo, T.B.	25	410	16.4	52	2
Giles, Jimmie, T.B.	25	349	14.0	80	1
Garrett, Alvin, Wash.	25	332	13.3	84	1
Hodge, Floyd, Atl.	25	280	11.2	t76	4
Scott, Lindsay, N.O.	24	274	11.4	35	0
Haddix, Michael, Phil.	23	254	11.0	34	0
Ring, Bill, S.F.	23	182	7.9	24	0
Margerum, Ken, Chi.	21	336	16.0	60	2
LeCount, Terry, Minn.	21	318	15.1	49	2
McCullum, Sam, Minn.	21	314	15.0	t49	2
Mowatt, Zeke, Giants	21	280	13.3	t46	1
Young, Rickey, Minn.	21	193	9.2	48	1
Williams, Byron, Giants	20	346	17.3	t43	1
McKinnon, Dennis, Chi.	20	326	16.3	t49	4
Casper, Dave, Hou.-Minn.	20	251	12.6	34	0
Warren, Don, Wash.	20	225	11.3	33	2
Wilson, Wayne, N.O.	20	178	8.9	24	2
Duckett, Kenny, N.O.	19	283	14.9	48	2
Moore, Jeff, S.F.	19	206	10.8	34	0
Donley, Doug, Dall.	18	370	20.6	47	2
Epps, Phillip, G.B.	18	313	17.4	45	0
Clark, Jessie, G.B.	18	279	15.5	t75	1
Newsome, Tim, Dall.	18	250	13.9	t52	4
Bell, Gerry, T.B.	18	200	11.1	33	1
Kab, Vyto, Phil.	18	195	10.8	25	1
Nehemiah, Renaldo, S.F.	17	236	13.9	27	1
Scott, Malcolm, Giants	17	206	12.1	24	0
Walker, Rick, Wash.	17	168	9.9	29	2
Riggs, Gerald, Atl.	17	149	8.8	25	0
Williams, Mike, Phil.	17	142	8.4	29	0
Gajan, Hokie, N.O.	17	130	7.6	26	1
Ramson, Eason, S.F.	17	125	7.4	16	1
Ellard, Henry, Rams	16	268	16.8	44	0

	No	Yards	Avg	Long	TD
Ivery, Eddie Lee, G.B.	16	139	8.7	17	1
Miller, Junior, Atl.	16	125	7.8	19	0
Meade, Mike, G.B.	16	110	6.9	t31	2
Jordan, Steve, Minn.	15	212	14.1	28	2
Cooper, Earl, S.F.	15	207	13.8	t73	3
Armstrong, Adger, T.B.	15	173	11.5	41	2
Owens, James, T.B.	15	81	5.4	11	1
Eddings, Floyd, Giants	14	231	16.5	33	0
Morris, Wayne, St L.	14	55	3.9	11	0
Jackson, Alfred, Atl.	13	220	16.9	t54	3
Mullady, Tom, Giants	13	184	14.2	35	1
Grant, Otis, Rams	12	221	18.4	57	1
Dupree, Billy Joe, Dall.	12	142	11.8	28	1
Lewis, Leo, Minn.	12	127	10.6	18	0
Saldi, Jay, Chi.	12	119	9.9	16	0
Robinson, Bo, Atl.	12	100	8.3	15	0
LaFleur, Greg, St L.	12	99	8.3	21	0
Rogers, George, N.O.	12	69	5.8	22	0
Lewis, Gary, G.B.	11	204	18.5	49	1
Jones, Gordon, Rams	11	172	15.6	46	0
Shumann, Mike, St L.	11	154	14.0	33	0
Hoover, Mel, Phil.	10	221	22.1	68	0
Huckleby, Harlan, G.B.	10	87	8.7	14	0
Rubick, Rob, Det.	10	81	8.1	15	1
Pittman, Danny, Giants-St L.	9	175	19.4	t40	1
Didier, Clint, Wash.	9	153	17.0	t40	4
Cox, Arthur, Atl.	9	83	9.2	19	1
King, Horace, Det.	9	76	8.4	14	0
Obradovich, Jim, T.B.	9	71	7.9	19	1
Montgomery, Wilbert, Phil.	9	53	5.9	13	0
Duinsmore, Pat, Chi.	8	102	12.8	24	0
Bussey, Dexter, Det.	8	49	6.1	t14	1
Miller, Mike, Giants	7	170	24.3	54	0
Young, Tyrone, N.O.	7	85	12.1	32	3
Mitchell, Stump, St L.	7	54	7.7	17	0
Tice, John, N.O.	7	33	4.7	t12	1
Jones, Mike, Minn.	6	95	15.8	47	0
Tyler, Andre, T.B.	6	77	12.8	21	0
Young, Benjamin, Atl.	6	74	12.3	19	1
Woodruff, Tony, Phil.	6	70	11.7	t29	2
Love, Randy, St L.	6	58	9.7	16	1
Scott, Fred, Det.	5	71	14.2	25	1
Baschnagel, Brian, Chi.	5	70	14.0	24	0
Riggins, John, Wash.	5	29	5.8	14	0
Dixon, Al, Phil.	4	54	13.5	22	0
Redden, Barry, Rams	4	30	7.5	9	0
Thompson, Vince, Det.	4	16	4.0	8	0
Young, Glen, Phil.	3	125	41.7	t71	1
Tuggle, John, Giants	3	50	16.7	27	0

	No	Yards	Avg	Long	TD
Matthews, Allama, Atl.	3	37	12.3	23	0
McDole, Mardye, Minn.	3	29	9.7	10	0
Harrell, Willard, St L.	3	25	8.3	13	0
Cain, Lynn, Atl.	3	24	8.0	11	0
Monroe, Carl, S.F.	2	61	30.5	50	0
Seay, Virgil, Wash.	2	55	27.5	t39	1
Bright, Leon, Giants	2	33	16.5	19	0
Thompson, Kenny, St L.	2	31	15.5	22	0
Mauti, Rich, N.O.	2	30	15.0	23	0
Hardy, Larry, N.O.	2	29	14.5	22	0
Sampleton, Lawrence, Phil.	2	28	14.0	19	0
Austin, Cliff, N.O.	2	25	12.5	18	0
Everett, Major, Phil.	2	18	9.0	11	0
Kane, Rick, Det.	2	15	7.5	9	0
Witte, Mark, T.B.	2	15	7.5	10	0
Thomas, Calvin, Chi.	2	13	6.5	7	0
Gentry, Dennis, Chi.	2	8	4.0	6	0
Morris, Joe, Giants	2	1	0.5	t6	1
Harrington, Perry, Phil.	1	19	19.0	19	0
McMahon, Jim, Chi.	1	18	18.0	t18	1
Curran, Willie, Atl.	1	15	15.0	15	0
White, Danny, Dall.	1	15	15.0	t15	1
Campfield, Billy, Giants	1	12	12.0	12	0
McGill, Eddie, St L.	1	11	11.0	11	0
Alexander, Robert, Rams	1	10	10.0	10	0
Kitson, Syd, G.B.	1	9	9.0	9	0
Morton, Michael, T.B.	1	9	9.0	9	0
Rafferty, Tom, Dall.	1	8	8.0	8	0
Smith, Ron, Phil.	1	8	8.0	8	0
McCall, Reese, Det.	1	6	6.0	6	0
McGrath, Mark, Wash.	1	6	6.0	6	0
Ahrens, Dave, Atl.	1	4	4.0	4	0
Redwine, Jarvis, Minn.	1	4	4.0	4	0
McDonald, James, Rams	1	1	1.0	t1	1

t=Touchdown
Leader based on most passes caught

NFC – TOP 25 PASS RECEIVERS BY YARDS

	Yards	No	Avg	Long	TD
Quick, Mike, Phil.	1409	69	20.4	t83	13
Lofton, James, G.B.	1300	58	22.4	t74	8
Green, Roy, St L.	1227	78	15.7	t71	14
Brown, Charlie, Wash.	1225	78	15.7	t75	8
Gray, Earnest, Giants	1139	78	14.6	62	5
Bailey, Stacey, Atl.	881	55	16.0	53	6
Clark, Dwight, S.F.	840	70	12.0	t46	8
Gault, Willie, Chi.	836	40	20.9	t87	8
Jefferson, John, G.B.	830	57	14.6	36	7
Coffman, Paul, G.B.	814	54	15.1	74	11
Hill, Tony, Dall.	801	49	16.3	t75	7
House, Kevin, T.B.	769	47	16.4	t74	5
Thompson, Leonard, Det.	752	41	18.3	t80	3
Monk, Art, Wash.	746	47	15.9	t43	5
Johnson, Billy, Atl.	709	64	11.1	t47	4
Carter, Gerald, T.B.	694	48	14.5	t56	2
Tilley, Pat, St L.	690	44	15.7	t71	5
Solomon, Freddie, S.F.	662	31	21.4	t77	4
Barber, Mike, Rams	657	55	11.9	t42	3
Nelson, Darrin, Minn.	618	51	12.1	68	0
Chadwick, Jeff, Det.	617	40	15.4	45	4
Andrews, William, Atl.	609	59	10.3	40	4
Payton, Walter, Chi.	607	53	11.5	t74	2
Ellis, Gerry, G.B.	603	52	11.6	56	2
Moorehead, Emery, Chi.	597	42	14.2	36	3

NFC – INDIVIDUAL INTERCEPTORS

	No	Yards	Avg	Long	TD
Murphy, Mark, Wash.	9	127	14.1	48	0
Reece, Beasley, Giants-T.B.	8	103	12.9	29	0
Washington, Lionel, St L.	8	92	11.5	26	0
Wright, Eric, S.F.	7	164	23.4	t60	2
Poe, Johnnie, N.O.	7	146	20.9	t31	1
Frazier, Leslie, Chi.	7	135	19.3	58	1
McNorton, Bruce, Det.	7	30	4.3	15	0
Thurman, Dennis, Dall.	6	49	8.2	34	0
Turner, John, Minn.	6	37	6.2	14	0
Jackson, Terry, Giants	6	20	3.3	17	0
Swain, John, Minn.	6	12	2.0	11	0
Fellows, Ron, Dall.	5	139	27.8	t58	1
Collins, Kirk, Rams	5	113	22.6	58	0
Lewis, Tim, G.B.	5	111	22.2	46	0
Anderson, John, G.B.	5	54	10.8	t27	1
Dean, Vernon, Wash.	5	54	10.8	26	0
Schmidt, Terry, Chi.	5	31	6.2	t32	1
Richardson, Mike, Chi.	5	9	1.8	6	0
Johnson, Johnnie, Rams	4	115	28.8	t60	2
Harris, Eric, Rams	4	100	25.0	45	0
Downs, Mike, Dall.	4	80	20.0	28	0
Brown, Cedric, T.B.	4	78	19.5	36	0
Walls, Everson, Dall.	4	70	17.5	37	0
Coffey, Ken, Wash.	4	62	15.5	29	0
Pridemore, Tom, Atl.	4	56	14.0	25	0
Williamson, Carlton, S.F.	4	51	12.8	26	0
Perrin, Benny, St L.	4	50	12.5	30	0
Watkins, Bobby, Det.	4	48	12.0	31	0
Irvin, LeRoy, Rams	4	42	10.5	22	0
Lee, Mark, G.B.	4	23	5.8	15	0
Lott, Ronnie, S.F.	4	22	5.5	22	0
Cobb, Garry, Det.	4	19	4.8	13	0
Washington, A., Wash.	4	12	3.0	8	0
Butler, Bobby, Atl.	4	12	3.0	12	0
Cromwell, Nolan, Rams	3	76	25.3	t43	1
Gary, Russell, N.O.	3	70	23.3	26	0
Griggs, Anthony, Phil.	3	61	20.3	32	0
Kinard, Terry, Giants	3	49	16.3	25	0
Holt, John, T.B.	3	43	14.3	25	0
Bess, Rufus, Minn.	3	38	12.7	19	0
Collier, Tim, S.F.	3	32	10.7	t32	1
Glazebrook, Bob, Atl.	3	30	10.0	25	0
Junior, E.J., St L.	3	27	9.0	19	0
Teal, Willie, Minn.	3	26	8.7	12	0
Mack, Cedric, St L.	3	25	8.3	25	0
Winston, Dennis, N.O.	3	21	7.0	15	0
Haynes, Mark, Giants	3	18	6.0	23	0

	No	Yards	Avg	Long	TD
Harris, Bob, St L.	3	10	3.3	10	0
Hicks, Dwight, S.F.	2	102	51.0	t62	2
Kaufman, Mel, Wash.	2	93	46.5	t70	1
Johnson, Bobby, N.O.	2	80	40.0	t70	1
Barnes, Roosevelt, Det.	2	70	35.0	70	0
Clinkscale, Dexter, Dall.	2	68	34.0	t68	1
Johnson, Kenny, Atl.	2	57	28.5	t31	2
Green, Hugh, T.B.	2	54	27.0	t33	2
Collins, Jim, Rams	2	46	23.0	29	0
Washington, Mike, T.B.	2	41	20.5	25	0
Currier, Bill, Giants	2	37	18.5	t30	1
Fencik, Gary, Chi.	2	34	17.0	20	0
Wattelet, Frank, N.O.	2	33	16.5	24	0
Williams, Greg, Wash.	2	25	12.5	25	0
Baker, Al, St L.	2	24	12.0	19	0
Milot, Rich, Wash.	2	20	10.0	20	0
Hall, Alvin, Det.	2	18	9.0	18	0
Leopold, Bobby, S.F.	2	13	6.5	9	0
Hill, Rod, Dall.	2	12	6.0	12	0
Reese, Booker, T.B.	2	11	5.5	11	0
Taylor, Lawrence, Giants	2	10	5.0	10	0
Green, Darrell, Wash.	2	7	3.5	7	0
Van Pelt, Brad, Giants	2	7	3.5	6	0
Gray, Johnny, G.B.	2	5	2.5	5	0
Paul, Whitney, N.O.	2	3	1.5	3	0
Smith, Wayne, St L.	2	3	1.5	3	0
Cotney, Mark, T.B.	2	1	0.5	1	0
Browner, Joey, Minn.	2	0	0.0	0	0
Fantetti, Ken, Det.	2	0	0.0	0	0
Castille, Jeremiah, T.B.	1	69	69.0	t69	1
Richardson, Al, Atl.	1	38	38.0	38	0
Harper, Willie, S.F.	1	37	37.0	37	0
Lee, Carl, Minn.	1	31	31.0	31	0
Bates, Bill, Dall.	1	29	29.0	29	0
Lewis, Reggie, N.O.	1	27	27.0	t27	1
Sternrick, Greg, N.O.	1	26	26.0	26	0
Andrews, George, Rams	1	22	22.0	22	0
Laughlin, Jim, G.B.	1	22	22.0	22	0
White, James, Minn.	1	22	22.0	22	0
Jordan, Curtis, Wash.	1	20	20.0	20	0
Flowers, Larry, Giants	1	19	19.0	19	0
Jones, Earl, Atl.	1	19	19.0	19	0
Ellis, Ray, Phil.	1	18	18.0	18	0
Galloway, David, St L.	1	17	17.0	17	0
Kelley, Brian, Giants	1	17	17.0	17	0
Pillers, Lawrence, S.F.	1	16	16.0	16	0
Olkewicz, Neal, Wash.	1	14	14.0	14	9
Jones, Ed, Dall.	1	12	12.0	12	0
Scott, Randy, G.B.	1	12	12.0	12	0

	No	Yards	Avg	Long	TD
Grooms, Elois, St L.	1	10	10.0	10	0
Dickerson, Anthony, Dall.	1	8	8.0	8	0
Nelson, Lee, St L.	1	8	8.0	8	0
Warren, Frank, N.O.	1	6	6.0	6	0
Wilson, Otis, Chi.	1	6	6.0	6	0
Carpenter, Brian, Wash.	1	2	2.0	2	0
Johnson, Charlie, Minn.	1	2	2.0	2	0
Ekern, Carl, Rams	1	1	1.0	1	0
Manley, Dexter, Wash.	1	1	1.0	1	0
Blair, Matt, Minn.	1	0	0.0	0	0
Brantley, Scot, T.B.	1	0	0.0	0	0
Breunig, Bob, Dall.	1	0	0.0	0	0
Dennis, Mike, Giants	1	0	0.0	0	0
Edwards, Herman, Phil.	1	0	0.0	0	0
Foules, Elbert, Phil.	1	0	0.0	0	0
Jackson, Rickey, N.O.	1	0	0.0	0	0
Jolly, Mike, G.B.	1	0	0.0	0	0
Latimer, Al, Det.	1	0	0.0	0	0
Logan, Randy, Phil.	1	0	0.0	0	0
Nord, Keith, Minn.	1	0	0.0	0	0
Singletary, Mike, Chi.	1	0	0.0	0	0
Young, Roynell, Phil.	1	0	0.0	0	0

t=Touchdown
Leader based on most interceptions

NFC – TEAM INTERCEPTIONS

	No	Yards	Avg	Long	TD
Washington	34	437	12.9	t70	1
St Louis	28	266	9.5	30	0
Dallas	27	467	17.3	t68	2
Minnesota	25	168	6.7	31	0
Los Angeles Rams	24	515	21.5	t60	3
San Francisco	24	437	18.2	t62	5
New Orleans	23	412	17.9	t70	3
New York Giants	23	210	9.1	t30	1
Tampa Bay	23	367	16.0	t69	3
Detroit	22	185	8.4	70	0
Chicago	21	215	10.2	58	2
Green Bay	19	227	11.9	46	1
Atlanta	15	212	14.1	38	2
Philadelphia	8	79	9.9	32	0
Conference Total	316	4197	—	t70	23
Conference Average	22.6	299.8	13.3	—	1.6

NFC – INDIVIDUAL PUNTERS

	No	Yards	Long	Avg	Total Punts	TB	Blk	Opp Ret	Ret Yds	In 20	Net Avg
Garcia, Frank, T.B.	95	4008	64	42.2	96	12	1	59	603	15	33.0
Runager, Max, Phil.	59	2459	55	41.7	59	5	0	37	339	12	34.2
Scribner, Bucky, G.B.	69	2869	70	41.6	70	7	1	43	384	11	33.5
Coleman, Greg, Minn.	91	3780	65	41.5	91	8	0	40	297	28	36.5
Birdsong, Carl, St L.	85	3529	59	41.5	85	7	0	47	307	14	36.3
Black, Mike, Det.	71	2911	60	41.0	72	9	1	39	302	17	33.7
Erxleben, Russell, N.O.	74	3034	60	41.0	74	9	0	49	571	10	30.9
Giacomarro, Ralph, Atl.	70	2823	57	40.3	71	8	1	34	179	18	35.0
Jennings, Dave, Giants	84	3386	66	40.3	85	5	1	47	283	29	35.3
Misko, John, Rams	82	3301	67	40.3	83	12	1	39	251	18	33.9
Orosz, Tom, S.F.	65	2552	61	39.3	66	6	1	38	278	16	32.6
Hayes, Jeff, Wash.	72	2796	56	38.8	72	2	0	41	407	29	32.6
Parsons, Bob, Chi.	79	2916	54	36.9	79	5	0	37	261	21	32.3
NON-QUALIFIERS											
Warren, John, Dall.	39	1551	54	39.8	39	1	0	24	283	7	32.0
White, Danny, Dall.	38	1543	50	40.6	39	3	1	26	233	6	32.1
Skladany, Tom, Phil.	27	1062	51	39.3	27	2	0	20	172	5	31.5
Stachowicz, Ray, Chi.	12	447	48	37.3	14	0	2	7	61	0	27.6
Miller, Jim, Dall.	5	178	43	35.6	5	0	0	3	72	1	21.2
Merkens, Guido, N.O.	4	144	45	36.0	4	1	0	2	2	0	30.5
McMahon, Jim, Chi.	1	36	36	36.0	1	0	0	0	0	0	36.0

Leader based on gross average, minimum 40 punts

NFC – TEAM PUNTING

	Total Punts	Yards	Long	Avg	TB	Blk	Opp Ret	Ret Yds	In 20	Net Avg
Tampa Bay	96	4008	64	41.8	12	1	59	603	16	33.0
Minnesota	91	3780	65	41.5	8	0	40	297	28	36.5
St Louis	85	3529	59	41.5	7	0	47	307	14	36.3
Green Bay	70	2869	70	41.0	7	1	43	384	11	33.5
Philadelphia	86	3521	55	40.9	7	0	57	511	17	33.4
New Orleans	78	3178	60	40.7	10	0	51	573	10	30.8
Detroit	72	2911	60	40.4	9	1	39	302	17	33.7
New York Giants	85	3386	66	39.8	5	1	47	283	29	35.3
Los Angeles Rams	83	3301	67	39.8	12	1	39	251	18	33.9
Atlanta	71	2823	57	39.8	8	1	34	179	18	35.0
Dallas	83	3272	54	39.4	4	1	53	588	14	31.4
Washington	72	2796	56	38.8	2	0	41	407	29	32.6
San Francisco	66	2552	61	38.7	6	1	38	278	16	32.6
Chicago	94	3399	54	36.2	5	2	44	322	21	31.7
Conference Total	1132	45325	70	—	102	10	632	5285	258	—
Conference Average	80.9	3237.5	—	40.0	7.3	0.7	45.1	377.5	18.4	33.6

NFC – INDIVIDUAL PUNT RETURNERS

	No	FC	Yards	Avg	Long	TD
Ellard, Henry, Rams	16	4	217	13.6	t72	1
McLemore, Dana, S.F.	31	6	331	10.7	t56	1
Johnson, Billy, Atl.	46	4	489	10.6	t71	1
Jenkins, Ken, Det.	23	1	230	10.0	43	0
McKinnon, Dennis, Chi.	34	3	316	9.3	t59	1
Epps, Phillip, G.B.	36	13	324	9.0	t90	1
Mitchell, Stump, St L.	38	1	337	8.9	34	0
Irvin, LeRoy, Rams	25	3	212	8.5	20	0
Shaw, Pete, Giants	29	4	234	8.1	27	0
Hill, Rod, Dall.	30	2	232	7.7	37	0
Tyler, Andre, T.B.	27	5	208	7.7	16	0
Nelms, Mike, Wash.	38	0	289	7.6	35	0
Bess, Rufus, Minn.	21	10	158	7.5	17	0
Groth, Jeff, N.O.	39	15	275	7.1	30	0
Bright, Leon, Giants	17	0	117	6.9	20	0
Sciarra, John, Phil.	22	3	115	5.2	14	0
(Non-Qualifiers)						
Martin, Robbie, Det.	15	3	183	12.2	t81	1
Johnson, Johnnie, Rams	14	1	109	7.8	26	0
Young, Glen, Phil.	14	3	93	6.6	23	0
Bird, Steve, St L.	14	2	76	5.4	16	0
Fisher, Jeff, Chi.	13	3	71	5.5	11	0
Fellows, Ron, Dall.	10	3	75	7.5	14	0
Bell, Theo, T.B.	10	2	48	4.8	11	0
Allen, Gary, Dall.	9	1	153	17.0	t68	1
Gault, Willie, Chi.	9	1	60	6.7	12	0
Reece, Beasley, Giants	9	2	26	2.9	7	0
Hall, Alvin, Det.	8	4	109	13.6	66	0
Hoover, Mel, Phil.	7	4	44	6.3	13	0
Seay, Virgil, Wash.	5	1	57	11.4	42	0
Holt, John, T.B.	5	0	43	8.6	17	0
Solomon, Freddie, S.F.	5	3	34	6.8	11	0
Harrell, Willard, St L.	5	1	31	6.2	11	0
Green, Darrell, Wash.	4	0	29	7.3	18	0
Lewis, Leo, Minn.	3	3	52	17.3	34	0
Giaquinto, Nick, Wash.	2	4	12	6.0	12	0
Gray, Johnny, G.B.	2	0	9	4.5	5	0
Ferrell, Earl, St L.	1	0	17	17.0	17	0
Foules, Elbert, Phil.	1	0	7	7.0	7	0
Donley, Doug, Dall.	1	0	1	1.0	1	0
Hood, Estus, G.B.	1	0	0	0.0	0	0
Lewis, Cliff, G.B.	1	0	0	0.0	0	0
Logan, Randy, Phil.	1	0	0	0.0	0	0
Newhouse, Robert, Dall.	1	0	0	0.0	0	0
Lee, Mark, G.B.	1	0	−4	−4.0	−4	0
Bell, Rick, Minn.	0	2	0	—	0	0

	No	FC	Yards	Avg	Long	TD
Latimer, Al, Det.	0	1	0	—	0	0
Pittman, Danny, Giants	0	1	0	—	0	0

t=Touchdown

Leader based on average return, minimum 16 returns

NFC – TEAM PUNT RETURNS

	No	FC	Yards	Avg	Long	TD
Detroit	46	9	522	11.3	t81	1
Atlanta	46	4	489	10.6	t71	1
San Francisco	36	9	365	10.1	t56	1
Los Angeles Rams	55	8	538	9.8	t72	1
Dallas	51	6	461	9.0	t68	1
Minnesota	24	15	210	8.8	34	0
Green Bay	41	13	329	8.0	t90	1
Chicago	56	7	447	8.0	t59	1
St Louis	58	4	461	7.9	34	0
Washington	49	5	387	7.9	42	0
Tampa Bay	42	7	299	7.1	17	0
New Orleans	39	15	275	7.1	30	0
New York Giants	55	7	377	6.9	27	0
Philadelphia	45	10	259	5.8	23	0
Conference Total	643	119	5419	—	t90	7
Conference Average	45.9	8.5	387.1	8.4	—	0.5

NFC – INDIVIDUAL KICKOFF RETURNERS

	No	Yards	Avg	Long	TD
Nelson, Darrin, Minn.	18	445	24.7	50	0
Morton, Michael, T.B.	30	689	23.0	50	0
Nelms, Mike, Wash.	35	802	22.9	41	0
Bright, Leon, Giants	21	475	22.6	36	0
Redwine, Jarvis, Minn.	38	838	22.1	41	0
Duckett, Kenny, N.O.	33	719	21.8	61	0
Mitchell, Stump, St.L.	36	778	21.6	66	0
Hall, Alvin, Det.	23	492	21.4	32	0
Young, Glen, Phil.	26	547	21.0	52	0
Jenkins, Ken, Det.	22	459	20.9	30	0
Williams, Richard, Atl.	23	461	20.0	34	0
Fellows, Ron, Dall.	43	855	19.9	53	0
Riggs, Gerald, Atl.	17	330	19.4	35	0
McLemore, Dana, S.F.	30	576	19.2	39	0
Owens, James, T.B.	20	380	19.0	31	0
Redden, Barry, Rams	19	358	18.8	43	0
Huckleby, Harlan, G.B.	41	757	18.5	57	0
Lewis, Tim, G.B.	20	358	17.9	30	0
Hutchison, Anthony, Chi.	17	259	15.2	28	0
(Non-Qualifiers)					
Ellard, Henry, Rams	15	314	20.9	44	0
Everett, Major, Phil.	14	275	19.6	46	0
Morris, Joe, Giants	14	255	18.2	26	0
Hill, Rod, Dall.	14	243	17.4	40	0
Gault, Willie, Chi.	13	276	21.2	38	0
Ferrell, Earl, St.L.	13	257	19.8	28	0
Alexander, Robert, Rams	13	222	17.1	30	0
Johnson, Kenny, Atl.	11	224	20.4	28	0
Cain, Lynn, Atl.	11	200	18.2	24	0
Gray, Johnny, G.B.	11	178	16.2	26	0
Evans, Reggie, Wash.	10	141	14.1	28	0
Wilson, Wayne, N.O.	9	239	26.6	52	0
Seay, Virgil, Wash.	9	218	24.2	50	0
Bird, Steve, St.L.	9	194	21.6	33	0
Tuggle, John, Giants	9	156	17.3	28	0
Campfield, Billy, Giants	9	154	17.1	23	0
Allen, Gary, Dall.	8	178	22.3	31	0
Monroe, Carl, S.F.	8	152	19.0	32	0
Mauti, Rich, N.O.	8	147	18.4	35	0
Martin, Robbie, Det.	8	140	17.5	51	0
Smith, Johnny Ray, T.B.	8	136	17.0	43	0
Gentry, Dennis, Chi.	7	130	18.6	28	0
Ellis, Ray, Phil.	7	119	17.0	25	0
Moore, Jeff, S.F.	7	117	16.7	46	0
Austin, Cliff, N.O.	7	112	16.0	27	0
Rogers, Jimmy, N.O.	7	103	14.7	25	0
Pittman, Danny, Giants	6	107	17.8	24	0
Watts, Rickey, Chi.	5	79	15.8	21	0

	No	Yards	Avg	Long	TD
Heater, Larry, Giants	5	71	14.2	26	0
Harrington, Perry, Phil.	4	79	19.8	26	0
Caver, Jim, Det.	4	71	17.8	33	0
Ring, Bill, S.F.	4	68	17.0	18	0
Schmitt, George, St.L.	4	41	10.3	19	0
Love, Randy, St.L.	3	71	23.7	23	0
Duerson, Dave, Chi.	3	66	22.0	24	0
Harrell, Willard, St.L.	3	62	20.7	26	0
Williams, Mike, Phil.	3	59	19.7	25	0
Haddix, Michael, Phil.	3	51	17.0	24	0
Cooper, Earl, S.F.	3	45	15.0	20	0
Baschnagel, Brian, Chi.	3	42	14.0	19	0
Huffman, Dave, Minn.	3	42	14.0	15	0
Spradlin, Danny, T.B.	3	35	11.7	24	0
Winters, Chet, G.B.	3	28	9.3	12	0
Young, Rickey, Minn.	3	27	9.0	15	0
Garrett, Alvin, Wash.	2	50	25.0	28	0
Bess, Rufus, Minn.	2	44	22.0	30	0
McKinnon, Dennis, Chi.	2	42	21.0	25	0
Wonsley, Otis, Wash.	2	36	18.0	20	0
Jones, Mike, Minn.	2	31	15.5	16	0
Miller, Mike, Giants	2	31	15.5	26	0
Guman, Mike, Rams	2	30	15.0	21	0
O'Steen, Dwayne, T.B.	2	30	15.0	16	0
Curran, Willie, Atl.	2	26	13.0	16	0
Carver, Mel, T.B.	2	24	12.0	13	0
Bell, Todd, Chi.	2	18	9.0	18	0
Cosbie, Doug, Dall.	2	17	8.5	10	0
Fitzsche, Jim, Phil.	2	17	8.5	15	0
Woolfolk, Butch, Giants	2	13	6.5	11	0
Cabral, Brian, Chi.	2	11	5.5	6	0
Rains, Dan, Chi.	2	11	5.5	11	0
Darby, Byron, Phil.	2	3	1.5	3	0
Glazebrook, Bob, Atl.	2	0	0.0	0	0
Dennis, Mike, Giants	1	54	54.0	54	0
Newsome, Tim, Dall.	1	28	28.0	28	0
Lewis, Leo, Minn.	1	25	25.0	25	0
Irvin, LeRoy, Rams	1	22	22.0	22	0
Smith, Leonard, St.L.	1	19	19.0	19	0
Young, Roynell, Phil.	1	18	18.0	18	0
Butler, Bobby, Atl.	1	17	17.0	17	0
Cronan, Pete, Wash.	1	17	17.0	17	0
Ivery, Eddie Lee, G.B.	1	17	17.0	17	0
McSwain, Chuck, Dall.	1	17	17.0	17	0
Richardson, Mike, Chi.	1	17	17.0	17	0
Washington, Joe, Wash.	1	16	16.0	16	0
Brock, Stan, N.O.	1	15	15.0	15	0
Sawyer, John, Wash.	1	15	15.0	15	0
Bell, Rick, Minn.	1	14	14.0	14	0

	No	Yards	Avg	Long	TD
Green, Roy, St L.	1	14	14.0	14	0
Springs, Ron, Dall.	1	13	13.0	13	0
Duda, Mark, St L.	1	12	12.0	12	0
Allerman, Kurt, St L.	1	11	11.0	11	0
King, Horace, Det.	1	11	11.0	11	0
Lee, Edward, Det.	1	11	11.0	11	0
Armstrong, Adger, T.B.	1	10	10.0	10	0
Middleton, Terdell, T.B.	1	10	10.0	10	0
Mayock, Mike, Giants	1	9	9.0	9	0
McLaughlin, Joe, Giants	1	8	8.0	8	0
Curley, August, Det.	1	7	7.0	7	0
Williams, Greg, Wash.	1	6	6.0	6	0
Wattelet, Frank, N.O.	1	4	4.0	4	0
Janata, John, Chi.	1	2	2.0	2	0
Drechsler, Dave, G.B.	1	1	1.0	1	0
Barnett, Doug, Rams	1	0	0.0	0	0
Giaquinto, Nick, Wash.	1	0	0.0	0	0
Huther, Bruce, Dall.	1	0	0.0	0	0
Kitson, Syd, G.B.	1	0	0.0	0	0
Lee, Mark, G.B.	1	0	0.0	0	0
Norris, Ulysses, Det.	1	0	0.0	0	0
Obradovich, Jim, T.B.	1	0	0.0	0	0
Simmons, Jeff, Rams	1	0	0.0	0	0

t=Touchdown
Leader based on average return, minimum 16 returns

NFC – TEAM KICKOFF RETURNS

	No	Yards	Avg	Long	TD
Minnesota	68	1466	21.6	50	0
Washington	63	1301	20.7	58	0
New Orleans	66	1339	20.3	61	0
St Louis	72	1459	20.3	66	0
Detroit	61	1191	19.5	51	0
Tampa Bay	68	1314	19.3	50	0
Dallas	71	1351	19.0	53	0
Philadelphia	62	1168	18.8	52	0
Atlanta	67	1258	18.8	35	0
New York Giants	71	1333	18.8	54	0
San Francisco	52	958	18.4	46	0
Los Angeles Rams	52	946	18.2	44	0
Green Bay	79	1339	16.9	57	0
Chicago	58	953	16.4	38	0
Conference Total	910	17376	—	66	0
Conference Average	65.0	1241.1	19.1	—	0.0

NFC – INDIVIDUAL SCORERS

KICKERS	XP	XPA	FG	FGA	PTS
Moseley, Mark, Wash.	62	63	33	47	161
Haji-Sheikh, Ali, Giants	22	23	35	42	127
Wersching, Ray, S.F.	51	51	25	30	126
Septien, Rafael, Dall.	57	59	22	27	123
Stenerud, Jan, G.B.	52	52	21	26	115
Murray, Ed, Det.	38	38	25	32	113
Ricardo, Benny, Minn.	33	34	25	33	108
Luckhurst, Mick, Atl.	43	45	17	22	94
Andersen, Morten, N.O.	37	38	18	23	91
O'Donoghue, Neil, St L.	45	47	15	28	90
Thomas, Bob, Chi.	35	38	14	25	77
Franklin, Tony, Phil.	24	27	15	26	69
Capece, Bill, T.B.	23	26	10	20	53
Nelson, Chuck, Rams	33	37	5	11	48
Lansford, Mike, Rams	9	9	6	9	27
Warnke, David, T.B.	1	2	0	1	1

NON-KICKERS	TD	TDR	TDP	TDM	PTS
Riggins, John, Wash.	24	24	0	0	144
Dickerson, Eric, Rams	20	18	2	0	120
Green, Roy, St L.	14	0	14	0	84
Quick, Mike, Phil.	13	0	13	0	78
Craig, Roger, S.F.	12	8	4	0	72
Andrews, William, Atl.	11	7	4	0	66
Brown, Ted, Minn.	11	10	1	0	66
Coffman, Paul, G.B.	11	0	11	0	66
Wilson, Wayne, N.O.	11	9	2	0	66
Dorsett, Tony, Dall.	9	8	1	0	54
Brown, Charlie, Wash.	8	0	8	0	48
Clark, Dwight, S.F.	8	0	8	0	48
Gault, Willie, Chi.	8	0	8	0	48
Lofton, James, G.B.	8	0	8	0	48
Marsh, Doug, St L.	8	0	8	0	48
Payton, Walter, Chi.	8	6	2	0	48
Riggs, Gerald, Atl.	8	8	0	0	48
Springs, Ron, Dall.	8	7	1	0	48
Hill, Tony, Dall.	7	0	7	0	42
Jefferson, John, G.B.	7	0	7	0	42
Jones, James, Det.	7	6	1	0	42
Norris, Ulysses, Det.	7	0	7	0	42
Sims, Billy, Det.	7	7	0	0	42
Anderson, Ottis, St L.	6	5	1	0	36
Bailey, Stacey, Atl.	6	0	6	0	36
Carpenter, Rob, Giants	6	4	2	0	36
Cosbie, Doug, Dall.	6	0	6	0	36
Ellis, Gerry, G.B.	6	4	2	0	36
Galbreath, Tony, Minn.	6	4	2	0	36

	TD	TDR	TDP	TDM	PTS
Newsome, Tim, Dall.	6	2	4	0	36
Owens, James, T.B.	6	5	1	0	36
Tyler, Wendell, S.F.	6	4	2	0	36
Washington, Joe, Wash.	6	0	6	0	36
Wilder, James, T.B.	6	4	2	0	36
Dennard, Preston, Rams	5	0	5	0	30
Didier, Clint, Wash.	5	0	4	1	30
Farmer, George, Rams	5	0	5	0	30
Gray, Earnest, Giants	5	0	5	0	30
House, Kevin, T.B.	5	0	5	0	30
Johnson, Billy, Atl.	5	0	5	0	30
McKinnon, Dennis, Chi.	5	0	4	1	30
Monk, Art, Wash.	5	0	4	1	30
Pearson, Drew, Dall.	5	0	5	0	30
Rogers, George, N.O.	5	5	0	0	30
Suhey, Matt, Chi.	5	4	1	0	30
Tilley, Pat, St L.	5	0	5	0	30
White, Danny, Dall.	5	4	1	0	30
Chadwick, Jeff, Det.	4	0	4	0	24
Evans, Reggie, Wash.	4	4	0	0	24
Francis, Russ, S.F.	4	0	4	0	24
Gajan, Hokie, N.O.	4	4	0	0	24
Guman, Mike, Rams	4	0	4	0	24
Hodge, Floyd, Atl.	4	0	4	0	24
Huckleby, Harlan, G.B.	4	4	0	0	24
Solomon, Freddie, S.F.	4	0	4	0	24
Thompson, Leonard, Det.	4	1	3	0	24
White, Sammy, Minn.	4	0	4	0	24
Woolfolk, Butch, Giants	4	4	0	0	24
Barber, Mike, Rams	3	0	3	0	18
Brenner, Hoby, N.O.	3	0	3	0	18
Carmichael, Harold, Phil.	3	0	3	0	18
Cooper, Earl, S.F.	3	0	3	0	18
Dickey, Lynn, G.B.	3	3	0	0	18
Hipple, Eric, Det.	3	3	0	0	18
Ivery, Eddie Lee, G.B.	3	2	1	0	18
Jackson, Alfred, Atl.	3	0	3	0	18
Johnson, Butch, Dall.	3	0	3	0	18
Love, Randy, St L.	3	2	1	0	18
McMahon, Jim, Chi.	3	2	1	0	18
Meade, Mike, G.B.	3	1	2	0	18
Mitchell, Stump, St L.	3	3	0	0	18
Moorehead, Emery, Chi.	3	0	3	0	18
Oliver, Hubert, Phil.	3	1	2	0	18
Young, Tyrone, N.O.	3	0	3	0	18
Armstrong, Adger, T.B.	2	0	2	0	12
Bell, Theo, T.B.	2	0	2	0	12
Bruer, Bob, Minn.	2	0	2	0	12
Carter, Gerald, T.B.	2	0	2	0	12

	TD	TDR	TDP	TDM	PTS
Donley, Doug, Dall.	2	0	2	0	12
Douglass, Mike, G.B.	2	0	0	2	12
Duckett, Kenny, N.O.	2	0	2	0	12
Fellows, Ron, Dall.	2	0	0	2	12
Goodlow, Eugene, N.O.	2	0	2	0	12
Green, Hugh, T.B.	2	0	0	2	12
Haddix, Michael, Phil.	2	2	0	0	12
Hicks, Dwight, S.F.	2	0	0	2	12
Hill, David, Rams	2	0	2	0	12
Johnson, Johnnie, Rams	2	0	0	2	12
Johnson, Kenny, Atl.	2	0	0	2	12
Jordan, Steve, Minn.	2	0	2	0	12
Kaufman, Mel, Wash.	2	0	0	2	12
LeCount, Terry, Minn.	2	0	2	0	12
Lewis, Gary, G.B.	2	1	1	0	12
Lomax, Neil, St L.	2	2	0	0	12
Margerum, Ken, Chi.	2	0	2	0	12
McCullum, Sam, Minn.	2	0	2	0	12
Montana, Joe, S.F.	2	2	0	0	12
Morris, Wayne, St L.	2	2	0	0	12
Redden, Barry, Rams	2	2	0	0	12
Ring, Bill, S.F.	2	2	0	0	12
Walker, Rick, Wash.	2	0	2	0	12
Warren, Don, Wash.	2	0	2	0	12
Woodruff, Tony, Phil.	2	0	2	0	12
Wright, Eric, S.F.	2	0	0	2	12
Young, Rickey, Minn.	2	2	0	0	12
Allen, Gary, Dall.	1	0	0	1	6
Anderson, John, G.B.	1	0	0	1	6
Bartkowski, Steve, Atl.	1	1	0	0	6
Bell, Jerry, T.B.	1	0	1	0	6
Board, Dwaine, S.F.	1	0	0	1	6
Bussey, Dexter, Det.	1	0	1	0	6
Cain, Lynn, Atl.	1	1	0	0	6
Carver, Mel, T.B.	1	0	1	0	6
Castille, Jeremiah, T.B.	1	0	0	1	6
Clark, Jessie, G.B.	1	0	1	0	6
Clark, Kelvin, N.O.	1	0	0	1	6
Clinkscale, Dextor, Dall.	1	0	0	1	6
Collier, Tim, S.F.	1	0	0	1	6
Cox, Arthur, Atl.	1	0	1	0	6
Cromwell, Nolan, Rams	1	0	0	1	6
Currier, Bill, Giants	1	0	0	1	6
Dean, Vernon, Wash.	1	0	0	1	6
Downs, Mike, Dall.	1	0	0	1	6
Dupree, Billy Joe, Dall.	1	0	1	0	6
Ellard, Henry, Rams	1	0	0	1	6
Epps, Phillip, G.B.	1	0	0	1	6
Evans, Vince, Chi.	1	1	0	0	6

	TD	TDR	TDP	TDM	PTS
Ferrell, Earl, St L.	1	1	0	0	6
Frazier, Leslie, Chi.	1	0	0	1	6
Gaison, Blane, Atl.	1	0	0	1	6
Garrett, Alvin, Wash.	1	0	1	0	6
Giaquinto, Nick, Wash.	1	1	0	0	6
Giles, Jimmie, T.B.	1	0	1	0	6
Grant, Otis, Rams	1	0	1	0	6
Grooms, Elois, St L.	1	0	0	1	6
Groth, Jeff, N.O.	1	0	1	0	6
Harrington, Perry, Phil.	1	1	0	0	6
Hartenstine, Mike, Chi.	1	0	0	1	6
Hegman, Mike, Dall.	1	0	0	1	6
Huffman, Dave, Minn.	1	0	0	1	6
Hutchison, Anthony, Chi.	1	1	0	0	6
Jackson, Terry, Giants	1	0	0	1	6
Jaworski, Ron, Phil.	1	1	0	0	6
Jenkins, Alfred, Atl.	1	0	1	0	6
Johnson, Bobby, N.O.	1	0	0	1	6
Johnson, Charlie, Minn.	1	0	0	1	6
Kab, Vyto, Phil.	1	0	1	0	6
Korte, Steve, N.O.	1	0	0	1	6
Lewis, Reggie, N.O.	1	0	0	1	6
Logan, Dave, T.B.	1	0	0	1	6
Martin, Robbie, Det.	1	0	0	1	6
McDonald, James, Rams	1	0	1	0	6
McLemore, Dana, S.F.	1	0	0	1	6
Moore, Jeff, S.F.	1	1	0	0	6
Morris, Joe, Giants	1	0	1	0	6
Mowatt, Zeke, Giants	1	0	1	0	6
Mullady, Tom, Giants	1	0	1	0	6
Nehemiah, Renaldo, S.F.	1	0	1	0	6
Nelson, Darrin, Minn.	1	1	0	0	6
Nelson, Lee, St L.	1	0	0	1	6
Nichols, Mark, Det.	1	0	1	0	6
Obradovich, Jim, T.B.	1	0	1	0	6
Perrin, Benny, St L.	1	0	0	1	6
Pittman, Danny, Giants	1	0	1	0	6
Poe, Johnnie, N.O.	1	0	0	1	6
Rade, John, Atl.	1	0	0	1	6
Ramson, Eason, S.F.	1	0	1	0	6
Rubick, Rob, Det.	1	0	1	0	6
Schmidt, Terry, Chi.	1	0	0	1	6
Scott, Fred, Det.	1	0	1	0	6
Seay, Virgil, Wash.	1	0	1	0	6
Theismann, Joe, Wash.	1	1	0	0	6
Thompson, Vince, Det.	1	1	0	0	6
Thurman, Dennis, Dall.	1	0	0	1	6
Tice, John, N.O.	1	0	1	0	6
Tuggle, John, Giants	1	1	0	0	6

	TD	TDR	TDP	TDM	PTS
Williams, Byron, Giants	1	0	1	0	6
Wilson, Dave, N.O.	1	1	0	0	6
Young, Benjamin, Atl.	1	0	1	0	6
Young, Glen, Phil.	1	0	1	0	6
English, Doug, Det.	0	0	0	0	*4
Boyd, Greg, G.B.	0	0	0	0	*2
Dickerson, Anthony, Dall.	0	0	0	0	*2
Fanning, Mike, Det.	0	0	0	0	*2
Galloway, David, St L.	0	0	0	0	*2
Mann, Charles, Wash.	0	0	0	0	*2
Marshall, Leonard, Giants	0	0	0	0	*2
Youngblood, Jack, Rams	0	0	0	0	*2
Yarno, George, T.B.	0	0	0	0	#1

* = Safety (also 2 Minn., 1 each Rams, Phil.)
# = Scored extra point

NFC – TEAM SCORING

	TD	TDR	TDP	TDM	XP	XPA	FG	FGA	SAF	PTS
Washington	63	30	29	4	62	63	33	47	1	541
Dallas	59	21	31	7	57	59	22	27	1	479
San Francisco	51	17	27	7	51	51	25	30	0	432
Green Bay	52	15	33	4	52	52	21	26	1	429
St Louis	47	15	29	3	45	47	15	28	1	374
Atlanta	46	17	24	5	43	45	17	22	0	370
Los Angeles Rams	47	20	23	4	42	47	11	20	2	361
Detroit	38	18	19	1	38	38	25	32	3	347
New Orleans	38	19	14	5	37	38	18	24	0	319
Minnesota	34	17	15	2	33	34	25	33	2	316
Chicago	39	14	21	4	35	39	14	25	0	311
New York Giants	23	9	12	2	22	23	35	42	1	267
Tampa Bay	31	9	18	4	25	31	10	24	0	241
Philadelphia	27	5	22	0	24	27	15	26	1	233
Conference Total	595	226	317	52	566	594	286	406	13	5020
Conference Average	42.5	16.1	22.6	3.7	40.4	42.4	20.4	29.0	0.9	358.6

NFC — TEAM-BY-TEAM SUMMARY 1983

OFFENSE	Atl.	Chi.	Dall.	Det.	G.B.
Rushes	492	583	519	513	439
Net Yds. Gained	2224	2727	2117	2181	1807
Avg. Gain	4.5	4.7	4.1	4.3	4.1
Avg. Yds. per Game	139.0	170.4	132.3	136.3	112.9
Passes Attempted	507	447	554	503	526
Completed	321	255	346	263	311
% Completed	63.3	57.0	62.5	52.3	59.1
Total Yds. Gained	3793	3461	4156	3297	4688
Times Sacked	55	53	37	45	42
Yds. Lost	389	358	314	342	323
Net Yds. Gained	3404	3103	3842	2955	4365
Avg. Yds. per Game	212.8	193.9	240.1	184.7	272.8
Net Yds. per Pass Play	6.06	6.21	6.50	5.39	7.68
Yds. Gained per Comp.	11.82	13.57	12.01	12.54	15.07
Combined Net Yds. Gained	5628	5830	5959	5136	6172
% Total Yds., Rushing	39.52	46.78	35.53	42.46	29.28
% Total Yds., Passing	60.48	53.22	64.47	57.54	70.72
Avg. Yds. per Game	351.8	364.4	372.4	321.0	385.8
Had Intercepted	10	22	25	23	32
Yds. Opp. Returned	94	291	358	241	337
Ret. by Opp. for TD	0	1	1	0	4
Punts	71	94	83	72	70
Yds. Punted	2823	3399	3272	2911	2869
Avg. Yds. per Punt	39.8	36.2	39.4	40.4	41.0
Punt Returns	46	56	51	46	41
Yds. Returned	489	447	461	522	329
Avg. Yds. per Return	10.6	8.0	9.0	11.3	8.0
Returned for TD	1	1	1	1	1
Kickoff Returns	67	58	71	61	79
Yds. Returned	1258	953	1351	1191	1339
Avg. Yds. per Return	18.8	16.4	19.0	19.5	16.9
Returned for TD	0	0	0	0	0
Total Points Scored	370	311	479	347	429
Total TDs	46	39	59	38	52
TDs Rushing	17	14	21	18	15
TDs Passing	24	21	31	19	33
TDs on Ret. and Rec.	5	4	7	1	4
Extra Points	43	35	57	38	52
Safeties	0	0	1	3	1
Field Goals Made	17	14	22	25	21
Field Goals Attempted	22	25	27	32	26
% Successful	77.3	56.0	81.5	78.1	80.8

Rams.	Minn.	N.O.	N.Y.G.	Phil.	St L.	S.F.	T.B.	Wash.
511	470	595	506	402	525	511	428	629
2253	1808	2461	1794	1417	2277	2257	1353	2625
4.4	3.8	4.1	3.5	3.5	4.3	4.4	3.2	4.2
140.8	113.0	153.8	112.1	88.6	142.3	141.1	84.6	164.1
489	555	425	575	486	460	528	528	463
286	310	243	284	252	267	339	300	278
58.5	55.9	57.2	49.4	51.9	58.0	64.2	56.8	60.0
3411	3514	2782	3854	3532	3309	4021	3490	3765
23	43	35	49	57	59	33	49	35
190	303	305	363	415	441	224	366	251
3221	3211	2477	3491	3117	2868	3797	3124	3514
201.3	200.7	154.8	218.2	194.8	179.3	237.3	195.3	219.6
6.29	5.37	5.38	5.59	5.74	5.55	6.77	5.41	7.06
11.93	11.34	11.45	13.57	14.02	12.39	11.86	11.63	13.54
5474	5019	4938	5285	4534	5145	6054	4477	6139
41.16	36.02	49.84	33.95	31.25	44.26	37.28	30.22	42.76
58.84	63.98	50.16	66.05	68.75	55.74	62.72	69.78	57.24
342.1	313.7	308.6	330.3	283.4	321.6	378.4	279.8	383.7
23	22	25	31	18	21	12	24	11
303	308	424	436	155	385	168	316	90
0	2	5	2	0	5	1	4	0
83	91	78	85	86	85	66	96	72
3301	3780	3178	3386	3521	3529	2552	4008	2796
39.8	41.5	40.7	39.8	40.9	41.5	38.7	41.8	38.8
·55	24	39	55	45	58	36	42	49
538	210	275	377	259	461	365	299	387
9.8	8.8	7.1	6.9	5.8	7.9	10.1	7.1	7.9
1	0	0	0	0	0	1	0	0
52	68	66	71	62	72	52	68	63
946	1466	1339	1333	1168	1459	958	1314	1301
18.2	21.6	20.3	18.8	18.8	20.3	18.4	19.3	20.7
0	0	0	0	0	0	0	0	0
361	316	319	267	233	374	432	241	541
47	34	38	23	27	47	51	31	63
20	17	19	9	5	15	17	9	30
23	15	14	12	22	29	27	18	29
4	2	5	2	0	3	7	4	4
42	33	37	22	24	45	51	25	62
2	2	0	1	1	1	0	0	1
11	25	18	35	15	15	25	10	33
20	33	24	42	26	28	30	24	47
55.0	75.8	75.0	83.3	57.7	53.6	83.3	41.7	70.2

NFC — TEAM-BY-TEAM SUMMARY 1983

DEFENSE

	Atl.	Chi.	Dall.	Det.	G.B.
Rushes	499	482	410	503	597
Net Yds. Gained	2309	2000	1499	2104	2641
Avg. Gain	4.6	4.1	3.7	4.2	4.4
Avg. Yds. per Game	144.3	125.0	93.7	131.5	165.1
Passes Attempted	493	490	558	515	518
Completed	313	249	299	297	300
% Completed	63.5	50.8	53.6	57.7	57.9
Total Yds. Gained	3734	3516	4365	3401	4033
Times Sacked	31	51	57	43	41
Yds. Lost	217	384	437	289	271
Net Yds. Gained	3517	3132	3928	3112	3762
Avg. Yds. per Game	219.8	195.8	245.5	194.5	235.1
Net Yds. per Pass Play	6.71	5.79	6.39	5.58	6.73
Yds. Gained per Comp	11.93	14.12	14.60	11.45	13.44
Combined Net Yds. Gained	5826	5132	5427	5216	6403
% Total Yds., Rushing	39.63	38.97	27.62	40.34	41.25
% Total Yds., Passing	60.37	61.03	72.38	59.66	58.75
Avg. Yds. per Game	364.1	320.8	339.2	326.0	400.2
Intercepted by	15	21	27	22	19
Yds. Returned by	212	215	467	185	227
Returned for TD	2	2	2	0	1
Punts	67	99	84	79	78
Yds. Punted	2812	3821	3515	3167	3052
Avg. Yds. per Punt	42.0	38.6	41.8	40.1	39.1
Punt Returns	34	44	53	39	43
Yds. Returned	179	322	588	302	384
Avg. Yds. per Return	5.3	7.3	11.1	7.7	8.9
Returned for TD	0	0	1	0	1
Kickoff Returns	60	66	78	71	78
Yds. Returned	1212	1229	1806	1146	1429
Avg. Yds. per Return	20.2	18.6	23.2	16.1	18.3
Returned for TD	0	0	0	0	0
Total Points Scored	389	301	360	286	439
Total TDs	49	36	42	33	55
TDs Rushing	20	20	12	11	28
TDs Passing	28	15	27	21	20
TDs on Ret. and Rec.	1	1	3	1	7
Extra Points	44	34	42	32	50
Safeties	0	0	0	1	1
Field Goals Made	17	17	22	18	19
Field Goals Attempted	26	23	30	26	29
% Successful	65.4	73.9	73.3	69.2	65.5

Rams	Minn.	N.O.	N.Y.G.	Phil.	St L.	S.F.	T.B.	Wash.
489	579	472	502	633	443	449	561	349
1781	2584	2000	1733	2655	1838	1936	2082	1289
3.6	4.5	4.2	3.5	4.2	4.1	4.3	3.7	3.7
111.3	161.5	125.0	108.3	165.9	114.9	121.0	130.1	80.6
556	478	496	493	430	519	526	490	570
319	263	271	283	247	290	322	300	301
57.4	55.0	54.6	57.4	57.4	55.9	61.2	61.2	52.8
3869	3229	3128	3584	3048	3635	3701	3624	4377
33	47	56	44	36	59	57	42	51
258	326	437	323	256	468	448	309	402
3611	2903	2691	3261	2792	3167	3253	3315	3975
225.7	181.4	168.2	203.8	174.5	197.9	203.3	207.2	248.4
6.13	5.53	4.88	6.07	5.99	5.48	5.58	6.23	6.40
12.13	12.28	11.54	12.66	12.34	12.53	11.49	12.08	14.54
5392	5487	4691	4994	5447	5005	5189	5397	5264
33.03	47.09	42.63	34.70	48.74	36.72	37.31	38.58	24.49
66.97	52.91	57.37	65.30	51.26	63.28	62.69	61.42	75.51
337.0	342.9	293.2	312.1	340.4	312.8	324.3	337.3	329.0
24	25	23	23	8	28	24	23	34
515	168	412	210	79	266	437	367	437
3	0	3	1	0	0	5	3	1
83	77	83	99	80	88	74	79	66
3465	3027	3473	3884	3020	3545	2993	3217	2748
41.7	39.3	41.8	39.2	37.8	40.3	40.4	40.7	41.6
39	40	51	47	57	47	38	59	41
251	297	573	283	511	307	278	603	407
6.4	7.4	11.2	6.0	9.0	6.5	7.3	10.2	9.9
0	0	2	0	0	0	0	1	1
71	70	44	67	45	66	78	50	91
1325	1392	938	1296	804	1300	1675	1039	1772
18.7	19.9	21.3	19.3	17.9	19.7	21.5	20.8	19.5
0	0	0	0	0	0	1	0	0
344	348	337	347	322	428	293	380	332
42	42	39	40	34	56	35	42	39
21	16	11	10	14	23	10	19	9
18	23	20	26	20	24	23	15	28
3	3	8	4	0	9	2	8	2
39	40	37	39	34	54	32	40	38
1	1	3	1	0	1	0	2	0
17	18	20	22	28	12	17	28	20
28	27	34	32	37	15	27	34	28
60.7	66.7	58.8	68.8	75.7	80.0	63.0	82.4	71.4

	AFC Offense Total	AFC Offense Average	AFC Defense Total	AFC Defense Average
First Downs	4376	312.6	4383	313.1
Rushing	1712	122.3	1749	124.9
Passing	2329	166.4	2291	163.6
Penalty	335	23.9	343	24.5
Rushes	7088	506.3	7243	517.4
Net Yds. Gained	28,821	2058.6	29,671	2119.4
Avg. Gain	—	4.1	—	4.1
Avg. Yds. per Game	—	128.7	—	132.5
Passes Attempted	7001	500.1	6915	493.9
Completed	3938	281.3	3939	281.4
% Completed	—	56.2	—	57.0
Total Yds. Gained	49,849	3560.6	49,678	3548.4
Times Sacked	600	42.9	567	40.5
Yds. Lost	4665	333.2	4424	316.0
Net Yds. Gained	45,184	3227.4	45,254	3232.4
Avg. Yds. per Game	—	201.7	—	202.0
Net Yds. per Pass Play	—	5.94	—	6.05
Yds. Gained per Comp.	—	12.66	—	12.61
Combined Net Yds. Gained	74,005	5286.1	74,925	5351.8
% Total Yds., Rushing	—	38.94	—	39.60
% Total Yds., Passing	—	61.06	—	60.40
Avg. Ydfs. per Game	—	330.4	—	334.5
Ball Control Plays	14,689	1049.2	14,725	1051.8
Avg. Yds. per Play	—	`5.0	—	5.1
Third Down Efficiency	—	40.0	—	39.8

SUMMARY 1983

NFC Offense Total	NFC Offense Average	NFC Defense Total	NFC Defense Average	NFL Total	NFL Average
4326	309.0	4319	308.5	8702	310.8
1695	121.1	1658	118.4	3407	121.7
2346	167.6	2384	170.3	4675	167.0
285	20.4	277	19.8	620	22.1
7123	508.8	6968	497.7	14,211	507.5
29,301	2092.9	28,451	2032.2	58,122	2075.8
—	4.1	—	4.1	—	4.1
—	130.8	—	127.0	—	129.7
7046	503.3	7132	509.4	14,047	501.7
4055	289.6	4054	289.6	7993	285.5
—	57.6	—	56.8	—	56.9
51,073	3648.1	51,244	3660.3	100,922	3604.4
615	43.9	648	46.3	1215	43.4
4584	327.4	4825	344.6	9249	330.3
46,489	3220.6	46,419	3315.6	91,673	3274.0
—	207.5	—	207.2	—	204.6
—	6.07	—	5.97	—	6.01
—	12.60	—	12.64	—	12.63
75,790	5413.6	74,870	5347.9	149,795	5349.8
—	38.66	—	38.00	—	38.80
—	61.34	—	62.00	—	61.20
—	338.3	—	334.2	—	334.4
14,784	1056.0	14,748	1053.4	29,473	1052.6
—	5.1	—	5.1	—	5.1
—	38.6	—	38.8	—	39.3

	AFC Offense Total	AFC Offense Average	AFC Defense Total	AFC Defense Average
Interceptions	304	21.7	321	22.9
Yds. Returned	4183	298.8	4474	319.6
Returned for TD	26	1.9	24	1.7
Punts	1117	79.8	1113	79.5
Yds. Punted	46,372	3312.3	45,958	3282.7
Avg. Yds. per Punt	—	41.5	—	41.3
Punt Returns	590	42.1	601	42.9
Yds. Returned	5191	370.8	5325	380.4
Avg. Yds. per Return	—	8.8	—	8.9
Returned for TD	5	0.4	6	0.4
Kickoff Returns	871	62.2	846	60.4
Yds. Returned	17,440	1245.7	16,453	1175.2
Avg. Yds. per Return	—	20.0	—	19.4
Returned for TD	3	0.2	2	0.1
Penalties	1476	105.4	1444	103.1
Yds. Penalized	12,527	894.8	12,236	874.0
Fumbles	475	33.9	473	33.8
Lost	246	17.6	244	17.4
Out of Bounds	32	2.3	30	2.1
Own Rec. for TD	1	0.1	1	0.1
Opp. Rec.	243	17.4	244	17.4
Opp. Rec. for TD	13	0.9	17	1.2
Total Points Scored	4759	339.9	4873	348.1
Total TD.	569	40.6	580	41.4
TDs Rushing	211	15.1	213	15.2
TDs Passing	308	22.0	317	22.6
TDs on Ret. and Rec.	50	3.6	50	3.6
Extra Points	538	38.4	549	39.2
Safeties	6	0.4	8	0.6
Field Goals Made	265	18.9	276	19.7
Field Goals Attempted	365	26.1	375	26.8
% Successful	—	72.6	—	73.6

NFC Offense Total	NFC Offense Average	NFC Defense Total	NFC Defense Average	NFL Total	NFL Average
316	22.6	299	21.4	620	22.1
4197	299.8	3906	279.0	8380	299.3
23	1.6	25	1.8	49	1.8
1132	80.9	1136	81.1	2249	80.3
45,325	3237.5	45,739	3267.1	91,697	3274.9
—	40.0	—	40.3	—	40.8
643	45.9	632	45.1	1233	44.0
5419	387.1	5285	377.5	10,610	378.9
—	8.4	—	8.4	—	8.6
7	0.5	6	0.4	12	0.4
910	65.0	935	66.8	1781	63.6
17,376	1241.1	18,363	1311.6	34,816	1243.4
—	19.1	—	19.6	—	19.5
0	0.0	1	0.1	3	0.1
1325	94.6	1357	96.9	2801	100.0
11,186	799.0	11,477	819.8	23,713	846.9
482	34.4	484	34.6	957	34.2
248	17.7	250	17.9	494	17.6
34	2.4	36	2.6	66	2.4
4	0.3	4	0.3	5	0.2
249	17.8	248	17.7	492	17.6
16	1.1	12	0.9	29	1.0
5020	358.6	4906	350.4	9779	349.3
595	42.5	584	41.7	1164	41.6
226	16.1	224	16.0	437	15.6
317	22.6	308	22.0	625	22.3
52	3.7	52	3.7	102	3.6
566	40.4	555	39.6	1104	39.4
13	0.9	11	0.8	19	0.7
286	20.4	275	19.6	551	19.7
406	29.0	396	28.3	771	27.5
—	70.4	—	69.4	—	71.5

CLUB LEADERS

	Offense	Defense
First Downs	S.D.361	Cin. 276
Rushing	Wash. 165	Wash.76
Passing	S.D. 230	Mia. 147
Penalty	Buff. & Den. 38	G.B. 8
Rushes	Wash. 629	Wash. 349
Net Yds. Gained	Chi. 2727	Wash. 1289
Avg. Gain	N.E. 4.8	N.Y.G. 3.5
Passes Attempted	K.C. 641	Hou. 424
Completed	K.C. & S.D. 369	Pitt. 238
%Completed	S.F. 64.2	Chi. 50.8
Total Yds. Gained	S.D. 4891	Phil. 3048
Times Sacked	Rams & Mia. 23	St L. 59
Yds. Lost	Rams & Mia. 190	Raid. 484
Net Yds. Gained	S.D. 4661	N.O. 2691
Net Yds. per Pass Play	G.B. 7.68	N.O. 4.88
Yds. Gained per Comp.	G.B. 15.07	Cin. 10.98
Combined Net Yds. Gained	S.D. 6197	Cin. 4327
%Total Yds. Rushing	Balt 53.71	Wash. 24.49
%Total Yds. Passing	K.C. 77.59	Hou. 5051
Ball Control Plays	N.Y.G. 1130	Wash. 970
Avg. Yds. per Play	G.B. 6.1	Cin. 4.4
Avg. Time of Poss.	Wash. 33.44	—
Third Down Efficiency	Atl. 48.4	N.Y.G. 30.3
Interceptions	—	Wash. 34
Yds. Returned	—	Rams 515
Returned for TD	—	S.F. 5
Punts	T.B. 96	—
Yds. Punted	Balt. 4124	—
Avg. Yds. per Punt	Balt. 45.3	—
Punt Returns	Raid. & St L. 58	Clev. 30
Yds. Returned	Raid. 666	Atl. 179
Avg. per Return	Raid. 11.5	Sea. 5.1
Returned for TD	By 12 teams 1	—
Kickoff Returns	Hou. 83	N.O. 44
Yds. Returned	Hou. 1676	Phil. 804
Avg. Yds. per Return	Mia. 23.1	Sea. 16.1
Returned for TD	Hou. 2	—
Total Points Scored	Wash. 541	Mia. 250
Total TDs	Wash. 63	N.E. 31
TDs Rushing	Wash. 30	N.E. & Wash. 9
TDs Passing	G.B. 33	Chi. & T.B. 15
TDs on Ret. and Rec.	Three with 7	Phil. 0
Extra Points	Wash. 62	N.E. 29
Safeties	Det. 3	—
Field Goals Made	N.Y.G. 35	Mia. 9
Field Goals Attempted	Wash. 47	Mia. & St L. 15
%Successful	Clev. 88.0	N.O. 58.8

CLUB RANKINGS BY YARDS

Team	OFFENSE			DEFENSE		
	Total	Rush	Pass	Total	Rush	Pass
Atlanta	8	11	11	25	22	20
Baltimore	21	2	28	23	17	21
Buffalo	25	24	18	24	24	18
Chicago	6	1	17	8	11t	12
Cincinnati	14	16	14	1	2t	3
Cleveland	10	19	6	9	14	9
Dallas	5	15	4	17	2t	27
Denver	26	23	20	21	10	23
Detroit	18	12	22	11	16	11
Green Bay	2	21	2	28	26	24
Houston	24	18	23	22	28	4
Kansas City	9	28	3	14	20	10
Los Angeles Raiders	7	10	9	4	4	13
Los Angeles Rams	12	9	12	15	6	22
Miami	16	13	19	7	13	8
Minnesota	20	20	13	19	25	6
New England	13	5	25	20	21	17
New Orleans	23	6	26	2	11t	1
New York Giants	15	22	8	5	5	16
New York Jets	11	17	10	13	23	7
Philadelphia	27	26	16	18	27	2
Pittsburgh	22	4	27	3	7	5
St Louis	17	7	24	6	8	14
San Diego	1	25	1	26	18	25
San Francisco	4	8	5	10	9	15
Seattle	19	14	21	27	19	26
Tampa Bay	28	27	15	16	15	19
Washington	3	3	7	12	1	28

t = Tie for position

SUPER BOWL RECORDS
RESULTS

Game	Date	Winner	Loser	Site	Attendance
XVIII	1-22-84	L.A. Raiders (AFC) 38	Washington (NFC) 9	Tampa	72,920
XVII	1-30-83	Washington (NFC) 27	Miami (AFC) 17	Pasadena	103,667
XVI	1-24-82	San Francisco (NFC) 26	Cincinnati (AFC) 21	Pontiac	81,270
XV	1-25-81	Oakland (AFC) 27	Philadelphia (NFC) 10	New Orleans	76,135
XIV	1-20-80	Pittsburgh (AFC) 31	Los Angeles (NFC) 19	Pasadena	103,985
XIII	1-21-79	Pittsburgh (AFC) 35	Dallas (NFC) 31	Miami	79,484
XII	1-15-78	Dallas (NFC) 27	Denver (AFC) 10	New Orleans	75,583
XI	1-9-77	Oakland (AFC) 32	Minnesota (NFC) 14	Pasadena	103,438
X	1-18-76	Pittsburgh (AFC) 21	Dallas (NFC) 17	Miami	80,187
IX	1-12-75	Pittsburgh (AFC) 16	Minnesota (NFC) 6	New Orleans	80,997
VIII	1-13-74	Miami (AFC) 24	Minnesota (NFC) 7	Houston	71,882
VII	1-14-73	Miami (AFC) 14	Washington (NFC) 7	Los Angeles	90,182
VI	1-16-72	Dallas (NFC) 24	Miami (AFC) 3	New Orleans	81,023
V	1-17-71	Baltimore (AFC) 16	Dallas (NFC) 13	Miami	79,204
IV	1-11-70	Kansas City (AFL) 23	Minnesota (NFL) 7	New Orleans	80,562
III	1-12-69	New York (AFL) 16	Baltimore (NFL) 7	Miami	75,389
II	1-14-68	Green Bay (NFL) 33	Oakland (AFL) 14	Miami	75,546
I	1-15-67	Green Bay (NFL) 35	Kansas City (AFL) 10	Los Angeles	61,946

SUPER BOWL COMPOSITE STANDINGS

	W	L	Pct	Pts	OP
Pittsburgh Steelers	4	0	1.000	103	73
Green Bay Packers	2	0	1.000	68	24
New York Jets	1	0	1.000	16	7
San Francisco 49ers	1	0	1.000	26	21
L.A./Oakland Raiders	3	1	.750	111	66
Baltimore Colts	1	1	.500	23	29
Kansas City Chiefs	1	1	.500	33	42
Miami Dolphins	2	2	.500	58	65
Dallas Cowboys	2	3	.400	112	85
Washington Redskins	1	2	.333	43	69
Cincinnati Bengals	0	1	.000	21	26
Denver Broncos	0	1	.000	10	27
Los Angeles Rams	0	1	.000	19	31
Philadelphia Eagles	0	1	.000	10	27
Minnesota Vikings	0	4	.000	34	95

SUPER BOWL RECORDS

1967: Super Bowl I	1973: Super Bowl VII	1979: Super Bowl XIII
1968: Super Bowl II	1974: Super Bowl VIII	1980: Super Bowl XIV
1969: Super Bowl III	1975: Super Bowl IX	1981: Super Bowl XV
1970: Super Bowl IV	1976: Super Bowl X	1982: Super Bowl XVI
1971: Super Bowl V	1977: Super Bowl XI	1983: Super Bowl XVII
1972: Super Bowl VI	1978: Super Bowl XII	1984: Super Bowl XVIII

INDIVIDUAL RECORDS

SERVICE

Most Games
5   Marv Fleming, Green Bay, 1967-68; Miami, 1972-74
     Larry Cole, Dallas, 1971-72, 1976, 1978-79
     Cliff Harris, Dallas, 1971-72, 1976, 1978-79
     D.D. Lewis, Dallas, 1971-72, 1976, 1978-79
     Preston Pearson, Baltimore, 1969; Pittsburgh, 1975; Dallas, 1976, 1978-79
     Charlie Waters, Dallas, 1971-72, 1976, 1978-79
     Rayfield Wright, Dallas, 1971-72, 1976, 1978-79
4   By many players

Most Games, Coach
5   Tom Landry, Dallas, 1971-72, 1976, 1978-79
     Don Shula, Baltimore, 1969; Miami, 1972-74, 1983
4   Bud Grant, Minnesota, 1970, 1974-75, 1977
     Chuck Noll, Pittsburgh, 1975-76, 1979-80

Most Games, Winning Team, Coach,
4   Chuck Noll, Pittsburgh, 1975-76, 1979-80
2   Vince Lombardi, Green Bay, 1967-68
     Tom Landry, Dallas, 1972, 1978
     Don Shula, Miami, 1973-74

SCORING

POINTS
Most Points, Career
24   Franco Harris, Pittsburgh, 4 games (4-td)
20   Don Chandler, Green Bay, 2 Games (8-pat, 4-fg)

Most Points, Game
15   Don Chandler, Green Bay vs. Oakland, 1968 (3-pat, 4-fg)

TOUCHDOWNS
Most Points, Game
4   Franco Harris, Pittsburgh, 4 games (4-r)
3   John Stallworth, Pittsburgh, 4 games (3-p)
     Lynn Swann, Pittsburgh, 4 games (3-p)

Most Touchdowns, Game
2   Max McGee, Green Bay vs. Kansas City, 1967 (2-p)
      Elijah Pitts, Green Bay vs. Kansas City, 1967 (2-r)
      Bill Miller, Oakland vs. Green Bay, 1968 (2-p)
      Larry Csonka, Miami vs. Minnesota, 1974 (2-r)
      Pete Banaszak, Oakland vs. Minnesota, 1977 (2-r)
      John Stallworth, Pittsburgh vs. Dallas, 1979 (2-p)
      Franco Harris, Pittsburgh vs. Los Angeles, 1980 (2-r)
      Cliff Branch, Oakland vs. Philadelphia, 1981 (2-p)
      Dan Ross, Cincinnati vs. San Francisco, 1982 (2-p)

FIELD GOALS

Field Goals, Attempted, Career
7   Roy Gerela, Pittsburgh, 3 games
6   Jim Turner, N.Y. Jets-Denver, 2 games

Most Field Goals, Attempted, Game
5   Jim Turner, N.Y. Jets vs. Baltimore, 1969
      Efren Herrera, Dallas vs. Denver, 1978

Most Field Goals, Career
4   Don Chandler, Green Bay, 2 games (4 att)
      Jim Turner, N.Y. Jets-Denver, 2 games (6 att)
      Ray Wersching, San Francisco, 1 game (4 att)
3   Mike Clark, Dallas, 2 games (3 att)
      Jan Stenerud, Kansas City, 1 game (3 att)

Most Field Goals, Game
4   Don Chandler, Green Bay vs. Oakland, 1968
      Ray Wersching, San Francisco vs. Cincinnati, 1982

Longest Field Goal
48   Jan Stenerud, Kansas City vs. Minnesota, 1970

RUSHING

ATTEMPTS

Most Attempts, Career
101   Franco Harris, Pittsburgh, 4 games
57   Larry Csonka, Miami, 3 games

Most Attempts, Game
38   John Riggins, Washington vs. Miami, 1983

YARDS GAINED

Most Yards Gained, Career
354   Franco Harris, Pittsburgh, 4 games
297   Larry Csonka, Miami, 3 games

Most Yards Gained, Game
191   Marcus Allen, L.A. Raiders vs. Washington, 1984

Longest Run From Scrimmage
74   Marcus Allen, L.A. Raiders vs. Washington, 1984

PASSING

ATTEMPTS
Most Passes Attempted, Career
98	Roger Staubach, Dallas, 4 games	
89	Fran Tarkenton, Minnesota, 3 games	

Most Passes Attempted, Game
38   Ron Jaworski, Philadelphia vs. Oakland, 1981

COMPLETIONS
Most Passes Completed, Career
61   Roger Staubach, Dallas, 4 games
49   Terry Bradshaw, Pittsburgh, 4 games

Most Passes Completed, Game
25   Ken Anderson, Cincinnati vs. San Francisco, 1982

Most Consecutive Completions, Game
8   Len Dawson, Kansas City vs. Green Bay, 1967
    Joe Theismann, Washington vs. Miami, 1983

YARDS GAINED
Most Yards Gained, Career
932   Terry Bradshaw, Pittsburgh, 4 games
734   Roger Staubach, Dallas, 4 games

Most Yards Gained, Game
318   Terry Bradshaw, Pittsburgh vs. Dallas, 1979

Longest Pass Completion
80   Jim Plunkett (to King), Oakland vs. Philadelphia, 1981 (TD)

TOUCHDOWNS
Most Touchdown Passes, Career
9   Terry Bradshaw, Pittsburgh, 4 games
8   Roger Staubach, Dallas, 4 games

Most Touchdown Passes, Game
4   Terry Bradshaw, Pittsburgh vs. Dallas, 1979

HAD INTERCEPTED
Lowest Percentage, Passes Had Intercepted, Career (40 attempts)
0.00   Jim Plunkett, L.A. Raiders, 2 games (46-0)
2.13   Bart Starr, Green Bay, 2 games (47-1)
4.08   Roger Staubach, Dallas, 4 games (98-4)

PASS RECEIVING

RECEPTIONS
Most Receptions, Career
16   Lynn Swann, Pittsburgh, 4 games
15   Chuck Foreman, Minnesota, 3 games

Most Receptions, Game
11   Dan Ross, Cincinnati vs. San Francisco, 1982

YARDS GAINED

Most Yards Gained, Career
364   Lynn Swann, Pittsburgh, 4 games
268   John Stallworth, Pittsburgh, 4 games

Most Yards Gained, Game
161   Lynn Swann, Pittsburgh vs. Dallas, 1976

Longest Reception
80   Kenny King (from Plunkett), Oakland vs. Philadelphia, 1981 (TD)

INTERCEPTIONS BY

Most Interceptions By, Career
3   Chuck Howley, Dallas, 2 games
      Rod Martin, Oakland, 1 game
2   Randy Beverly, N.Y. Jets, 1 game
      Jake Scott, Miami, 3 games
      Mike Wagner, Pittsburgh, 3 games
      Mel Blount, Pittsburgh, 4 games

Most Interceptions By, Game
3   Rod Martin, Oakland vs. Philadelphia, 1981

Longest Return
75   Willie Brown, Oakland vs. Minnesota, 1977 (TD)

PUNTING

Most Punts, Game
9   Ron Widby, Dallas vs. Baltimore, 1971

Longest Punt
61   Jerrel Wilson, Kansas City vs. Green Bay, 1967

PUNT RETURNS

Most Punt Returns, Career
6   Willie Wood, Green Bay, 2 games
      Jake Scott, Miami, 3 games
      Theo Bell, Pittsburgh, 2 games
      Mike Nelms, Washington, 1 game
4   By seven players

Most Punt Returns, Game
6   Mike Nelms, Washington vs. Miami, 1983

YARDS GAINED
Most Yards Gained, Career
52   Mike Nelms, Washington, 1 game
45   Jake Scott, Miami, 3 games

Most Yards Gained, Game
52   Mike Nelms, Washington vs. Miami, 1983

Longest Return
34   Darrell Green, Washington vs. L.A. Raiders, 1984

KICKOFF RETURNS

Most Kickoff Returns, Career
8   Larry Anderson, Pittsburgh, 2 games
7   Preston Pearson, Baltimore-Pittsburgh-Dallas, 5 games

Most Kickoff Returns, Game
5   Larry Anderson, Pittsburgh vs. Los Angeles, 1980
      Billy Campfield, Philadelphia vs. Oakland, 1981
      David Verser, Cincinnati vs. San Francisco, 1982

YARDS GAINED
Most Yards Gained, Career
207   Larry Anderson, Pittsburgh, 2 games
190   Fulton Walker, Miami, 1 game

Most Yards Gained, Game
190   Fulton Walker, Miami vs. Washington, 1983

Longest Return
98   Fulton Walker, Miami vs. Washington, 1983 (TD)

COMBINED NET YARDS GAINED

ATTEMPTS
Most Attempts, Career
108   Franco Harris, Pittsburgh, 4 games
60   Larry Csonka, Miami, 3 games

Most Attempts, Game
39   John Riggins, Washington vs. Miami, 1983

YARDS GAINED
Most Yards Gained, Career
468   Franco Harris, Pittsburgh, 4 games
391   Lynn Swann, Pittsburgh, 4 games

Most Yards Gained, Game
209   Marcus Allen, L.A. Raiders vs. Washington, 1984

TEAM RECORDS

GAMES, VICTORIES, DEFEATS

Most Games
5   Dallas, 1971-72, 1976, 1978-79

Most Games Won
4   Pittsburgh, 1975-76, 1979-80

Most Games Lost
4   Minnesota, 1970, 1974-75, 1977

SCORING

Most Points, Game
38   L.A. Raiders vs. Washington, 1984

Fewest Points, Game
3   Miami vs. Dallas, 1972

Most Points, Both Teams, Game
66   Pittsburgh (35) vs. Dallas (31), 1979

Fewest Points, Both Teams, Game
21   Washington (7) vs. Miami (14), 1973

TOUCHDOWNS
Most Touchdowns, Game
5   Green Bay vs. Kansas City, 1967
      Pittsburgh vs. Dallas, 1979

Fewest Touchdowns, Game
0   Miami vs. Dallas, 1972

Most Touchdowns, Both Teams, Game
9   Pittsburgh (5) vs. Dallas (4), 1979

Fewest Touchdowns, Both Teams, Game
2   Baltimore (1) vs. N.Y. Jets (1), 1969

FIELD GOALS
Most Field Goals Attempted, Game
5   N.Y. Jets vs. Baltimore, 1969
      Dallas vs. Denver, 1978

Most Field Goals Attempted, Both Teams, Game
7   N.Y. Jets (5) vs. Baltimore (2), 1969

Fewest Field Goals Attempted, Both Teams, Game
1   Minnesota (0) vs. Miami (1), 1974

Most Field Goals, Game
4   Green Bay vs. Oakland, 1968
      San Francisco vs. Cincinnati, 1982

Most Field Goals, Both Teams, Game
4   Green Bay (4) vs. Oakland (0), 1968
      San Francisco (4) vs. Cincinnati (0), 1982

Fewest Field Goals, Both Teams, Game
0   Miami vs. Washington, 1973
      Pittsburgh vs. Minnesota, 1975

NET YARDS GAINED RUSHING AND PASSING

Most Yards Gained, Game
429   Oakland vs. Minnesota, 1977

Fewest Yards Gained, Game
119   Minnesota vs. Pittsburgh, 1975

Most Yards Gained, Both Teams, Game
782   Oakland (429) vs. Minnesota (353), 1977

Fewest Yards Gained, Both Teams, Game
452   Minnesota (119) vs. Pittsburgh (333), 1975

RUSHING

ATTEMPTS
Most Attempts, Game
57   Pittsburgh vs. Minnesota, 1975

Fewest Attempts, Game
19   Kansas City vs. Green Bay, 1967
      Minnesota vs. Kansas City, 1970

Most Attempts, Both Teams, Game
81   Washington (52) vs. Miami (29), 1983

Fewest Attempts, Both Teams, Game
52   Kansas City (19) vs. Green Bay (33), 1967

YARDS GAINED
Most Yards Gained, Game
276   Washington vs. Miami, 1983

Fewest Yards Gained, Game
17   Minnesota vs. Pittsburgh, 1975

Most Yards Gained, Both Teams, Game
372   Washington (276) vs. Miami (96), 1983

Fewest Yards Gained, Both Teams, Game
171   Baltimore (69) vs. Dallas (102), 1971

PASSING

ATTEMPTS
Most Passes Attempted, Game
44   Minnesota vs. Oakland, 1977

Fewest Passes Attempted, Game
7   Miami vs. Minnesota, 1974

Most Passes Attempted, Both Teams, Game
70   Baltimore (41) vs. N.Y. Jets (29), 1969

Fewest Passes Attempted, Both Teams, Game
35   Miami (7) vs. Minnesota (28), 1974

COMPLETIONS
Most Passes Completed, Game
25   Cincinnati vs. San Francisco, 1982

Fewest Passes Completed, Game
4   Miami vs. Washington, 1983

Most Passes Completed, Both Teams, Game
39   Cincinnati (25) vs. San Francisco (14), 1982

Fewest Passes Completed, Both Teams, Game
19   Miami (4) vs. Washington (15), 1983

YARDS GAINED
Most Yards Gained, Game
309   Pittsburgh vs. Los Angeles, 1980

Fewest Yards Gained, Game
35   Denver vs. Dallas, 1978

Most Yards Gained, Both Teams, Game
551   Philadelphia (291) vs. Oakland (260), 1981

Fewest Yards Gained, Both Teams, Game
156   Miami (69) vs. Washington (87), 1973

TIMES SACKED
Most Times Sacked, Game
7   Dallas vs. Pittsburgh, 1976

Fewest Times Sacked, Game
0   Baltimore vs. N.Y. Jets, 1969; vs. Dallas, 1971
    Minnesota vs. Pittsburgh, 1975
    Pittsburgh vs. Los Angeles, 1980
    Philadelphia vs. Oakland, 1981

Most Times Sacked, Both Teams, Game
9   Kansas City (6) vs. Green Bay (3), 1967
    Dallas (7) vs. Pittsburgh (2), 1976
    Dallas (5) vs. Denver (4), 1978
    Dallas (5) vs. Pittsburgh (4), 1979

Fewest Times Sacked, Both Teams, Game
1   Philadelphia (0) vs. Oakland (1), 1981

INTERCEPTIONS BY

Most Interceptions By, Game
4   N.Y. Jets vs. Baltimore, 1969
    Dallas vs. Denver, 1978

Most Interceptions By, Both Teams, Game
6   Baltimore (3) vs. Dallas (3), 1971

PUNTING

Most Punts, Game
9   Dallas vs. Baltimore, 1971

Fewest Punts, Game
2   Pittsburgh vs. Los Angeles, 1980

Most Punts, Both Teams, Game
15   Washington (8) vs. L.A. Raiders (7), 1984

Fewest Punts, Both Teams, Game
6   Oakland (3) vs. Philadelphia (3), 1981

PUNT RETURNS

Most Punt Returns, Game
6   Washington vs. Miami, 1983

Fewest Punt Returns, Game
0   Minnesota vs. Miami, 1974

Most Punt Returns, Both Teams, Game
9   Pittsburgh (5) vs. Minnesota (4), 1975

Fewest Punt Returns, Both Teams, Game
2   Dallas (1) vs. Miami (1), 1972

YARDS GAINED
Most Yards Gained, Game
52   Washington vs. Miami, 1983

Fewest Yards Gained, Game
−1   Dallas vs. Miami, 1972

Most Yards Gained, Both Teams, Game
74   Washington (52) vs. Miami (22), 1983

Fewest Yards Gained, Both Teams, Game
13   Miami (4) vs. Washington (9), 1973

KICKOFF RETURNS

Most Kickoff Returns, Game
7   Oakland vs. Green Bay, 1968
      Minnesota vs. Oakland, 1977
      Cincinnati vs. San Francisco, 1982

Fewest Kickoff Returns, Game
1   N.Y. Jets vs. Baltimore, 1969

Most Kickoff Returns, Both Teams, Game
11   Los Angeles (6) vs. Pittsburgh (5), 1980

Fewest Kickoff Returns, Both Teams, Game
5   N.Y. Jets (1) vs. Baltimore (4), 1969
      Miami (2) vs. Washington (3), 1973

YARDS GAINED
Most Yards Gained, Game
222   Miami vs. Washington, 1983

Fewest Yards Gained, Game
25   N.Y. Jets vs. Baltimore, 1969

Most Yards Gained, Both Teams, Game
279   Miami (222) vs. Washington (57), 1983

Fewest Yards Gained, Both Teams, Game
78   Miami (33) vs. Washington (45), 1973

AFC-NFC Pro Bowl Results — NFC leads series 9-5

Year	Date	Winner	Loser	Site	Attendance
1984	Jan. 29	NFC 45	AFC 3	Honolulu	50,445
1983	Feb. 6	NFC 20	AFC 19	Honolulu	47,201
1982	Jan. 31	AFC 16	NFC 13	Honolulu	49,521
1981	Feb. 1	NFC 21	AFC 7	Honolulu	47,879
1980	Jan. 27	NFC 37	AFC 27	Honolulu	48,060
1979	Jan. 29	NFC 13	AFC 7	Los Angeles	46,281
1978	Jan. 23	NFC 14	AFC 13	Tampa	51,337
1977	Jan. 17	AFC 24	NFC 14	Seattle	64,151
1976	Jan. 26	NFC 23	AFC 20	New Orleans	30,546
1975	Jan. 20	NFC 17	AFC 10	Miami	26,484
1974	Jan. 20	AFC 15	NFC 13	Kansas City	66,918
1973	Jan. 21	AFC 33	NFC 28	Dallas	37,091
1972	Jan. 23	AFC 26	NFC 13	Los Angeles	53,647
1971	Jan. 24	NFC 27	AFC 6	Los Angeles	48,222

NUMBER – ONE DRAFT CHOICES

Season	Team	Player	Position	College
1984	New England	Irving Fryar	WR	Nebraska
1983	Baltimore	John Elway	QB	Stanford
1982	New England	Kenneth Sims	DT	Texas
1981	New Orleans	George Rogers	RB	South Carolina
1980	Detroit	Billy Sims	RB	Oklahoma
1979	Buffalo	Tom Cousineau	LB	Ohio State
1978	Houston	Earl Campbell	RB	Texas
1977	Tampa Bay	Ricky Bell	RB	So. Carolina
1976	Tampa Bay	Lee Roy Selmon	DE	Oklahoma
1975	Atlanta	Steve Bartkowski	QB	California
1974	Dallas	Ed Jones	DE	Tennessee State
1973	Houston	John Matuszak	DE	Tampa
1972	Buffalo	Walt Patulski	DE	Notre Dame
1971	New England	Jim Plunkett	QB	Stanford
1970	Pittsburgh	Terry Bradshaw	QB	Louisiana Tech
1969	Buffalo (AFL)	O.J. Simpson	RB	So. California
1968	Minnesota	Ron Yary	T	So. California
1967	Baltimore	Bubba Smith	DT	Michigan State
1966	Atlanta	Tommy Nobis	LB	Texas
	Miami (AFL)	Jim Grabowski	RB	Illinois
1965	N.Y. Giants	Tucker Frederickson	RB	Auburn
	Houston (AFL)	Lawrence Elkins	E	Baylor
1964	San Francisco	Dave Parks	E	Texas Tech
	Boston (AFL)	Jack Concannon	QB	Boston College
1963	Los Angeles Rams	Terry Baker	QB	Oregon State
	Kansas City (AFL)	Buck Buchanan	DT	Grambling

Season	Team	Player	Position	College
1962	Washington	Ernie Davis	RB	Syracuse
	Oakland (AFL)	Roman Gabriel	QB	N. Carolina State
1961	Minnesota	Tommy Mason	RB	Tulane
	Buffalo (AFL)	Ken Rice	G	Auburn
1960	Los Angeles Rams	Billy Cannon	RB	LSU
	(AFL had no formal first pick)			
1959	Green Bay	Randy Duncan	QB	Iowa
1958	Chi. Cardinals	King Hill	QB	Rice
1957	Green Bay	Paul Hornung	HB	Notre Dame
1956	Pittsburgh	Gary Glick	DB	Colorado A&M
1955	Baltimore	George Shaw	QB	Oregon
1954	Cleveland	Bobby Garrett	QB	Stanford
1953	San Francisco	Harry Babcock	E	Georgia
1952	Los Angeles Rams	Bill Wade	QB	Vanderbilt
1951	N.Y. Giants	Kyle Rote	HB	SMU
1950	Detroit	Leon Hart	E	Notre Dame
1949	Philadelphia	Chuck Bednarik	C	Pennsylvania
1948	Washington	Harry Gilmer	QB	Alabama
1947	Chi. Bears	Bob Fenimore	HB	Oklahoma A&M
1946	Boston	Frank Dancewicz	QB	Notre Dame
1945	Chi. Cardinals	Charley Trippi	HB	Georgia
1944	Boston	Angelo Bertelli	QB	Notre Dame
1943	Detroit	Frank Sinkwich	HB	Georgia
1942	Pittsburgh	Bill Dudley	HB	Virginia
1941	Chi. Bears	Tom Harmon	HB	Michigan
1940	Chi. Cardinals	George Cafego	HB	Tennessee
1939	Chi. Cardinals	Ki Aldrich	C	TCU
1938	Cleveland	Corbett Davis	FB	Indiana
1937	Philadelphia	Sam Francis	FB	Nebraska
1936	Philadelphia	Jay Berwanger	HB	Chicago

1984 COLLEGIATE DRAFT

ROUND 1

No.	Team	Name	Pos.	College
1	NEW ENGLAND from Tampa Bay through Cincinnati	Fryar, Irving	WR	Nebraska
2	HOUSTON	Steinkuhler, Dean	T	Nebraska
3	N.Y. GIANTS	Banks, Carl	LB	Michigan State
4	PHILADELPHIA	Jackson, Kenny	WR	Penn State
5	KANSAS CITY	Maas, Bill	DT	Pittsburgh
6	SAN DIEGO	Cade, Mossy	DB	Texas
7	CINCINNATI	Hunley, Ricky	LB	Arizona
8	COLTS	Coleman, Leonard	DB	Vanderbilt
9	ATLANTA	Bryan, Rick	DT	Oklahoma
10	N.Y. JETS	Carter, Russell	DB	Southern Methodist
11	CHICAGO	Marshall, Wilber	LB	Florida
12	GREEN BAY	Carreker, Alphonso	DE	Florida State
13	MINNESOTA	Millard, Keith	DE	Washington State
14	MIAMI from Buffalo	Shipp, Jackie	LB	Oklahoma
15	N.Y. JETS from New Orleans	Faurot, Ron	DE	Arkansas
16	CINCINNATI from New England	Koch, Pete	DE	Maryland
17	ST. LOUIS	Duncan, Clyde	WR	Tennessee
18	CLEVELAND	Rogers, Don	DB	UCLA
19	COLTS from Denver	Solt, Ron	G	Maryland
20	DETROIT	Lewis, David	TE	California
21	KANSAS CITY from L.A. Rams	Alt, John	T	Iowa
22	SEATTLE	Taylor, Terry	DB	Southern Illinois
23	PITTSBURGH	Lipps, Louis	WR	So. Mississippi
24	SAN FRANCISCO	Shell, Todd	LB	Brigham Young
25	DALLAS	Cannon, Billy Jr.	LB	Texas A&M
26	BUFFALO from Miami	Bell, Greg	RB	Notre Dame
27	N.Y. GIANTS from Washington	Roberts, Bill	T	Ohio State
28	CINCINNATI from L.A. Raiders through New England	Blados, Brian	T	North Carolina

ROUND 2

No.	Team	Name	Pos.	College
1	HOUSTON	Smith, Doug	DE	Auburn
2	TAMPA BAY	Browner, Keith	LB	Southern California
3	WASHINGTON from N.Y. Giants	Slater, Bob	DT	Oklahoma
4	ATLANTA from Philadelphia	Case, Scott	DB	Oklahoma
5	SAN DIEGO	Guendling, Mike	LB	Northwestern
6	KANSAS CITY	Radecic, Scott	LB	Penn State
7	COLTS	Winter, Blaise	DT	Syracuse
8	ATLANTA	Benson, Thomas	LB	Oklahoma
9	N.Y. JETS	Sweeney, Jim	C	Pittsburgh
10	CINCINNATI	Esiason, Boomer	QB	Maryland
11	N.Y. JETS from Green Bay through San Diego	Dennison, Glenn	TE	Miami
12	DALLAS from Minnesota through Houston	Scott, Victor	DB	Colorado

No.	Team	Name	Pos.	College
13	BUFFALO	Richardson, Eric	WR	San Jose State
14	NEW ORLEANS	Geathers, James	DE	Wichita State
15	NEW ENGLAND	Williams, Ed	LB	Texas
16	CHICAGO	Rivera, Ron	LB	California
17	ST LOUIS	Dawson, Doug	G	Texas
18	DENVER	Townsend, Andre	DE	Mississippi
19	DETROIT	Mandley, Pete	WR	Northern Arizona
20	CLEVELAND from L.A. Rams	Rockins, Chris	DB	Oklahoma State
21	SEATTLE	Turner, Daryl	WR	Michigan State
22	CLEVELAND	Davis, Bruce	WR	Baylor
23	L.A. RAIDERS from San Francisco	Jones, Sean	DE	Northeastern
24	PITTSBURGH	Kolodziejski, Chris	TE	Wyoming
25	MIAMI	Brophy, Jay	LB	Miami
26	HOUSTON from Dallas	Eason, Bo	DB	Cal-Davis
27	WASHINGTON	Hamilton, Steve	DE	East Carolina
28	SAN FRANCISCO from L.A. Raiders	Frank, John	TE	Ohio State

ROUND 3

No.	Team	Name	Pos.	College
1	TAMPA BAY	Acorn, Fred	DB	Texas
2	HOUSTON	Meads, Johnny	LB	Nicholls State
3	N.Y. GIANTS	Hostetler, Jeff	QB	West Virginia
4	PHILADELPHIA	Russell, Rusty	T	South Carolina
5	KANSAS CITY	Heard, Herman	RB	Southern Colorado
6	DETROIT from San Diego through St. Louis	Williams, Eric	DT	Washington State
7	ATLANTA	McSwain, Rod	DB	Clemson
8	N.Y. JETS	Clifton, Kyle	LB	Texas Christian
9	CINCINNATI	Jennings, Stanford	RB	Furman
10	COLTS	Scott, Chris	DT	Purdue
11	MINNESOTA	Anderson, Alfred	RB	Baylor
12	NEW ORLEANS from Buffalo	Hoage, Terry	DB	Georgia
13	NEW ORLEANS	Anthony, Tyrone	RB	North Carolina
14	NEW ENGLAND	Williams, Jon	RB	Penn State
15	CHICAGO	Humphries, Stefan	G	Michigan
16	GREEN BAY	Humphrey, Donnie	DT	Auburn
17	SAN FRANCISCO from St. Louis	McIntyre, Guy	G	Georgia
18	DETROIT	Anderson, Ernest	RB	Oklahoma State
19	DETROIT from L.A. Rams	Baack, Steve	DE	Oregon
20	SEATTLE	Young, Fred	LB	New Mexico State
21	BUFFALO from Cleveland	Bellinger, Rodney	DB	Miami
22	DENVER	Lilly, Tony	DB	Florida
23	BUFFALO from Pittsburgh through Miami	McNanie, Sean	DE	San Diego State
24	ST LOUIS from San Francisco	McIvor, Rick	QB	Texas
25	DALLAS	Cornwell, Fred	TE	Southern California
26	BUFFALO from Miami	Neal, Speedy	RB	Miami
27	WASHINGTON	Schroeder, Jay	QB	UCLA
28	L.A. RAIDERS	McCall, Joe	RB	Pittsburgh

1984 Collegiate Draft *continued*
ROUND 4

No.	Team	Name	Pos.	College
1	HOUSTON	Studaway, Mark	DE	Tennessee
2	SEATTLE from Tampa Bay through San Francisco	Hagood, Rickey	DT	South Carolina
3	N.Y. GIANTS	Goode, Conrad	T	Missouri
4	PHILADELPHIA	Cooper, Evan	DB	Michigan
5	DENVER from San Diego through Tampa Bay	Robbins, Randy	DB	Arizona
6	KANSAS CITY	Robinson, Mark	DB	Penn State
7	N.Y. JETS	Bell, Bobby	LB	Missouri
8	CINCINNATI	Farley, John	RB	Cal State-Sacramento
9	COLTS	Curry, Craig	DB	Texas
10	ATLANTA	Malancon, Rydell	LB	Louisiana State
11	BUFFALO	Brookins, Mitchell	WR	Illinois
12	CLEVELAND from New Orleans through Denver	Bolden, Rickey	TE	Southern Methodist
13	NEW ORLEANS from New England	Hilgenberg, Joel	C	Iowa
14	CHICAGO	Andrews, Tom	G	Louisville
15	GREEN BAY	Dorsey, John	LB	Connecticut
16	HOUSTON from Minnesota	Allen, Patrick	DB	Utah State
17	ST. LOUIS	Bayless, Martin	DB	Bowling Green
18	WASHINGTON from L.A. Rams through Houston	Smith, Jimmy	RB	Elon
19	COLTS from Seattle	Wonsley, George	RB	Mississippi State
20	CLEVELAND	Brennan, Brian	WR	Boston College
21	N.Y. GIANTS from Denver	Reasons, Gary	LB	N.W. Louisiana
22	DETROIT	D'Addio, Dave	RB	Maryland
23	TAMPA BAY from San Francisco through San Diego	Gunter, Michael	RB	Tulsa
24	PITTSBURGH	Thompson, Weegie	WR	Florida State
25	MIAMI	Carter, Joe	RB	Alabama
26	DALLAS	DeOssie, Steve	LB	Boston College
27	PITTSBURGH from Washington	Long, Terry	G	East Carolina
28	TAMPA BAY from L.A. Raiders	Heller, Ron	T	Penn State

ROUND 5

No.	Team	Name	Pos.	College
1	DALLAS from Tampa Bay	Pelluer, Steve	QB	Washington
2	HOUSTON	Lyles, Robert	LB	Texas Christian
3	N.Y. GIANTS	Harris, Clint	DB	East Carolina
4	PHILADELPHIA	Hardy, Andre	RB	St. Mary's, California
5	KANSAS CITY	Holle, Eric	DE	Texas
6	SAN DIEGO	James, Lionel	KR	Auburn
7	CINCINNATI	Bussey, Barney	DB	South Carolina State
8	COLTS	Tate, Golden	WR	Tennessee State
9	SAN FRANCISCO from Atlanta	Carter, Michael	DT	Southern Methodist
10	N.Y. JETS	Armstrong, Tron	WR	Eastern Kentucky
11	NEW ORLEANS	Fields, Jitter	DB	Texas
12	NEW ENGLAND	Fairchild, Paul	G	Kansas
13	WASHINGTON from Chicago through San Diego, Seattle & N.Y. Giants	Pegues, Jeff	LB	East Carolina

234

No.	Team	Name	Pos.	College
14	GREEN BAY	Flynn, Tom	DB	Pittsburgh
15	L.A. RAIDERS from Minnesota	Parker, Andy	TE	Utah
16	BUFFALO	Kidd, John	P	Northwestern
17	ST LOUIS	Leiding, Jeff	LB	Texas
18	COLTS from Seattle	Call, Kevin	T	Colorado State
19	CLEVELAND	Piepkorn, Dave	T	North Dakota State
20	ATLANTA from Denver through San Francisco	Benson, Cliff	TE	Purdue
21	L.A. RAMS from Detroit	Stephens, Hal	DE	East Carolina
22	KANSAS CITY from L.A. Rams	Paine, Jeff	LB	Texas A&M
23	PITTSBURGH	Hughes, Van	DT	S.W. Texas State
24	ST LOUIS from San Francisco	Goode, John	TE	Youngstown
25	DALLAS	Granger, Norm	RB	Iowa
26	MIAMI	May, Dean	QB	Louisville
27	SAN FRANCISCO from Washington through L.A. Raiders	Fuller, Jeff	LB	Texas A&M
28	MINNESOTA from L.A. Raiders	Rice, Allen	RB	Baylor

ROUND 6

No.	Team	Name	Pos.	College
1	HOUSTON	Grimsley, John	LB	Kentucky
2	TAMPA BAY	Washington, Chris	LB	Iowa State
3	N.Y. GIANTS	Scott, Jim	DE	Clemson
4	PHILADELPHIA	Raridon, Scott	T	Nebraska
5	SAN DIEGO	Guthrie, Keith	DT	Texas A&M
6	KANSAS CITY	Stevens, Rufus	WR	Grambling
7	COLTS	Beverly, Dwight	RB	Illinois
8	ATLANTA	Bennett, Ben	QB	Duke
9	N.Y. JETS	Paige, Tony	RB	Virginia Tech
10	CINCINNATI	Kern, Don	TE	Arizona State
11	NEW ENGLAND	Gibson, Ernest	DB	Furman
12	DALLAS from Chicago	Lockhart, Eugene	LB	Houston
13	GREEN BAY	Wright, Randy	QB	Wisconsin
14	MINNESOTA	Collins, Dwight	WR	Pittsburgh
15	BUFFALO	Slaton, Tony	C	Southern California
16	NEW ORLEANS	Thorp, Don	DT	Illinois
17	ST LOUIS	Clark, Rod	LB	S.W. Texas State
18	CLEVELAND	Nugent, Terry	QB	Colorado State
19	DENVER	Smith, Aaron	LB	Utah State
20	DETROIT	Witkowski, John	QB	Columbia
21	HOUSTON from L.A. Rams	Mullins, Eric	WR	Stanford
22	SEATTLE	Kaiser, John	LB	Arizona
23	ATLANTA from San Francisco	Ralph, Dan	DT	Oregon
24	PITTSBURGH	Brown, Chris	DB	Notre Dame
25	MIAMI	Tatum, Rowland	LB	Ohio State
26	DALLAS	Levelis, Joe	G	Iowa
27	WASHINGTON	Singer, Curt	T	Tennessee
28	L.A. RAIDERS	Toran, Stacey	DB	Notre Dame

San Diego selected ahead of Philadelphia which passed

1984 Collegiate Draft *continued*
ROUND 7

No.	Team	Name	Pos.	College
1	TAMPA BAY	Carroll, Jay	TE	Minnesota
2	HOUSTON	Joyner, Willie	RB	Maryland
3	N.Y. GIANTS	Manuel, Lionel	WR	Pacific
4	PHILADELPHIA	Hayes, Joe	RB	Central State, Oklahoma
5	KANSAS CITY	Ross, Kevin	DB	Temple
6	SAN DIEGO	Bendross, Jesse	WR	Alabama
7	ATLANTA	Dodge, Kirk	LB	Nevada-Las Vegas
8	N.Y. JETS	Hamilton, Harry	DB	Penn State
9	CINCINNATI	Barker, Leo	LB	New Mexico State
10	DETROIT from Colts	Carter, Jimmie	LB	New Mexico
11	CHICAGO	Robertson, Nakita	RB	Central Arkansas
12	GREEN BAY	Jones, Daryll	DB	Georgia
13	MINNESOTA	Haines, John	DT	Texas
14	BUFFALO	David, Stan	DB	Texas Tech
15	L.A. RAIDERS from New Orleans	Willis, Mitch	DE	Southern Methodist
16	NEW ENGLAND	Kallmeyer, Bruce	K	Kansas
17	ST LOUIS	Walker, Quentin	RB	Virginia
18	DENVER	Kay, Clarence	TE	Georgia
19	DETROIT	Atkins, Renwick	T	Kansas
20	L.A. RAMS	Radachowsky, George	DB	Boston College
21	SEATTLE	Slater, Sam	T	Weber State
22	CLEVELAND	Dumont, Jim	LB	Rutgers
23	PITTSBURGH	Campbell, Scott	QB	Purdue
24	NEW ENGLAND from San Francisco	Williams, Derwin	WR	New Mexico
25	DALLAS	Martin, Ed	LB	Indiana State
26	MIAMI	Carvalho, Bernard	G	Hawaii
27	WASHINGTON	Smith, Mark	WR	North Carolina
28	MINNESOTA from L.A. Raiders	Lewis, Loyd	G	Texas A&I

Minnesota selected ahead of Green Bay which passed

ROUND 8

No.	Team	Name	Pos.	College
1	HOUSTON	Baugh, Kevin	WR	Penn State
2	TAMPA BAY	Robinson, Fred	DE	Miami
3	SAN DIEGO from N.Y. Giants	Woodard, Raymond	DT	Texas
4	PHILADELPHIA	Matsakis, Manny	K	Capital
5	ST LOUIS from San Diego	Noga, Falaniko	LB	Hawaii
6	KANSAS CITY	Clark, Randy	DB	Florida
7	N.Y. JETS	Griggs, Billy	TE	Virginia
8	CINCINNATI	Reimers, Bruce	T	Iowa State
9	COLTS	Daniel, Eugene	DB	Louisiana State
10	ATLANTA	Jackson, Jeff	LB	Auburn
11	DENVER from Green Bay	Hood, Winford	T	Georgia
12	MINNESOTA	Sverchek, Paul	DT	Cal Poly-Obispo
13	BUFFALO	Rayfield, Stacy	DB	Texas-Arlington
14	NEW ORLEANS	Terrell, Clemon	RB	So. Mississippi
15	NEW ENGLAND	Keyton, James	T	Arizona State

No.	Team	Name	Pos.	College
16	CHICAGO	Anderson, Brad	WR	Arizona
17	ST. LOUIS	Paulling, Bob	K	Clemson
18	DETROIT	Jones, David	C	Texas
19	L.A. RAMS	Brady, Ed	LB	Illinois
20	SEATTLE	Puzar, John	C	Cal State-Long Beach
21	N.Y. JETS from Cleveland	Wright, Brett	P	S.E. Louisiana
22	DENVER	Garnett, Scott	DT	Washington
23	SAN DIEGO from San Francisco	Craighead, Bob	RB	N.E. Louisiana
24	PITTSBURGH	Rasmussen, Randy	C	Minnesota
25	MIAMI	Landry, Ronnie	RB	McNeese State
26	DALLAS	Revell, Mike	RB	Bethune-Cookman
27	WASHINGTON	Smith, Jeff	DB	Missouri
28	L.A. RAIDERS	Seale, Sam	WR	Western State, Colorado

ROUND 9

No.	Team	Name	Pos.	College
1	TAMPA BAY	Mallory, Rick	G	Washington
2	HOUSTON	Donaldson, Jeff	DB	Colorado
3	HOUSTON from N.Y. Giants	Johnson, Mike	DE	Illinois
4	CLEVELAND from Philadelphia	Jones, Don	WR	Texas A&M
5	KANSAS CITY	Auer, Scott	T	Michigan State
6	SAN DIEGO	Barnes, Zack	DT	Alabama State
7	CINCINNATI	Kozerski, Bruce	C	Holy Cross
8	DALLAS from Colts	Hunt, John	G	Florida
9	ATLANTA	Howe, Glen	T	So. Mississippi
10	N.Y. JETS	Baldwin, Tom	DT	Tulsa
11	MINNESOTA	Kidd, Keith	WR	Arkansas
12	BUFFALO	Howell, Leroy	DE	Appalachian State
13	NEW ORLEANS	Hansen, Brian	P	Sioux Falls, S. D.
14	NEW ENGLAND	Bolzan, Scott	T	Northern Illinois
15	SAN FRANCISCO from Chicago	Miller, Lee	DB	Cal State-Fullerton
16	KANSAS CITY from Green Bay	Hestera, Dave	TE	Colorado
17	ST. LOUIS	Walker, John	RB	Texas
18	L.A. RAMS	Reynolds, George	P	Penn State
19	SEATTLE	Schreiber, Adam	G	Texas
20	CHICAGO from Cleveland	Casale, Mark	QB	Montclair State
21	DENVER	Brewer, Chris	RB	Arizona
22	DETROIT	Hollins, Rich	WR	West Virginia
23	PITTSBURGH	Erenberg, Rich	RB	Colgate
24	SAN FRANCISCO	Harmon, Derrick	RB	Cornell
25	DALLAS	Maune, Neil	G	Notre Dame
26	MIAMI	Boyle, Jim	T	Tulane
27	NEW ENGLAND from Washington	Windham, David	LB	Jackson State
28	HOUSTON from L.A. Raiders	Russell, Mike	LB	Toledo

Cleveland selected ahead of Houston which passed

ROUND 10

No.	Team	Name	Pos.	College
1	L.A. RAMS from Houston	Vann, Norwood	TE	East Carolina
2	TAMPA BAY	Gallery, Jim	K	Minnesota
3	N.Y. GIANTS	Jordan, David	G	Auburn
4	PHILADELPHIA	Thomas, John	DB	Texas Christian
5	N.Y. GIANTS from San Diego	Golden, Heyward	DB	South Carolina State
6	KANSAS CITY	Wenglikowski, Al	LB	Pittsburgh
7	DETROIT from Colts	Frizzell, William	DB	N. Carolina Central
8	ATLANTA	Franklin, Derrick	DB	Fresno State
9	N.Y. JETS	Cone, Ronny	RB	Georgia Tech
10	CINCINNATI	Jackson, Aaron	LB	North Carolina
11	BUFFALO	Azelby, Joe	LB	Harvard
12	NEW ORLEANS	Gray, Paul	LB	Western Kentucky
13	CINCINNATI from New England	Ziegler, Brent	RB	Syracuse
14	CHICAGO	Vestman, Kurt	TE	Idaho
15	GREEN BAY	Hoffman, Gary	T	Santa Clara
16	MINNESOTA	Spencer, James	LB	Oklahoma State
17	ST. LOUIS	Smythe, Mark	DT	Indiana
18	SEATTLE	Morris, Randall	RB	Tennessee
19	CHICAGO from Cleveland	Gayle, Shaun	DB	Ohio State
20	DENVER	Micho, Bobby	TE	Texas
21	DETROIT	Thaxton, James	DB	Louisiana Tech
22	L.A. RAMS	Dooley, Joe	C	Ohio State
23	SAN FRANCISCO	Moritz, Dave	WR	Iowa
24	PITTSBURGH	McJunkin, Kirk	T	Texas
25	MIAMI	Chesley, John	TE	Oklahoma State
26	DALLAS	Salonen, Brian	TE	Montana
27	WASHINGTON	Griffin, Keith	RB	Miami
28	CLEVELAND from L.A. Raiders	Byner, Earnest	RB	East Carolina

ROUND 11

No.	Team	Name	Pos.	College
1	TAMPA BAY	Kiel, Blair	QB	Notre Dame
2	L.A. RAIDERS from Houston	Williams, Gardner	DB	St. Mary's, Calif.
3	N.Y. GIANTS	Cephous, Frank	RB	UCLA
4	PHILADELPHIA	Robertson, John	T	East Carolina
5	KANSAS CITY	Johnson, Bobby	RB	San Jose State
6	SAN DIEGO	McGee, Buford	RB	Mississippi
7	ATLANTA	Norman, Tommy	WR	Jackson State
8	N.Y. JETS	Martin, Dan	T	Iowa State
9	CINCINNATI	McKeaver, Steve	RB	Central State, Oklahoma
10	COLTS	Stowe, Bob	T	Illinois
11	NEW ORLEANS	Bourgeau, Michel	DE	Boise State
12	NEW ENGLAND	Flager, Charlie	G	Washington State
13	L.A. RAMS from Chicago	Harper, Michael	RB	Southern California
14	GREEN BAY	Cannon, Mark	C	Texas-Arlington
15	MINNESOTA	Pickett, Edgar	LB	Clemson

No.	Team	Name	Pos.	College
16	BUFFALO	White, Craig	WR	Missouri
17	ST LOUIS	Mackey, Kyle	QB	East Texas State
18	CHICAGO from Cleveland	Butkus, Mark	DT	Illinois
19	DENVER	Lang, Gene	RB	Louisiana State
20	DETROIT	Saxon, Mike	P	San Diego State
21	L.A. RAMS	Love, Dwyane	RB	Houston
22	SEATTLE	Gemza, Steve	T	UCLA
23	PITTSBURGH	Veals, Elton	RB	Tulane
24	SAN FRANCISCO	Pendleton, Kirk	WR	Brigham Young
25	DALLAS	Aughtman, Dowe	DT	Auburn
26	MIAMI	Brown, Bud	DB	So. Mississippi
27	WASHINGTON	Jones, Anthony	TE	Wichita State
28	MINNESOTA from			
	L.A. Raiders	Thompson, Lawrence	WR	Miami

St. Louis, Chicago and Denver selected before Buffalo which passed.
Dallas, Miami and Washington selected before San Francisco which passed.

ROUND 12

No.	Team	Name	Pos.	College
1	L.A. RAMS from Houston	Fisher, Rod	DB	Oklahoma State
2	TAMPA BAY	Jemison, Thad	WR	Ohio State
3	N.Y. GIANTS	Green, Lawrence	LB	Tenn.-Chattanooga
4	PHILADELPHIA	McFadden, Paul	K	Youngstown
5	GREEN BAY from			
	San Diego	Taylor, Lenny	WR	Tennessee
6	KANSAS CITY	Lang, Mark	LB	Texas
7	N.Y. JETS	Roberson, David	WR	Houston
8	CINCINNATI	Raquet, Steve	LB	Holy Cross
9	COLTS	Hathaway, Steve	LB	West Virginia
10	ATLANTA	Holmes, Don	WR	Mesa, Colo
11	NEW ENGLAND	Howell, Harper	TE	UCLA
12	MIAMI from Chicago			
	through San Francisco	Devane, William	DT	Clemson
13	GREEN BAY	Emans, Mark	LB	Bowling Green
14	MINNESOTA	Jones, Mike	RB	North Carolina A&T
15	BUFFALO	Davis, Russell	WR	Maryland
16	NEW ORLEANS	Nelson, Byron	T	Arizona
17	ST LOUIS	Parker, Paul	G	Oklahoma
18	DENVER	Jarmin, Murray	WR	Clemson
19	DETROIT	Streno, Glenn	C	Tennessee
20	L.A. RAMS	Bias, Moe	LB	Illinois
21	SEATTLE	Windham, Theodis	DB	Utah State
22	CHICAGO from Cleveland	Jordan, Donald	RB	Houston
23	SAN DIEGO from			
	San Francisco	Harper, Maurice	WR	La Verne
24	PITTSBURGH	Gillespie, Fernanda	RB	William Jewell
25	MIAMI	Weingrad, Mike	LB	Illinois
26	DALLAS	Lewis, Carl	WR	Houston
27	WASHINGTON	Thomas, Curtland	WR	Missouri
28	L.A. RAIDERS	Essington, Randy	QB	Colorado

Minnesota and Buffalo selected ahead of Green Bay which passed

THE NCAA FOOTBALL STATISTICS

DIVISION I-A INDIVIDUAL LEADERS

Rushing

	CL	G	CAR	YDS	AVG	TD	YDSPG
Mike Rozier, Nebraska	Sr	12	275	2148	7.8	29	179.0
Shawn Faulkner, Western Mich.	Sr	11	394	1668	4.2	7	151.6
Napoleon McCallum, Navy	Jr	11	331	1587	4.8	10	144.3
Curtis Adams, Central Mich.	Jr	11	267	1431	5.4	15	130.1
Allen Pinkett, Notre Dame	So	11	252	1394	5.5	16	126.7
Kirby Warren, Pacific	Sr	12	304	1423	4.7	12	118.6
Reggie Dupard, SMU	So	11	197	1249	6.3	9	113.5
Johnnie Jones, Tennessee	Jr	10	191	1116	5.8	5	111.6
Steve Bartalo, Colorado St.	Fr	10	292	1113	3.8	8	111.3
Bo Jackson, Auburn	So	11	158	1213	7.7	12	110.3
Darryl Richardson, No. III	So	11	236	1204	5.1	10	109.5
Michael Gunter, Tulsa	Sr	11	226	1198	5.3	14	108.9
Alfred Anderson, Baylor	Sr	11	226	1046	4.6	10	104.6
Greg Allen, Florida St.	Jr	11	200	1134	5.7	13	103.1
Keith Byars, Ohio State	So	11	207	1126	5.4	19	102.4
Eric Denson, Wichita St.	So	10	163	1017	6.2	9	101.7
Ethan Horton, North Carolina	Jr	11	200	1107	5.5	8	100.6

Passing

	CL	G	ATT	CMP	CMP %	INT	INT %	YDS	YDS. ATT	TD	TD %	RATING POINTS
Steve Young, Brigham Young	Sr	11	429	306	71.33	10	2.33	3902	9.10	33	7.69	168.5
Chuck Long, Iowa	Jr	10	236	144	61.02	8	3.39	2434	10.31	14	5.93	160.4
Mike Eppley, Clemson	Jr	11	166	99	59.64	9	5.42	1410	8.49	13	7.83	146.0
Cody Carlson, Baylor	Fr	11	180	98	54.44	7	3.89	1617	8.98	12	6.67	144.1
Rick Neuheisel, UCLA	Sr	11	236	163	69.07	10	4.24	1947	8.25	9	3.81	142.5
Randall Cunningham, Nev.-LV	Jr	11	316	189	59.81	8	2.53	2545	8.05	18	5.70	141.2
Marlon Adler, Missouri	Jr	11	175	102	58.29	13	7.43	1603	9.16	11	6.29	141.1
Brad Baumberger, Wyoming	Sr	12	189	112	59.26	7	3.70	1551	8.21	10	5.29	138.2
Jack Trudeau, Illinois	So	11	324	203	62.65	13	4.01	2446	7.55	18	5.56	136.4
Raphel Cherry, Hawaii	Jr	11	299	170	56.86	15	5.02	2478	8.29	18	6.02	136.3
Mike Tomczak, Ohio State	Jr	10	205	116	56.59	12	5.85	1716	8.37	12	5.85	134.5
Ricky Turner, Washington St.	Sr	10	172	100	58.14	5	2.91	1351	7.85	8	4.65	133.7
Doug Strang, Penn State	Jr	12	259	134	51.74	7	2.70	1944	7.51	19	7.34	133.6
Boomer Esiason, Maryland	Sr	10	294	163	55.44	8	2.72	2322	7.90	15	5.10	133.2
Steve Pelluer, Washington	Sr	11	317	213	67.19	8	2.52	2212	6.98	11	3.47	132.2
Jeff Hostetler, West Virginia	Sr	11	287	163	56.79	10	3.48	2257	7.86	14	4.88	132.0
Scott Stankavage, N. Carolina	Sr	11	249	147	59.04	8	3.21	1721	6.91	16	6.43	131.9

Receiving

	CL	G	CT	YDS	TD	CTPG
Keith Edwards, Vanderbilt	Jr	11	97	909	0	8.8
Ricky Edwards, Northwestern	Sr	11	83	570	0	7.5
Tracy Henderson, Iowa State	So	11	81	1051	8	7.4
Chuck Scott, Vanderbilt	Jr	11	70	971	9	6.4
Mark Dowdell, Bowling Green	Jr	11	70	679	5	6.4
Ed Washington, Ohio	Sr	11	68	866	5	6.2

	CL	G					
Brian Brennan, Boston Col.	Sr	11	67	1168	8	6.1
Mike Leuck, Ball State	Jr	11	67	667	4	6.1
Mike Grayson, Duke	Sr	11	66	582	2	6.0
Dave Naumcheff, Ball State	Sr	11	65	1065	6	5.9
Jason Jacobs, Iowa State	Sr	11	64	584	3	5.8
Jim Sandusky, San Diego St.	Sr	12	69	1171	6	5.7
Keli McGregor, Colorado St.	Jr	12	69	717	2	5.7
Stan Hunter, Bowling Green	So	11	63	1107	6	5.7
Larry Willis, Fresno St.	Jr	11	63	1009	6	5.7
Mark Militello, Duke	Sr	11	63	682	3	5.7
Gerald McNeil, Baylor	Sr	11	62	1034	8	5.6

Scoring

	CL	G	TD	XP	FG	PTS	PTPG
Mike Rozier, Nebraska	Sr	12	29	0	0	174	14.5
Keith Byars, Ohio State	So	11	20	0	0	120	10.9
Luis Zendejas, Arizona St.	Jr	11	0	28	28	112	10.2
Allen Pinkett, Notre Dame	So	11	18	2	0	110	10.0
Max Zendejas, Arizona	So	11	0	39	20	99	9.0
Bruce Kallmeyer, Kansas	Sr	11	0	26	24	98	8.9
Curtis Adams, Central Mich.	Jr	11	16	0	0	96	8.7
Marty Louthan, Air Force	Sr	11	16	0	0	96	8.7
Paul Woodside, W. Virginia	Jr	11	0	35	19	92	8.4
Bob Bergeron, Michigan	Sr	9	0	30	15	75	8.3
Bob Paulling, Clemson	Sr	11	0	36	18	90	8.2
Randy Pratt, California	Sr	11	0	24	22	90	8.2
Bobby Raymond, Florida	Jr	11	0	29	20	89	8.1
Jeff Jaeger, Washington	Fr	11	0	27	20	87	7.9
Lee Johnson, Brigham Young	Jr	11	0	52	11	85	7.7
Bo Jackson, Auburn	So	11	14	0	0	84	7.6
Michael Gunter, Tulsa	Sr	11	14	0	0	84	7.6

All-Purpose Runners

	CL	G	RUSH	REC	PR	KOR	YDS	YDSPG
Napoleon McCallum, Navy	Jr	11	1587	166	272	360	2385	216.8
Mike Rozier, Nebraska	Sr	12	2148	106	0	232	2486	207.2
Shawn Faulkner, Western Mich.	Sr	11	1668	221	0	0	1889	171.7
Curtis Adams, Central Mich.	Jr	11	1431	86	0	234	1751	159.2
Jim Sandusky, San Diego St.	Sr	12	-15	1171	381	340	1877	156.4
Alan Pinkett, Notre Dame	So	11	1394	288	0	0	1682	152.9
Ricky Edwards, Northwestern	Sr	11	561	570	0	523	1654	150.4
Steve Bartalo, Colorado St.	Fr	10	1113	284	0	0	1397	139.7
Keith Byars, Ohio State	So	11	1126	338	0	37	1501	136.5
Mike Grayson, Duke	Sr	11	785	582	110	22	1499	136.3
Elton Akins, Army	Jr	10	712	156	0	455	1323	132.3
Darryl Clack, Arizona St.	So	10	932	299	0	92	1323	132.3
Bo Jackson, Auburn	So	11	1213	73	0	163	1449	131.7
Casey Tiumalu, Brigham Young	Sr	11	851	583	0	0	1434	130.4
Kirby Warren, Pacific	Sr	12	1423	70	0	0	1493	124.4
Kim Locklin, New Mexico St.	Jr	11	727	279	0	360	1366	124.2
Louis Lipps, Southern Miss.	Sr	11	72	800	462	0	1334	121.3

COLLEGE BOWL RESULTS

Regular season records are indicated in brackets.

COLLEGE FOOTBALL BOWLS

Dec. 10
Independence Bowl: Air Force (8-2) 9 vs. Mississippi (6-5) 3
Dec. 17
Citrus Bowl: Maryland (8-3) 23 vs. Tennessee (8-3) 30
Dec. 22
Hall of Fame Bowl: West Virginia (8-3) 20 vs. Kentucky (6-4-1) 16
Dec. 23
Holiday Bowl: Brigham Young (10-1) 21 vs. Missouri (7-4) 17
Dec. 24
Sun Bowl: Alabama (7-3) 28 vs. Southern Methodist (10-1) 7
Dec. 26
Aloha Bowl: Penn State (7-4-1) 13 vs. Washington (8-3) 10
Dec. 29
Liberty Bowl: Notre Dame (6-5) 19 vs. Boston College (9-2) 18
Dec. 30
Peach Bowl: North Carolina (8-3) 3 vs. Florida State (6-4) 28
Gator Bowl: Iowa (9-2) 6 vs. Florida (7-2-1) 14
Dec. 31
Bluebonnet Bowl: Baylor (7-3-1) 14 vs. Oklahoma State (7-4-1) 24
Jan. 2
Cotton Bowl: Georgia (9-1-1) 10 vs. Texas (11-0) 9
Fiesta Bowl: Ohio State (8-3) 28 vs. Pittsburgh (8-2-1) 23
Rose Bowl: Illinois (10-1) 9 vs. UCLA (6-4-1) 45
Orange Bowl: Nebraska (12-0) 30 vs. Miami (10-1) 31
Sugar Bowl: Auburn (9-1) 9 vs. Michigan (9-2) 7

HEISMAN TROPHY WINNERS

1983 – Mike Rozier, Nebraska, TB
1982 – Herschel Walker, Georgia, TB
1981 – Marcus Allen, Southern Cal, TB
1980 – George Rogers, South Carolina, HB
1979 – Charles White, Southern Cal, TB
1978 – Billy Sims, Oklahoma, HB
1977 – Earl Campbell, Texas, FB
1976 – Tony Dorsett, Pittsburgh, HB
1975 – Archie Griffin, Ohio State, HB
1974 – Archie Griffin, Ohio State, HB
1973 – John Cappelletti, Penn State, HB
1972 – Johnny Rogers, Nebraska, FL
1971 – Pat Sullivan, Auburn, QB

1970 – Jim Plunkett, Stanford, QB
1969 – Steve Owens, Oklahoma, HB
1968 – O.J. Simpson, Southern Cal, TB
1967 – Gary Beban, UCLA, QB
1966 – Steve Spurrier, Florida, QB
1965 – Mike Garrett, Southern Cal, TB
1964 – John Huarte, Notre Dame, QB
1963 – Roger Staubach, Navy, QB
1962 – Terry Baker, Oregon State, QB
1961 – Ernie Davis, Syracuse, HB
1960 – Joe Bellino, Navy, HB
1959 – Billy Cannon, LSU, HB
1958 – Pete Dawkins, Army, HB
1957 – John David Crow, Texas A & M, HB
1956 – Paul Hornung, Notre Dame, QB
1955 – Howard Cassady, Ohio State, HB
1954 – Alan Ameche, Wisconsin, FB
1953 – John Lattner, Notre Dame, HB
1952 – Billy Vessels, Oklahoma, HB
1951 – Dick Kazmaier, Princeton, HB
1950 – Vic Janowicz, Ohio State, HB
1949 – Leon Hart, Notre Dame, E
1948 – Doak Walker, SMU, HB
1947 – John Lujack, Notre Dame, QB
1946 – Glenn Davis, Army, HB
1945 – Doc Blanchard, Army, HB
1944 – Les Horvath, Ohio State, QB
1943 – Angelo Bertelli, Notre Dame, QB
1942 – Frank Sinkwich, Georgia, HB
1941 – Bruce Smith, Minnesota, HB
1940 – Tom Harmon, Michigan, HB
1939 – Nile Kinnick, Iowa, HB
1938 – Davey O' Brien, TCU, QB
1937 – Clint Frank, Yale, HB
1936 – Larry Kelley, Yale, E
1935 – Jay Berwanger, Chicago, HB

1983 SEASON RESULTS

WEEK 1
SUNDAY, SEPTEMBER 4
Atlanta Falcons at Chicago Bears ....20 – 17
Baltimore Colts at New England Patriots ....29 – 23
Denver Broncos at Pittsburgh Steelers ....14 – 10
Detroit Lions at Tampa Bay Buccaneers ....11 – 0
Green Bay Packers at Houston Oilers ....41 – 38
Los Angeles Raiders at Cincinnati Bengals ....20 – 10
Los Angeles Rams at New York Giants ....16 – 6
Miami Dolphins at Buffalo Bills ....12 – 0
Minnesota Vikings at Cleveland Browns ....27 – 21
New York Jets at San Diego Chargers ....41 – 29
Philadelphia Eagles at San Francisco 49ers ....22 – 17
St Louis Cardinals at New Orleans Saints ....17 – 28
Seattle Seahawks at Kansas City Chiefs ....13 – 17
MONDAY, SEPTEMBER 5
Dallas Cowboys at Washington Redskins ....31 – 30

WEEK 2
THURSDAY, SEPTEMBER 8
San Francisco 49ers at Minnesota Vikings ....48 – 17
SUNDAY, SEPTEMBER 11
Buffalo Bills at Cincinnati Bengals ....10 – 6
Cleveland Browns at Detroit Lions ....31 – 26
Dallas Cowboys at St Louis Cardinals ....34 – 17
Denver Broncos at Baltimore Colts ....17 – 10
Houston Oilers at Los Angeles Raiders ....6 – 20
New England Patriots at Miami Dolphins ....24 – 34
New Orleans Saints at Los Angeles Rams ....27 – 30
New York Giants at Atlanta Falcons ....16 – 13
Pittsburgh Steelers at Green Bay Packers ....25 – 21
Seattle Seahawks at New York Jets ....17 – 10
Tampa Bay Buccaneers at Chicago Bears ....10 – 17
Washington Redskins at Philadelphia Eagles ....23 – 13
MONDAY, SEPTEMBER 12
San Diego Chargers at Kansas City Chiefs ....17 – 14

WEEK 3
THURSDAY, SEPTEMBER 15
Cincinnati Bengals at Cleveland Browns ....7 – 17
SUNDAY, SEPTEMBER 18
Atlanta Falcons at Detroit Lions ....30 – 14
Baltimore Colts at Buffalo Bills ....23 – 28
Chicago Bears at New Orleans Saints ....31 – 34
Kansas City Chiefs at Washington Redskins ....12 – 27
Los Angeles Rams vs. Green Bay Packers at Milw ....24 – 27
Minnesota Vikings at Tampa Bay Buccaneers ....19 – 16
New York Giants at Dallas Cowboys ....13 – 28
New York Jets at New England Patriots ....13 – 23
Philadelphia Eagles at Denver Broncos ....13 – 10
Pittsburgh Steelers at Houston Oilers ....40 – 28
San Diego Chargers at Seattle Seahawks ....31 – 34
San Francisco 49ers at St Louis Cardinals ....42 – 27

MONDAY, SEPTEMBER 19
Miami Dolphins at Los Angeles Raiders ....14 – 27

WEEK 4
SUNDAY, SEPTEMBER 25
Atlanta Falcons at San Francisco 49ers ....20 – 24
Chicago Bears at Baltimore Colts ....19 – 22
Cincinnati Bengals at Tampa Bay Buccaneers ....23 – 17
Cleveland Browns at San Diego Chargers ....30 – 24
Detroit Lions at Minnesota Vikings ....17 – 20
Houston Oilers at Buffalo Bills ....13 – 30
Kansas City Chiefs at Miami Dolphins .... 6 – 14
Los Angeles Raiders at Denver Broncos ....22 – 7
Los Angeles Rams at New York Jets ....24 – 27
New England Patriots at Pittsburgh Steelers ....28 – 23
New Orleans Saints at Dallas Cowboys ....20 – 21
St Louis Cardinals at Philadelphia Eagles ....14 – 11
Washington Redskins at Seattle Seahawks ....27 – 17
MONDAY, SEPTEMBER 26
Green Bay Packers at New York Giants .... 3 – 27

WEEK 5
SUNDAY, OCTOBER 2
Baltimore Colts at Cincinnati Bengals ....34 – 31
Dallas Cowboys at Minnesota Vikings ....37 – 24
Denver Broncos at Chicago Bears ....14 – 31
Detroit Lions at Los Angeles Rams ....10 – 21
Houston Oilers at Pittsburgh Steelers ....10 – 17
Los Angeles Raiders at Washington Redskins ....35 – 37
Miami Dolphins at New Orleans Saints .... 7 – 17
Philadelphia Eagles at Atlanta Falcons ....28 – 24
St Louis Cardinals at Kansas City Chiefs ....14 – 38
San Diego Chargers at New York Giants ....41 – 34
San Francisco 49ers at New England Patriots ....33 – 13
Seattle Seahawks at Cleveland Browns ....24 – 9
Tampa Bay Buccaneers at Green Bay Packers ....14 – 55
MONDAY, OCTOBER 3
New York Jets at Buffalo Bills ....34 – 10

WEEK 6
SUNDAY, OCTOBER 9
Buffalo Bills at Miami Dolphins ....38 – 35
Denver Broncos at Houston Oilers ....26 – 14
Green Bay Packers at Detroit Lions ....14 – 38
Kansas City Chiefs at Los Angeles Raiders ....20 – 21
Los Angeles Rams at San Francisco 49ers ....10 – 7
Minnesota Vikings at Chicago Bears ....23 – 14
New England Patriots at Baltimore Colts .... 7 – 12
New Orleans Saints at Atlanta Falcons ....19 – 17
New York Jets at Cleveland Browns .... 7 – 10
Philadelphia Eagles at New York Giants ....17 – 13
Seattle Seahawks at San Diego Chargers ....21 – 28
Tampa Bay Buccaneers at Dallas Cowboys ....24 – 27
Washington Redskins at St Louis Cardinals ....38 – 14
MONDAY, OCTOBER 10
Pittsburgh Steelers at Cincinnati Bengals ....24 – 14

WEEK 7
SUNDAY, OCTOBER 16

Atlanta Falcons at Los Angeles Rams	21 – 27
Buffalo Bills at Baltimore Colts	30 – 7
Chicago Bears at Detroit Lions	17 – 31
Cincinnati Bengals at Denver Broncos	17 – 24
Cleveland Browns at Pittsburgh Steelers	17 – 44
Houston Oilers at Minnesota Vikings	14 – 34
Los Angeles Raiders at Seattle Seahawks	36 – 38
Miami Dolphins at New York Jets	32 – 14
New York Giants at Kansas City Chiefs	17 – 38
Philadelphia Eagles at Dallas Cowboys	7 – 37
St Louis Cardinals at Tampa Bay Buccaneers	34 – 27
San Diego Chargers at New England Patriots	21 – 37
San Francisco 49ers at New Orleans Saints	32 – 13

MONDAY, OCTOBER 17

Washington Redskins at Green Bay Packers	47 – 48

WEEK 8
SUNDAY, OCTOBER 23

Atlanta Falcons at New York Jets	27 – 21
Chicago Bears at Philadelphia Eagles	7 – 6
Cleveland Browns at Cincinnati Bengals	21 – 28
Detroit Lions at Washington Redskins	17 – 38
Kansas City Chiefs at Houston Oilers	13 – 10
Los Angeles Raiders at Dallas Cowboys	40 – 38
Miami Dolphins at Baltimore Colts	21 – 7
Minnesota Vikings at Green Bay Packers	20 – 17
New England Patriots at Buffalo Bills	31 – 0
New Orleans Saints at Tampa Bay Buccaneers	24 – 21
Pittsburgh Steelers at Seattle Seahawks	27 – 21
San Diego Chargers at Denver Broncos	6 – 14
San Francisco 49ers at Los Angeles Rams	45 – 35

MONDAY, OCTOBER 24

New York Giants at St Louis Cardinals	20 – 20

WEEK 9
SUNDAY, OCTOBER 30

Baltimore Colts at Philadelphia Eagles	22 – 21
Dallas Cowboys at New York Giants	38 – 20
Detroit Lions at Chicago Bears	38 – 17
Green Bay Packers at Cincinnati Bengals	14 – 34
Houston Oilers at Cleveland Browns	19 – 25
Kansas City Chiefs at Denver Broncos	24 – 27
Los Angeles Rams at Miami Dolphins	14 – 30
Minnesota Vikings at St Louis Cardinals	31 – 41
New England Patriots at Atlanta Falcons	13 – 24
New Orleans Saints at Buffalo Bills	21 – 27
New York Jets at San Francisco 49ers	27 – 13
Seattle Seahawks at Los Angeles Raiders	34 – 21
Tampa Bay Buccaneers at Pittsburgh Steelers	12 – 17

MONDAY, OCTOBER 31

Washington Redskins at San Diego Chargers	27 – 24

WEEK 10
SUNDAY, NOVEMBER 6
Atlanta Falcons at New Orleans Saints .... 10 – 27
Baltimore Colts at New York Jets .... 17 – 14
Buffalo Bills at New England Patriots .... 7 – 21
Chicago Bears at Los Angeles Rams .... 14 – 21
Cincinnati Bengals at Houston Oilers .... 55 – 14
Cleveland Browns vs. Green Bay Packers at Milw .... 21 – 35
Dallas Cowboys at Philadelphia Eagles .... 27 – 20
Denver Broncos at Seattle Seahawks .... 19 – 27
Los Angeles Raiders at Kansas City Chiefs .... 28 – 20
Miami Dolphins at San Francisco 49ers .... 20 – 17
St Louis Cardinals at Washington Redskins .... 7 – 45
San Diego Chargers at Pittsburgh Steelers .... 3 – 26
Tampa Bay Buccaneers at Minnesota Vikings .... 17 – 12
MONDAY, NOVEMBER 7
New York Giants at Detroit Lions .... 9 – 15

WEEK 11
SUNDAY, NOVEMBER 13
Buffalo Bills at New York Jets .... 24 – 17
Cincinnati Bengals at Kansas City Chiefs .... 15 – 20
Dallas Cowboys at San Diego Chargers .... 23 – 24
Denver Broncos at Los Angeles Raiders .... 20 – 22
Detroit Lions at Houston Oilers .... 17 – 27
Green Bay Packers at Minnesota Vikings .... 29 – 21
Miami Dolphins at New England Patriots .... 6 – 17
New Orleans Saints at San Francisco 49ers .... 0 – 27
Philadelphia Eagles at Chicago Bears .... 14 – 17
Pittsburgh Steelers at Baltimore Colts .... 24 – 13
Seattle Seahawks at St Louis Cardinals .... 28 – 33
Tampa Bay Buccaneers at Cleveland Browns .... 0 – 20
Washington Redskins at New York Giants .... 33 – 17
MONDAY, NOVEMBER 14
Los Angeles Rams at Atlanta Falcons .... 36 – 13

WEEK 12
SUNDAY, NOVEMBER 20
Baltimore Colts at Miami Dolphins .... 0 – 37
Chicago Bears at Tampa Bay Buccaneers .... 27 – 0
Cleveland Browns at New England Patriots .... 30 – 0
Detroit Lions vs. Green Bay Packers at Milw .... 23 – 20
Houston Oilers at Cincinnati Bengals .... 10 – 38
Kansas City Chiefs at Dallas Cowboys .... 21 – 41
Los Angeles Raiders at Buffalo Bills .... 27 – 24
Minnesota Vikings at Pittsburgh Steelers .... 17 – 14
New York Giants at Philadelphia Eagles .... 23 – 0
San Diego Chargers at St Louis Cardinals .... 14 – 44
San Francisco 49ers at Atlanta Falcons .... 24 – 28
Seattle Seahawks at Denver Broncos .... 27 – 38
Washington Redskins at Los Angeles Rams .... 42 – 20
MONDAY, NOVEMBER 21
New York Jets at New Orleans Saints .... 31 – 28

WEEK 13
THURSDAY, NOVEMBER 24
Pittsburgh Steelers at Detroit Lions . . . . 3 – 45
St Louis Cardinals at Dallas Cowboys . . . . .17 – 35
SUNDAY, NOVEMBER 27
Baltimore Colts at Cleveland Browns . . . . .23 – 41
Buffalo Bills at Los Angeles Rams . . . . .17 – 41
Denver Broncos at San Diego Chargers . . . . 7 – 31
Green Bay Packers at Atlanta Falcons . . . . .41 – 47
Houston Oilers at Tampa Bay Buccaneers . . . . .24 – 33
Kansas City Chiefs at Seattle Seahawks . . . . .48 – 51
Minnesota Vikings at New Orleans Saints . . . . .16 – 17
New England Patriots at New York Jets . . . . 3 – 26
New York Giants at Los Angeles Raiders . . . . .12 – 27
Philadelphia Eagles at Washington Redskins . . . . .24 – 28
San Francisco 49ers at Chicago Bears . . . . 3 – 13
MONDAY, NOVEMBER 28
Cincinnati Bengals at Miami Dolphins . . . . .14 – 38
WEEK 14
THURSDAY, DECEMBER 1
Los Angeles Raiders at San Diego Chargers . . . . .42 – 10
SUNDAY, DECEMBER 4
Atlanta Falcons at Washington Redskins . . . . .21 – 37
Buffalo Bills at Kansas City Chiefs . . . . .14 – 9
Chicago Bears at Green Bay Packers . . . . .28 – 31
Cincinnati Bengals at Pittsburgh Steelers . . . . .23 – 10
Cleveland Browns at Denver Broncos . . . . 6 – 27
Dallas Cowboys at Seattle Seahawks . . . . .35 – 10
Los Angeles Rams at Philadelphia Eagles . . . . 9 – 13
Miami Dolphins at Houston Oilers . . . . .24 – 17
New Orleans Saints at New England Patriots . . . . 0 – 7
New York Jets at Baltimore Colts . . . . .10 – 6
St Louis Cardinals at New York Giants . . . . .10 – 6
Tampa Bay Buccaneers at San Francisco 49ers . . . . .21 – 35
MONDAY, DECEMBER 5
Minnesota Vikings at Detroit Lions . . . . 2 – 13
WEEK 15
SATURDAY, DECEMBER 10
Atlanta Falcons at Miami Dolphins . . . . .24 – 31
Pittsburgh Steelers at New York Jets . . . . .34 – 7
SUNDAY, DECEMBER 11
Baltimore Colts at Denver Broncos . . . . .19 – 21
Chicago Bears at Minnesota Vikings . . . . .19 – 13
Cleveland Browns at Houston Oilers . . . . .27 – 34
Detroit Lions at Cincinnati Bengals . . . . 9 – 17
Kansas City Chiefs at San Diego Chargers . . . . .38 – 41
New England Patriots at Los Angeles Rams . . . . .21 – 7
New Orleans Saints at Philadelphia Eagles . . . . .20 – 17
St Louis Cardinals at Los Angeles Raiders . . . . .34 – 24
San Francisco 49ers at Buffalo Bills . . . . .23 – 10
Seattle Seahawks at New York Giants . . . . .17 – 12
Washington Redskins at Dallas Cowboys . . . . .31 – 10

MONDAY, DECEMBER 12
Green Bay Packers at Tampa Bay Buccaneers ....12 – 9

WEEK 16
FRIDAY, DECEMBER 16
New York Jets at Miami Dolphins ....14 – 34
SATURDAY, DECEMBER 17
Cincinnati Bengals at Minnesota Vikings ....14 – 20
New York Giants at Washington Redskins ....22 – 31
SUNDAY, DECEMBER 18
Buffalo Bills at Atlanta Falcons ....14 – 31
Denver Broncos at Kansas City Chiefs ....17 – 48
Green Bay Packers at Chicago Bears ....21 – 23
Houston Oilers at Baltimore Colts ....10 – 20
Los Angeles Rams at New Orleans Saints ....26 – 24
New England Patriots at Seattle Seahawks ....6 – 24
Philadelphia Eagles at St Louis Cardinals ....7 – 31
Pittsburgh Steelers at Cleveland Browns ....17 – 30
San Diego Chargers at Los Angeles Raiders ....14 – 30
Tampa Bay Buccaneers at Detroit Lions ....20 – 23
MONDAY, DECEMBER 19
Dallas Cowboys at San Francisco 49ers ....17 – 42
FIRST ROUND PLAYOFF GAMES
SATURDAY, DECEMBER 24
American Football Conference
Denver Broncos at Seattle Seahawks ....7 – 31
MONDAY, DECEMBER 26
National Football Conference
Los Angeles Rams at Dallas Cowboys ....24 – 17

DIVISIONAL PLAYOFF GAMES
SATURDAY, DECEMBER 31
American Football Conference
Seattle Seahawks at Miami Dolphins ....27 – 20
National Football Conference
Detroit Lions at San Francisco 49ers ....23 – 24
SUNDAY, JANUARY 1
American Football Conference
Pittsburgh Steelers at Los Angeles Raiders ....10 – 38
National Football Conference
Los Angeles Rams at Washington Redskins ....7 – 51

CONFERENCE CHAMPIONSHIP GAMES, SUPER BOWL XVIII, AND AFC-NFC PRO BOWL
SUNDAY, JANUARY 8
American Football Conference Championship Game
Seattle Seahawks at Los Angeles Raiders ....14 – 30
National Football Conference Championship Game
San Francisco 49ers at Washington Redskins ....21 – 24
SUNDAY, JANUARY 22
Super Bowl XVIII at Tampa Stadium, Tampa, Florida
Los Angeles Raiders vs. Washington Redskins ....38 – 9
SUNDAY, JANUARY 29
AFC-NFC Pro Bowl at Honolulu, Hawaii ....3 – 45

1983 FINAL STANDINGS

AFC WEST

	W	L	T	PF	PA
L.A. Raiders	12	4	0	442	338
Seattle Seahawks	9	7	0	403	397
Denver Broncos	9	7	0	302	327
San Diego Chargers	6	10	0	358	462
Kansas City Chiefs	6	10	0	386	367

AFC CENTRAL

	W	L	T	PF	PA
Pittsburgh Steelers	10	6	0	355	303
Cleveland Browns	9	7	0	356	342
Cincinnati Bengals	7	9	0	346	302
Houston Oilers	2	14	0	288	460

AFC EAST

	W	L	T	PF	PA
Miami Dolphins	12	4	0	389	250
New England Patriots	8	8	0	274	289
Buffalo Bills	8	8	0	283	351
Baltimore Colts	7	9	0	264	354
N.Y. Jets	7	9	0	313	331

NFC WEST

	W	L	T	PF	PA
San Francisco 49ers	10	6	0	432	293
L.A. Rams	9	7	0	361	344
New Orleans Saints	8	8	0	319	337
Atlanta Falcons	7	9	0	370	389

NFC CENTRAL

	W	L	T	PF	PA
Detroit Lions	9	7	0	347	286
Green Bay Packers	8	8	0	429	439
Chicago Bears	8	8	0	311	301
Minnesota Vikings	8	8	0	316	348
Tampa Bay Buccaneers	2	14	0	241	380

NFC EAST

	W	L	T	PF	PA
Washington Redskins	14	2	0	541	332
Dallas Cowboys	12	4	0	479	360
St Louis Cardinals	8	7	1	374	428
Philadelphia Eagles	5	11	0	233	322
N.Y. Giants	3	12	1	267	347

1984 SEASON SCHEDULE

WEEK 1

Result

Sunday, September 2

Atlanta Falcons at New Orleans Saints. . . . . ____--____
Cincinnati Bengals at Denver Broncos . . . . ____--____
Cleveland Browns at Seattle Seahawks. . . . . ____--____
Kansas City Chiefs at Pittsburgh Steelers . . . . ____--____
Los Angeles Raiders at Houston Oilers. . . . . ____--____
Miami Dolphins at Washington Redskins . . . . ____--____
New England Patriots at Buffalo Bills . . . . ____--____
New York Jets at Indianapolis Colts . . . . ____--____
Philadelphia Eagles at New York Giants . . . . ____--____
St Louis Cardinals at Green Bay Packers. ____--____
San Diego Chargers at Minnesota Vikings . . . . ____--____
San Francisco 49ers at Detroit Lions . . . . ____--____
Tampa Bay Buccaneers at Chicago Bears . . . . ____--____

Monday, September 3

Dallas Cowboys at Los Angeles Rams . . . . ____--____

WEEK 2

Thursday, September 6

Pittsburgh Steelers at New York Jets . . . . ____--____

Sunday, September 9

Buffalo Bills at St Louis Cardinals. . . . . ____--____
Cleveland Browns at Los Angeles Rams. . . . . ____--____
Dallas Cowboys at New York Giants . . . . ____--____
Denver Broncos at Chicago Bears . . . . ____--____
Detroit Lions at Atlanta Falcons. . . . . ____--____
Green Bay Packers at Los Angeles Raiders . . . . ____--____
Indianapolis Colts at Houston Oilers . . . . ____--____
Kansas City Chiefs at Cincinnati Bengals . . . . ____--____
Minnesota Vikings at Philadelphia Eagles . . . . ____--____
New England Patriots at Miami Dolphins . . . . ____--____
San Diego Chargers at Seattle Seahawks. ____--____
Tampa Bay Buccaneers at New Orleans Saints . . . . ____--____

Monday, September 10

Washington Redskins at San Francisco 49ers. . . . . ____--____

WEEK 3

Sunday, September 16

Atlanta Falcons at Minnesota Vikings. . . . . ____--____
Chicago Bears at Green Bay Packers . . . . ____--____
Cincinnati Bengals at New York Jets . . . . ____--____
Denver Broncos at Cleveland Browns . . . . ____--____
Detroit Lions at Tampa Bay Buccaneers . . . . ____--____
Houston Oilers at San Diego Chargers . . . . ____--____
Los Angeles Raiders at Kansas City Chiefs . . . . ____--____
Los Angeles Rams at Pittsburgh Steelers. ____--____
New Orleans Saints at San Francisco 49ers. . . . . ____--____
New York Giants at Washington Redskins . . . . ____--____
Philadelphia Eagles at Dallas Cowboys . . . . ____--____
St Louis Cardinals at Indianapolis Colts . . . . ____--____
Seattle Seahawks at New England Patriots . . . . ____--____

Monday, September 17

Miami Dolphins at Buffalo Bills. . . . . ____--____

WEEK 4

Sunday, September 23   Result

Chicago Bears at Seattle Seahawks . . . . ___—___
Green Bay Packers at Dallas Cowboys . . . . ___—___
Houston Oilers at Atlanta Falcons . . . . ___—___
Indianapolis Colts at Miami Dolphins . . . . ___—___
Kansas City Chiefs at Denver Broncos . . . . ___—___
Los Angeles Rams at Cincinnati Bengals . . . . ___—___
Minnesota Vikings at Detroit Lions . . . . ___—___
New York Jets at Buffalo Bills . . . . ___—___
Pittsburgh Steelers at Cleveland Browns . . . . ___—___
St Louis Cardinals at New Orleans Saints . . . . ___—___
San Francisco 49ers at Philadelphia Eagles . . . . ___—___
Tampa Bay Buccaneers at New York Giants . . . . ___—___
Washington Redskins at New England Patriots . . . . ___—___
Monday, September 24
San Diego Chargers at Los Angeles Raiders . . . . ___—___

WEEK 5

Sunday, September 30

Atlanta Falcons at San Francisco 49ers . . . . ___—___
Buffalo Bills at Indianapolis Colts . . . . ___—___
Cleveland Browns at Kansas City Chiefs . . . . ___—___
Dallas Cowboys at Chicago Bears . . . . ___—___
Detroit Lions at San Diego Chargers . . . . ___—___
Green Bay Packers at Tampa Bay Buccaneers . . . . ___—___
Los Angeles Raiders at Denver Broncos . . . . ___—___
Miami Dolphins at St Louis Cardinals . . . . ___—___
New England Patriots at New York Jets . . . . ___—___
New Orleans Saints at Houston Oilers . . . . ___—___
New York Giants at Los Angeles Rams . . . . ___—___
Philadelphia Eagles at Washington Redskins . . . . ___—___
Seattle Seahawks at Minnesota Vikings . . . . ___—___
Monday, October 1
Cincinnati Bengals at Pittsburgh Steelers . . . . ___—___

WEEK 6

Sunday, October 7

Atlanta Falcons at Los Angeles Rams . . . . ___—___
Denver Broncos at Detroit Lions . . . . ___—___
Houston Oilers at Cincinnati Bengals . . . . ___—___
Miami Dolphins at Pittsburgh Steelers . . . . ___—___
Minnesota Vikings at Tampa Bay Buccaneers . . . . ___—___
New England Patriots at Cleveland Browns . . . . ___—___
New Orleans Saints at Chicago Bears . . . . ___—___
New York Jets at Kansas City Chiefs . . . . ___—___
Philadelphia Eagles at Buffalo Bills . . . . ___—___
St Louis Cardinals at Dallas Cowboys . . . . ___—___
San Diego Chargers at Green Bay Packers . . . . ___—___
Seattle Seahawks at Los Angeles Raiders . . . . ___—___
Washington Redskins at Indianapolis Colts . . . . ___—___
Monday, October 8
San Francisco 49ers at New York Giants . . . . ___—___

WEEK 7   **Result**
Sunday, October 14
Buffalo Bills at Seattle Seahawks. . . . . ___—___
Chicago Bears at St. Louis Cardinals . . . . ___—___
Cincinnati Bengals at New England Patriots . . . . ___—___
Dallas Cowboys at Washington Redskins . . . . ___—___
Houston Oilers at Miami Dolphins . . . . ___—___
Indianapolis Colts at Philadelphia Eagles. . . . . ___—___
Los Angeles Rams at New Orleans Saints . . . . ___—___
Minnesota Vikings at Los Angeles Raiders . . . . ___—___
New York Giants at Atlanta Falcons . . . . ___—___
New York Jets at Cleveland Browns. . . . . ___—___
Pittsburgh Steelers at San Francisco 49ers . . . . ___—___
San Diego Chargers at Kansas City Chiefs . . . . ___—___
Tampa Bay Buccaneers at Detroit Lions. . . . . ___—___
Monday, October 15
Green Bay Packers at Denver Broncos . . . . ___—___

WEEK 8
Sunday, October 21
Chicago Bears at Tampa Bay Buccaneers . . . . ___—___
Cleveland Browns at Cincinnati Bengals . . . . ___—___
Denver Broncos at Buffalo Bills . . . . ___—___
Detroit Lions at Minnesota Vikings . . . . ___—___
Kansas City Chiefs at New York Jets. . . . . ___—___
Los Angeles Raiders at San Diego Chargers . . . . ___—___
Miami Dolphins at New England Patriots . . . . ___—___
New Orleans Saints at Dallas Cowboys . . . . ___—___
New York Giants at Philadelphia Eagles. . . . . ___—___
Pittsburgh Steelers at Indianapolis Colts . . . . ___—___
San Francisco 49ers at Houston Oilers. . . . . ___—___
Seattle Seahawks vs. Green Bay Packers at Milwaukee . . . . ___—___
Washington Redskins at St. Louis Cardinals . . . . ___—___
Monday, October 22
Los Angeles Rams at Atlanta Falcons. . . . . ___—___

WEEK 9
Sunday, October 28
Atlanta Falcons at Pittsburgh Steelers . . . . ___—___
Buffalo Bills at Miami Dolphins. . . . . ___—___
Cincinnati Bengals at Houston Oilers . . . . ___—___
Denver Broncos at Los Angeles Raiders . . . . ___—___
Detroit Lions at Green Bay Packers . . . . ___—___
Indianapolis Colts at Dallas Cowboys . . . . ___—___
Minnesota Vikings at Chicago Bears. . . . . ___—___
New Orleans Saints at Cleveland Browns. . . . . ___—___
New York Jets at New England Patriots . . . . ___—___
St. Louis Cardinals at Philadelphia Eagles . . . . ___—___
San Francisco 49ers at Los Angeles Rams. . . . . ___—___
Tampa Bay Buccaneers at Kansas City Chiefs . . . . ___—___
Washington Redskins at New York Giants . . . . ___—___
Monday, October 29
Seattle Seahawks at San Diego Chargers. . . . . ___—___

Sunday, November 4
Cincinnati Bengals at San Francisco 49ers .... ____—____
Cleveland Browns at Buffalo Bills .... ____—____
Green Bay Packers at New Orleans Saints.................. ____—____
Houston Oilers at Pittsburgh Steelers..................... ____—____
Kansas City Chiefs at Seattle Seahawks .... ____—____
Los Angeles Raiders at Chicago Bears .... ____—____
Los Angeles Rams at St Louis Cardinals .... ____—____
Miami Dolphins at New York Jets......................... ____—____
New England Patriots at Denver Broncos .... ____—____
New York Giants at Dallas Cowboys .... ____—____
Philadelphia Eagles at Detroit Lions .... ____—____
San Diego Chargers at Indianapolis Colts .... ____—____
Tampa Bay Buccaneers at Minnesota Vikings.............. ____—____
Monday, November 5
Atlanta Falcons at Washington Redskins.................. ____—____

WEEK 11
Sunday, November 11
Buffalo Bills at New England Patriots .... ____—____
Chicago Bears at Los Angeles Rams...................... ____—____
Dallas Cowboys at St Louis Cardinals .... ____—____
Denver Broncos at San Diego Chargers .... ____—____
Detroit Lions at Washington Redskins..................... ____—____
Houston Oilers at Kansas City Chiefs .... ____—____
Indianapolis Colts at New York Jets .... ____—____
Minnesota Vikings vs. Green Bay Packers at Milwaukee.... ____—____
New Orleans Saints at Atlanta Falcons.................... ____—____
New York Giants at Tampa Bay Buccaneers .... ____—____
Philadelphia Eagles at Miami Dolphins.................... ____—____
Pittsburgh Steelers at Cincinnati Bengals.................. ____—____
San Francisco 49ers at Cleveland Browns .... ____—____
Monday, November 12
Los Angeles Raiders at Seattle Seahawks .... ____—____

WEEK 12
Sunday, November 18
Cleveland Browns at Atlanta Falcons .... ____—____
Dallas Cowboys at Buffalo Bills .... ____—____
Detroit Lions at Chicago Bears.......................... ____—____
Kansas City Chiefs at Los Angeles Raiders .... ____—____
Los Angeles Rams vs. Green Bay Packers at Milwaukee..... ____—____
Miami Dolphins at San Diego Chargers.................... ____—____
Minnesota Vikings at Denver Broncos..................... ____—____
New England Patriots at Indianapolis Colts .... ____—____
New York Jets at Houston Oilers .... ____—____
St Louis Cardinals at New York Giants .... ____—____
Seattle Seahawks at Cincinnati Bengals................... ____—____
Tampa Bay Buccaneers at San Francisco 49ers .... ____—____
Washington Redskins at Philadelphia Eagles............... ____—____
Monday, November 19
Pittsburgh Steelers at New Orleans Saints................. ____—____

WEEK 13   **Result**
Thursday, November 22
Green Bay Packers at Detroit Lions . . . . ____—____
New England Patriots at Dallas Cowboys . . . . ____—____
Sunday, November 25
Atlanta Falcons at Cincinnati Bengals . . . . ____—____
Buffalo Bills at Washington Redskins . . . . ____—____
Chicago Bears at Minnesota Vikings . . . . ____—____
Indianapolis Colts at Los Angeles Raiders . . . . ____—____
Houston Oilers at Cleveland Browns . . . . ____—____
Kansas City Chiefs at New York Giants . . . . ____—____
Los Angeles Rams at Tampa Bay Buccaneers . . . . ____—____
Philadelphia Eagles at St. Louis Cardinals . . . . ____—____
San Diego Chargers at Pittsburgh Steelers . . . . ____—____
San Francisco 49ers at New Orleans Saints . . . . ____—____
Seattle Seahawks at Denver Broncos . . . . ____—____
Monday, November 26
New York Jets at Miami Dolphins . . . . ____—____

WEEK 14
Thursday, November 29
Washington Redskins at Minnesota Vikings . . . . ____—____
Sunday, December 2
Cincinnati Bengals at Cleveland Browns . . . . ____—____
Dallas Cowboys at Philadelphia Eagles . . . . ____—____
Denver Broncos at Kansas City Chiefs . . . . ____—____
Detroit Lions at Seattle Seahawks . . . . ____—____
Indianapolis Colts at Buffalo Bills . . . . ____—____
Los Angeles Raiders at Miami Dolphins . . . . ____—____
New Orleans Saints at Los Angeles Rams . . . . ____—____
New York Giants at New York Jets . . . . ____—____
Pittsburgh Steelers at Houston Oilers . . . . ____—____
St Louis Cardinals at New England Patriots . . . . ____—____
San Francisco 49ers at Atlanta Falcons . . . . ____—____
Tampa Bay Buccaneers at Green Bay Packers . . . . ____—____
Monday, December 3
Chicago Bears at San Diego Chargers . . . . ____—____

WEEK 15
Saturday, December 8
Buffalo Bills at New York Jets . . . . ____—____
Minnesota Vikings at San Francisco 49ers . . . . ____—____
Sunday, December 9
Atlanta Falcons at Tampa Bay Buccaneers . . . . ____—____
Cincinnati Bengals at New Orleans Saints . . . . ____—____
Cleveland Browns at Pittsburgh Steelers . . . . ____—____
Green Bay Packers at Chicago Bears . . . . ____—____
Houston Oilers at Los Angeles Rams . . . . ____—____
Miami Dolphins at Indianapolis Colts . . . . ____—____
New England Patriots at Philadelphia Eagles . . . . ____—____
New York Giants at St Louis Cardinals . . . . ____—____
San Diego Chargers at Denver Broncos . . . . ____—____
Seattle Seahawks at Kansas City Chiefs . . . . ____—____
Washington Redskins at Dallas Cowboys . . . . ____—____
Monday, December 10
Los Angeles Raiders at Detroit Lions . . . . ____—____

WEEK 16   **Result**
Friday, December 14
Los Angeles Rams at San Francisco 49ers..................................____—____
Saturday, December 15
Denver Broncos at Seattle Seahawks ....____—____
New Orleans Saints at New York Giants.....................................____—____
Sunday, December 16
Buffalo Bills at Cincinnati Bengals...____—____
Chicago Bears at Detroit Lions...____—____
Cleveland Browns at Houston Oilers..____—____
Green Bay Packers at Minnesota Vikings....................................____—____
Indianapolis Colts at New England Patriots..................................____—____
Kansas City Chiefs at San Diego Chargers...................................____—____
New York Jets at Tampa Bay Buccaneers....................................____—____
Philadelphia Eagles at Atlanta Falcons......................................____—____
Pittsburgh Steelers at Los Angeles Raiders..................................____—____
St Louis Cardinals at Washington Redskins..................................____—____
Monday, December 17
Dallas Cowboys at Miami Dolphins...____—____

FIRST ROUND PLAYOFF GAMES
Sunday, December 23, 1984
American Football Conference

_____at_____

National Football Conference

_____at_____

DIVISIONAL PLAYOFF GAMES
Saturday, December 29, 1984
American Football Conference

_____at_____

National Football Conference

_____at_____

Sunday, December 30, 1984
American Football Conference

_____at_____

National Football Conference

_____at_____

CONFERENCE CHAMPIONSHIP GAMES, SUPER BOWL XIX, AND AFC-NFC PRO BOWL
Sunday, January 6, 1985
American Football Conference Championship Game

_____at_____

National Football Conference Championship Game

_____at_____

Sunday, January 20, 1985
Super Bowl XIX at Stanford Stadium, Palo Alto, California

_____vs_____

Sunday, January 27, 1985
AFC-NFC Pro Bowl at Honolulu, Hawaii

AFC_____ vs. NFC_____